Rome
Shortlist

timeout.com / rome

96

110

Contents

Piazza del Popolo

ABOUT THE GUIDE

The *Time Out Rome Shortlist* is one of a series of pocket guides to cities around the globe. Drawing on the expertise of local authors, it distils their knowledge into a handy, easy-to-use format that ensures you get the most from your trip, whether you're a first-time or a return visitor.

Time Out Rome Shortlist is divided into four sections:

Welcome to Rome introduces the city and provides inspiration for your visit.

Rome Day by Day helps you plan your trip with an events calendar and customised itineraries.

Rome by Area is the main visitor section of the guide. It includes detailed listings and reviews for the very best sights and museums; restaurants ⑩; cafés, bars and pubs ⑩; bakeries, pasticcerie and gelaterie ⑩; shops and services ⑩, and entertainment venues ⑩, all organised by area with a corresponding street map. To help navigation, each area of Rome has been assigned its own colour.

Rome Essentials provides practical visitor information, including accommodation options and details of public transport.

Shortlists & highlights

We have selected a Shortlist of stand-out venues in each area, which are marked with a heart ♥ in the text. The very best of these appear in the Highlights feature (*see p10*) and receive extended coverage in the guide.

Maps

There's an overview map on *p8* and individual street maps for each area of the city. Venues featured in the guide have been given a grid reference so that you can find them easily on the maps and on the ground.

Prices

All our **restaurant listings** are marked with a euro symbol category from budget to blow-out (€-€€€€), indicating the price you should expect to pay for two courses (from *antipasto, primo, secondo* and *dolce*) plus wine: € = under €20; €€ = €20-€40; €€€ = €40-€60; €€€€ = over €60.

A similar system is used in our **Accommodation** chapter based on the hotel's standard prices for one night in a double room, mid-week and mid-season: **Budget** = up to €100; **Moderate** = €100-€250; **Expensive** = €250-€400; **Luxury** = over €400.

Introduction

Whether you're here for a long weekend or a lifetime, there's so much to love about Rome: its colours, raking mid-season light and sunsets; its agelessness, artistic wealth and cocksure sense that it is the world's most beautiful city.

There's quite a lot to rile you too: traffic chaos, stroppy shopkeepers and less-than-reliable public transport. The Eternal City and its eternal contradictions can be challenging for first-time visitors. But Rome more than repays the effort of getting to know it: once you've got a handle on this city, you'll find there's so, so much to revel in.

There are few places in the world that offer such artistic riches on a plate, many of them free to enjoy. Six magnificent Caravaggios, for example, hang in three of Rome's churches, gratis. Music rings out around Rome – from churches and obscure institutions, to the magnificent Auditorium-Parco della Musica. Any stroll around the city centre (and central Rome, being small, is great for walking) is likely to take you past millennia of architecture, from the Pantheon (AD 126) to Richard Meier's shell for the Ara Pacis (2006), from the Roman Forum's Temple of Vesta (seventh century BC) to the MAXXI contemporary art and architecture gallery (2010).

Add to all this some very fine food and wine, some extremely chic shopping and much scope for pavement-table lounging and people-watching, and the impulse to moan about life-threatening driving styles will fade away.

Take it as it is – rough, ready and infinitely fascinating – and you too will enjoy this infuriating, fabulous city.

Welcome to Rome

Palazzo Valentini Domus

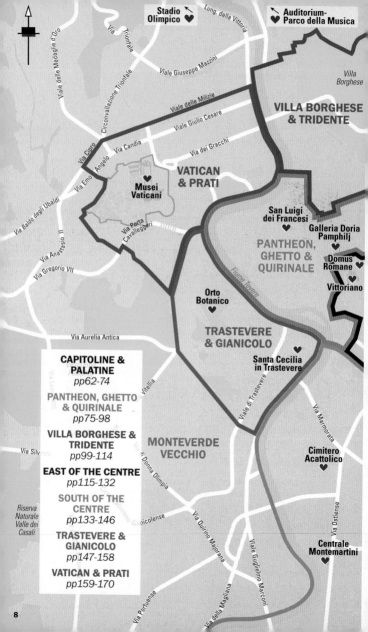

Stadio
Olimpico ❤

Auditorium-
❤ Parco della Musica

Lung. della Vittoria

Viale Giuseppe Mazzini

Viale delle Medaglie d'Oro

Via Trionfale

Circonvallazione Trionfale

Viale delle Milizie

Viale Giulio Cesare

Via Cipro

Via Candia

Via dei Gracchi

**VILLA BORGHESE
& TRIDENTE**

Villa
Borghese

Via Angelo Emo

Via Baldo degli Ubaldi

Via Anastasio II

Via Gregorio VII

Via Emo

**VATICAN
& PRATI**

❤
Musei
Vaticani

Via di Porta
Cavalleggeri

San Luigi
dei Francesi
❤

Galleria Doria
Pamphilj
❤

**PANTHEON,
GHETTO &
QUIRINALE**

Domus
Romane ❤

Vittoriano ❤

Fiume Tevere

❤
Orto
Botanico

**TRASTEVERE
& GIANICOLO**

❤
Santa Cecilia
in Trastevere

Via Aurelia Antica

Via di Trastevere

Via Marmorata

Via Vitellia

**MONTEVERDE
VECCHIO**

Via di Donna Olimpia

Circonvallazione Gianicolense

Via Silveri

Riserva
Naturale
Valle dei
Casali

Via di Quirino Majorana

Cimitero
Acattolico
❤

Via Ostiense

Centrale
Montemartini
❤

Viale Guglielmo Marconi

Via Portuense

Via della Magliana

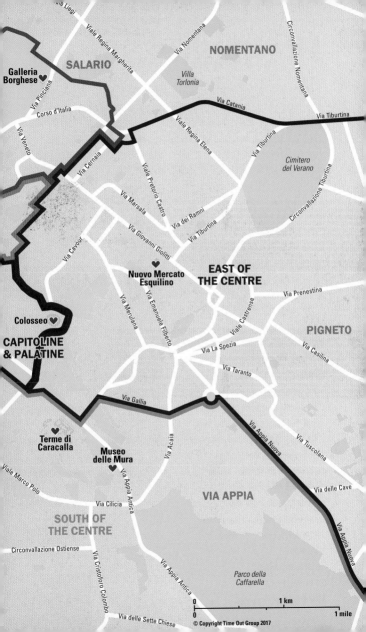

Highlights

From ancient Rome's Colosseo to contemporary Rome's Auditorium-Parco della Musica; from the artistic treasures of the Musei Vaticani to the multicultural flavours of the Nuovo Mercato Esquilino, we count down the unmissable sights and experiences of the Eternal City.

01

Colosseo *p70*

No other landmark says 'Rome' quite like the Flavian Amphitheatre – aka the Colosseo (Colosseum) – a symbol of influence, clout and skilful manipulation of the people, in an architectural marvel that has withstood the passage of time. Inaugurated in AD 80 with 100 days of wild-animal carnage, the 50,000-seater Colosseum kept social unrest at bay with free gory entertainment.

02

Centrale Montemartini *p141*

A decommissioned power station hosting a beautifully displayed collection of ancient statuary, the Centrale Montemartini is arguably Rome's most under-visited, under-appreciated gem. Admittedly, it's less than central. But the striking setting and the glorious selection of pieces – including the engaging muse Polimnia and a remarkable ivory doll with jointed limbs – make it unique.

03

Cimitero Acattolico *p139*

Rome's utterly lovely non-catholic cemetery celebrated its 300th anniversary in 2016. Nestling beneath the Pyramid and sheltered by umbrella pines, this is the flower-filled final resting place of poets (Keats, Shelley, Gregory Corso), philosophers (Antonio Gramsci) and Grand Tourists galore. For atmosphere, the cemetery is hard to beat, especially at sunset, bathed with golden light through the pines.

04

A match at the Stadio Olimpico *p46*

For sheer decibels, matches at the Stadio Olimpico are cup winners. Whether you're here to see SS Lazio (diehard fans in the Curva Nord) or AS Roma (Curva Sud), for a Serie A match or the Coppa Italia, you'll enjoy great crowd choreography and – in general – much audience camaraderie, at surprisingly low ticket prices.

05

Galleria Borghese *p104*

A superb container for a superlative collection, Galleria Borghese is the 17th-century pleasure house where Cardinal Scipione Borghese stashed his Bernini statues and Caravaggio paintings. Two Bernini works alone – Daphne turning into a bay tree as she flees lustful Apollo, and Pluto seizing the grain goddess Proserpina – make the (obligatory) process of pre-booking a visit worthwhile.

06

Musei Vaticani p164

Sprawling, overwhelming and with something for everyone, the Musei Vaticani (Vatican Museums) offer far more than the Sistine Chapel and a handful of Raphael frescoes. There are sections covering – among other things – Egypt (complete with mummies), the Etruscans, ethnographical artefacts collected by adventuring missionaries, and modern art.

07

Auditorium-Parco della Musica p43

The three beetle-shaped blocks of this pulsating performing arts centre in the northern suburbs are the venue for music concerts from classical to contemporary, for meetings with authors, science festivals, Rome's annual film fest and endless other events. The outdoor *cavea* (enclosure) is a skating rink in winter and the perfect concert spot in summer.

08

Museo delle Mura p145

With 12.5km (7.5 miles) of the third-century BC Aurelian walls still standing, you'll come face to face with them all over the city. Only in this overlooked little museum can you walk on them. From the San Sebastiano gatehouse – where exhibits explaining ancient wall and road construction will fascinate detail-orientated visitors – there's access to a 350m (1150ft) stretch with magnificent views.

09

Nuovo Mercato Esquilino *p120*

Strolling the streets of central Rome, you may wonder at the city's lack of ethnic mix. But not in the Esquilino district. At the heart of this vibrant multicultural zone lies the Nuovo Mercato Esquilino – still known as piazza Vittorio market after its venue until 2002 – where stalls purvey ingredients from all over the globe to clients of every nationality.

10

Domus Romane *p65*

Archaeological wonders never cease coming to light in Rome. Recently added to the roster, the Domus Romane – remains of several richly decorated ancient Roman houses – stands out for its superb use of avant-garde technology to enhance our appreciation of the ancient. Computer-generated images 'grow' up the monumental brick walls, adding Roman Empire decor and filling the spaces with the sounds of inhabitants.

11

San Luigi dei Francesi *p83*

The dramatic *Scenes from the Life of St Matthew* (1600-1602) painting cycle by Caravaggio is the biggest draw in the French national church in Rome. But visitors to the 16th-century church often overlook a series of lovely depictions of *Histories of Cecilia* (1615), the patron saint of music, by Domenichino.

12

Opera at Terme di Caracalla *p59*

The beetling ruins of Emperor Caracalla's great bath complex never fail to impress, but seen on a summer's night, startlingly illuminated, to the notes of an opera, concert or dance performance, they are sheer magic. Gone are the heydays of *Turandot* complete with elephants, but productions remain impressive.

13

Santa Cecilia in Trastevere *p152*

Reputedly built over the home of St Cecilia, this church – of fifth-century origins with later additions – is a treasure trove. From the Cosmatesque decoration in the crypt, to Stefano Maderno's moving sculpture of St Cecilia beneath the altar, to the magnificent *Last Judgement* (c1300) mural by proto-Renaissance dark horse Pietro Cavallini upstairs in the choir, it's an essential stopover.

14

Gelato *p31*

Ice-cream is Rome's great leveller. From scurrying nuns to pompous politicians and chic boutique staff... everyone can be caught slurping a cone on a hot day. Recent years have seen a revolution in gelato culture. Sure, you can still get the highly coloured processed variety; but now there's also organic, gluten- and lactose-free and gourmet to choose from.

15

Orto Botanico *p155*

Plants have been cultivated since the 13th century in the area where Rome's botanical garden now flourishes, and the Orto has a lush timelessness to it that restores the spirits after an overdose of sightseeing. Officially it's a university research department, but the vibe is more genteel disarray than scientific rigour. There's a scent garden for visually impaired garden-lovers.

16

Galleria Doria Pamphilj *p81*

The Doria Pamphilj family is part of Rome's papal aristocracy, with a *centro storico* palace covering a whole city block and a superlative art collection still in private hands. Besides the Velazquez portrait of the Pamphilj pope Innocent X, there are works by Caravaggio and Titian, Filippino Lippi and Lorenzo Lotto... plus sumptuous interiors fit for a *principe*.

17

Vittoriano *p73*

This monument to Italian unification is a jingoistic bit of kitsch, glaringly out of whack with its surroundings. Exhibition spaces in its cavernous interior host so-so events. But slog up its daunting white steps or – even better – whizz in the glass lift up to the roof of the pile for a magical experience: Rome laid out in glory below.

View from St Peter's

Sightseeing

Rome can be overwhelming: in this centre of the ancient world – and chaotic example of the contemporary – there's simply too much to do. You'll discover a densely built-up network of cobbled streets, medieval and Renaissance churches and palaces, and opulent Baroque piazzas, with traces of the Imperial city permeating the entire area.
So make sure that your Eternal City bucket list includes 'sitting at pavement cafés watching people go by' and 'strolling aimlessly through the alleys of the *centro storico*'. Relaxation and musing will restore your strength for the next instalment of the city's museums, galleries and archaeological gems.

Most breathtaking views
Gianicolo hill *p148*
Pincio *p100*
Vittoriano *p73*

Oases of calm
Cimitero Acattolico *p139*
Orto Botanico *p155*

Best of ancient Rome
Colosseo *p70*
Domus Romane *p65*
Foro Romano *p68*
Museo delle Mura *p145*

Best for communing with God
Gesù *p88*
San Luigi dei Francesi *p83*
Santa Cecilia in Trastevere *p152*
St Peter's *p163*

Best for Grand Masters
Centrale Montemartini *p141*
Galleria Borghese *p104*
Galleria Doria Pamphilj *p81*
Musei Vaticani *p164*

The *centro storico* (historic centre) is probably where you'll be spending most of your time. The two most important of the seven hills upon which ancient Rome was built, the **Capitoline** and **Palatine**, are separated by a valley containing the Roman Forum, where you'll find some of the world's best archaeological remains. To the north-east, the area around the **Pantheon** was first incorporated into the city limits by Augustus and is littered with imperial monuments; while the picturesque tangle of cobbled streets around the **Ghetto** and campo de' Fiori is crammed with late medieval apartment buildings, punctuated by elegant Renaissance *palazzi*. The **Quirinale** hill and area surrounding the Fontana di Trevi has a mass of Baroque treasures and art galleries to be discovered.

A stone's throw from the cobbled streets of the *centro storico* is the vast **Villa Borghese** park, providing acres of green and splendid views. Below lies the elegant sweep of the via Veneto and the **Tridente**, the heartland of high-end shopping with a significant portion of ancient heritage.

East of the city centre is Termini railway station and the districts of **Monti** and **Esquilino**. In ancient times the Esquiline hill was a grand residential district, but today it's a little rough around the edges. Monti was the ancient city's slum; today its cobbled streets are full of hip boutiques. South-east of the Colosseum is the altogether less-touristed area of **Celio**, with the delightful Villa Celimontana park and some of Rome's finest early Christian churches. Further east sits Rome's cathedral, San Giovanni in Laterano.

South of the *centro storico* is the **Aventine** hill, whose residential grandeur contrasts with the noisy atmosphere at the foot of the hill in **Testaccio**. Testaccio remains a solidly salt-of-the-earth neighbourhood with an excellent market. Further south is student-heavy **Ostiense**, with its buzzing nightlife. Beyond the Aurelian walls, the bucolic sites of the **Appian Way** are there to explore.

On the west side of the river Tiber, **Trastevere** retains a villagey vibe; its cobbled streets and ancient churches are full of charm. Climb nearby **Gianicolo** hill for great views of the city. North of here, the **Vatican City**, seat of the Pope, is surrounded by the stolidly elegant avenues of the **Prati**, which exudes a certain fin de siècle bourgeois pomposity.

Pantheon *p80*

Art in the Eternal City

An aesthetic education

Roman art offers a stirring aesthetic experience – and a great education, embracing as it does quality and stunning chronological range. That the city displays art covering nearly 3,000 years is staggering; that almost all of it was produced right here, even more so.

Art of the Romans

From the third century BC new structural techniques gave birth to daring and spacious buildings. The Romans were responsible for monumental forms that blur the boundary between architecture and art, such as the triumphal arch ornamented with reliefs and the independent column ornamented with a spiral band.

Much of the best classical art is now concentrated in a few major museums. The sculptures in the Musei Capitolini (see p72) are an essential accompaniment to the ruins of the Forum. The Palazzo Altemps (see p77) and the Palazzo Massimo alle Terme (see p117) also house important works of Roman painting and sculpture. The sheer size of the classical collection at the Vatican Museums (see p164) can be demoralising, but one sculpture there gives modern tourists the same frisson that countless other classical works imparted to 18th-century visitors: this is *Laocoön and His Sons* (AD c27-68), a Hellenistic sculpture showing a powerful man and his sons struggling for their lives against serpents. It remains perhaps the most dynamic statue in the whole history of art.

Holy inspiration

Christian art flourished in Rome after AD 313, as Rome was transformed from a city of temples to one of churches. Little of the devotional apparatus of the newly recognised religion survives, but stunning mosaics decorate a number of venerable churches: including Santa Maria Maggiore (fifth century; see p117). Later medieval art can be enjoyed in Santa Cecilia in Trastevere (see p152).

From 1309 to 1377 the papacy was based in Avignon; Rome withered, and only a fraction of the population remained. Thus the Gothic is largely absent in the Eternal City. The lack of late-medieval art, however, is compensated for by the wealth of High Renaissance art from the 15th and 16th centuries.

High Renaissance

In the 16th century art and architecture took a monumental turn. In painting, the human figure grew in relation to the pictorial field: the busy backgrounds of 15th-century art were eliminated. Florentine Michelangelo (1475-1564) first worked in Rome from 1496 to 1501 for clerics and businessmen, carving his first *Pietà* (1499, now in St Peter's) for a French cardinal. In this sculpture, Michelangelo positions the dead Christ gracefully in his mother's lap, creating an eternal meditation on death.

Under Julius II (1503-13) papal patronage called ever greater artists to work on ever larger projects at the Vatican, including the ceiling of the Sistine Chapel and the new basilica of St Peter's.

The Sack of Rome in 1527 halted the artistic boom of the High Renaissance, as frightened artists sought employment elsewhere.

The spread of the Protestant Reformation prompted a more hardened, pessimistic spirit that gave preference to mannerist art, a style of exaggerated proportions and contorted poses that developed out of the mature work of Raphael and Michelangelo.

Going for Baroque

In the second half of the 16th century, Baroque emerged through the works of Annibale Carracci (1560-1609) and the shocking naturalism of Michelangelo Merisi, better known as Caravaggio (1571-1610). Carracci is best experienced at the Galleria Doria Pamphilj (see p81), while Caravaggio left paintings throughout the city during his stormy career. His masterpiece may be the *Calling of St Matthew* (c1599-1602) in the church of San Luigi dei Francesi (see p83). The Galleria Borghese (see p104) houses a fine nucleus of Caravaggio paintings, from the coy secular works of his early years to the brooding religious canvases of his maturity, notably the powerful *David*

with the Head of Goliath (c1609), in which the severed head is Caravaggio's self-portrait.

The consummate artist of the Roman Baroque, however, was primarily a sculptor: Gian Lorenzo Bernini (1598-1680). The confident energy inherent in Baroque art is revealed in Bernini's greatest religious sculpture: the *Ecstasy of St Theresa* (1647-52) in Santa Maria della Vittoria (see p116) brilliantly captures a split second of sensual rapture.

Art moves on

The final great artistic movement born in Rome was neo-classicism, an 18th-century celebration of ancient Greek art, expressed in stark white statues and reliefs.

Later movements of the 19th and 20th centuries can be seen at the Galleria Nazionale d'Arte Moderna (see p101). For contemporary art, the MAXXI (see p112) and MACRO (see p112) galleries show that – at least as far as exhibiting goes – the city isn't entirely trapped in its past.

Santa Maria Maggiore

Laocoön and His Sons

Colosseum p70

Sights of Rome

The area of the city with the greatest density of ancient remains lies between the Palatine, Capitoline, Esquiline and Quirinale hills. Located here are the Colosseum, the Roman Forum and ancient Rome's most desirable residential area, the Palatine. But ancient Rome doesn't stop there: the **Museo Nazionale Romano** group (*see p121*) houses a positively mind-boggling collection of ancient statuary and art. There is plenty more to admire in the **Vatican** and **Capitoline museums** (*see p164* and *p72*) too. And the **Pantheon** (*see p80*) is a work of art in itself.

Down the centuries, popes, princes and aristocrats all commissioned architects and artists to build and adorn their preferred places of worship, with the result that central Rome is home to more than 400 churches, containing endless artistic treasures to explore. Unmissable churches include **San Luigi dei Francesi** (*see p83*), with its glorious Caravaggio, the Cosmatesque-heavy **Santa Cecilia in Trastevere** (*see p152*) and, of course, **St Peter's** (*see p163*).

Rome has long boasted some of the world's greatest galleries and museums. Recent years have seen the sprucing up of old showcases and the construction of a

couple of new repositories too. Classical, Renaissance and Baroque art dominate, of course – for some of the best examples, visit the stunning **Galleria Borghese** (*see p104*) and **Galleria Doria Pamphilj** (*see p81*). However, it's the juxtaposition of ancient and modern – in power station **Centrale Montemartini** (*see p141*), or through museum **Domus Romane**'s use of technology (*see p65*) – that showcases antiquity in a different light. *See also p20* Art in the Eternal City.

Getting around

Although Rome undeniably suffers from chronic traffic congestion, much of the compact central area is either pedestrianised or has restricted access to traffic, which means that walking is by far the best and most pleasant way to get around.

When you do use public transport, the bus is your best bet; the atac.roma.it journey planner and the **Roma Bus** app (www.muovi.roma.it) are useful. The metro currently has only two main lines through the centre and is far from exhaustive. There are, however, some strategic central stops (Spagna, Barberini, Colosseo). Children travel free on Rome's city transport until their tenth birthday; older children pay the full price. *See also p181.*

Tickets & tourist passes

Tickets for concerts of all descriptions, sporting events, cultural happenings and queue-free or guided visits to artistic or archaeological sites can be booked online through a number of agencies, the largest of which are: **Ticket One** (www.ticketone.it, 892 101), **Hello Ticket** (www.helloticket.it, 800 907 080) and **Coop Culture** (www. coopculture.it).

The **Roma Pass** (€38.50, www.romapass.it) is a three-day pass including buses and metro, free entrance to two sites and reduced entrance to many more. There is also a seven-day **Archeologia Card** (€23, €13 reductions), which is great value if you're visiting several sites and want to avoid queues; for details, see 060608.it.

On the first Sunday of the month, entrance to all Italian state museums is free; save the packed Colosseum for another day and take advantage at less-busy sites.

Tourist information

Rome's city council operates a number of green-painted tourist information kiosks (**PIT**) that are open 9.30am-7.30pm daily. The excellent, exhaustive 060608.it website is the city council's one-stop shop for information on museums, galleries, events, hotels and much more besides.

Tours

The most popular sites for guided tours are the Vatican Museums and the Colosseum/Forum archeological areas. Both sites are vast and can be confusing; a good guided tour will help you maximise your time. **Context Travel** (www.contexttravel.com) runs tours led by highly qualified guides, largely archaeologists and art historians. **Understanding Rome** (www.understandingrome.com) tailor-makes private tours of Rome, including 'off the beaten track' itineraries.

To take an open top bus, **City Sightseeing Roma** and **Roma Cristiana** (*see p182* Tour buses) are the best of the bunch, the latter especially for visiting slightly further-flung churches if you'd rather not take the metro.

Eating & Drinking

Rome has always taken its food seriously, valuing substance over style where eating is concerned. So, although plenty of high-end and design-driven restaurants exist, most Romans, even the well-heeled ones, will opt for tradition and hearty portions over fusion and fashion. Simple, good-value restaurants (which generally go by the name of trattoria or osteria) remain the stalwarts of Rome's eating scene – more and more as times get harder. Some are unreconstructed family-run operations that have been serving up the same dishes for generations – but still do them so well that they pack in the punters day after day. Others are revamped old-school trattorias or bistros – places that take a tried-and-tested formula (informal service, unfussy cooking based on market-fresh ingredients) but give it a twist by upping the creativity quotient in the kitchen and offering a range of fine wines.

Best traditional Italian
Armando al Pantheon *p82*
Da Enzo al 29 *p153*
Flavio al Velavevodetto *p138*

Best blow-out restaurants
Antico Arco *p153*
Glass Hostaria *p154*
Il Sanlorenzo *p91*

Best for a glass of red
Ai Tre Scalini *p125*
Il Goccetto *p92*
Terre e Domus Enoteca della
Provincia di Roma *p74*

Best street food
Da Simo Pane e Vino *p84*
Pizzarium *p169*
I Supplì *p154*
Trapizzino *p138*

Best for your morning caffè
Barberini *p140*
Caffè Sant'Eustachio *p84*

Best for an aperitivo
Hotel Locarno Bar *p113*
Masto *p138*
Tram Depot *p140*

Eat like a Roman

With only 150 years of unification under its belt, the food in Italy has remained primarily regional. The Italians' inherent respect for tradition is usually manifested on the menu, and the history and landscape of each region uniquely shapes the ingredients and preparation of its signature dishes. *Cucina romana* takes its lead from the produce historically available in the Lazio countryside; namely *pecorino romano* (sheep's cheese) and *guanciale* (cured pork jowl) which form the basis for the classic Roman pasta quartet of *carbonara*, *amatriciana*, *gricia* and *cacio e pepe* (*see p195* Menu Reader).

The slaughterhouse of Rome, which was situated in Testaccio throughout the 20th century, also greatly influenced eating habits among the lower-classes as offal became popular as a cheap and nutritious meal: *trippa* (tripe), *coda* (oxtail), *pajata* (calf intestine) and *cervello* (brain) can still often be found in Roman trattorias, usually accompanied by locally grown seasonal greens such as *cicoria* (chicory) or *broccoletti* (turnip tops). Rome's Jewish population, which can be traced back more than 2,000 years, also contributed its own recipes to the city's cuisine. Roman favourites such as *carciofi alla giudia* (deep-fried artichokes), *fiori di zucca* (stuffed, battered courgette flowers), *filetti di baccalà* (battered salt cod) and *torta di ricotta e visciole* (cherry and ricotta pie) all have their roots in the Jewish Ghetto.

The standard Roman running order is: *antipasto* (hors d'oeuvre), *primo* (usually pasta, sometimes soup or risotto), *secondo* (the meat or fish course) with optional *contorno* (vegetables or salad, served separately), and *dolce* (dessert). You're under no obligation to order four courses – few locals do. It's perfectly normal, for example, to order a pasta course followed by a simple *contorno*. Top-flight places sometimes offer a *menu degustazione* (tasting menu) in the evening, but most venues offering a *menu turistico* should be avoided.

Central restaurants tend to be packed on Friday and Saturday nights and Sunday lunchtime, so do book ahead. Romans eat late (usually around 8.30-9pm) so proper restaurants open at 7-7.30pm. Places that open earlier are usually aimed at tourists, offering poor food at high prices.

Flavio al Velavevodetto

In the know
Price codes

Average restaurant prices are what you are likely to spend per person for two courses (from *antipasto*, *primo*, *secondo* and *dolce*) plus wine; while for pizzerias they cover a starter (such as bruschetta), a pizza and a medium beer.

€ = under €20

€€ = €20-€40

€€€ = €40-€60

€€€€ = over €60

Il Goccetto *p92*

The street food revolution

As Romans increasingly search for dining options that are not only delicious but easy on the wallet, the city has seen an invasion of street food establishments. **Da Simo Pane e Vino** (*see p84*) has repackaged traditionally home-cooked dishes in sandwich form, while Stefano Callegari's **Trapizzino** (*see p138*) brand has expanded from humble beginnings to become a worldwide export with branches in Japan and the US. The humble *pizza al taglio* (pizza-by-the-slice) has been revamped by superstar pizzamaker Gabriele Bonci of **Pizzarium** (*see p169*) whose focus on prime ingredients and creative combinations have prompted a loyal following.

Cafés, bars & pubs

Almost every Italian starts their day with a coffee and *cornetto* (breakfast pastry) in their local café or bar (in Italy these amount to the same thing since alcohol and coffee are served all day long in both) and will often make several trips throughout the day for a galvanising *caffè* (espresso), to grab a snack or sandwich or merely to catch up on the local gossip after work over an *aperitivo* or *digestivo*.

The action takes place at the counter with most locals preferring to stand. This is partly to participate in the lively banter but also because it is considerably cheaper than sitting down. There are usually two price lists at the bar: *al banco* (at the counter) and *al tavolo* (at the table), with the latter often costing twice or three times the former. Protocol is vague but common practice when consuming standing up is to pay first at the cash desk and then take your receipt to the counter; be prepared to stand your ground and catch the eye of

Open Baladin *p90*

the *barista* as there is no discernible queue system. Table service should involve somebody coming to take your order but again, in busy spots, you may have to work hard to gain their attention.

With the exception of the ever-present Irish pub, until recently the *enoteca* (*see p30*) was the backbone of drinking culture in wine-centred Italy. However, the global trend for artisanal beers has not passed Rome by and locals are now searching out more than the usual Peroni or Moretti. Italian-style pubs such as **Open Baladin** (*see p90*) is a good place to start.

Enoteche

The term *enoteca* encompasses everything *vino*-related: from dusty old bottle shops, to modern wine bars. Confusingly, restaurants in Italy may also be referred to as *enoteche*, generally denoting that they have a particular focus on the wine list or double as a wine bar. The small, charming *enoteche* of the *centro storico* offer a glimpse of local life as well as serving good-value wines *alla mescita* (by the glass). Where the food is particularly good *enoteche* have been listed here as restaurants; if it is better to stick to drinking they can be found listed under bars. Wine lists in *enoteche* and restaurants are organised by region and can be somewhat overwhelming to the uninitiated so don't be afraid to ask for recommendations.

Bakeries, pasticcerie & gelaterie

Every *zona* of Rome has its *forni* (bakeries) and *pasticcerie* (cake shops) selling freshly baked goodies including bread, pizza, pastries, cakes and biscuits. Many *pasticcerie* are also bars where a sweet pick-me-up can be consumed in situ accompanied by coffee or drinks. There can be huge variations, however, in quality and freshness; the places listed here are always reliable.

Gelato is sold on almost every corner of the city, particularly in summer. Sadly, the majority of city centre *gelaterie* cut corners by preparing industrial gelato mixes packed with colourings and chemicals. Real gelato is a truly memorable experience and it is worth hunting down the good stuff (*see p31* Gelato). Ice-cream is served in a *cono* (cone) or *coppetta* (tub) of varying sizes, usually costing from €2 to €4.

💜 Gelato

No trip to Rome would be complete without gelato. Although thought to have been invented in 17th-century Florence, the Romans are serious fans of the icy stuff and there are now over 2,000 *gelaterie* throughout the city, albeit of varying degrees of quality. Real gelato, made the proper way with fresh ingredients, is a true joy. As a general rule Italian gelato is made with more milk and less cream than conventional ice-cream, it is lower in fat but a higher sugar content makes it sweeter. Most fruit flavours contain no dairy, placing them closer to sorbet in both flavour and texture.

Sadly, as tourism in Rome boomed, so did the number of quick-fix gelato shops strategically placed by the main attractions and aimed at weary tourists. These eschewed traditional methods and fresh ingredients for time-saving, money-making industrial chemical mixes and machinery. Thankfully, the last two decades have seen a gradual shift towards

higher quality options. **Il Gelato di San Crispino** (*see p98*) revolutionised the Romans' expectation of gelato when it opened in 1992; small chains such as **Fatamorgana** (*see p125*) have opened multiple branches, and their experimental, often weird and wonderful, flavours are now held in just as high regard as the old-style stalwarts such as **Alberto Pica** (*see p92*).

Luckily there are some tell-tale signs that help punters to spot the bad stuff: unnaturally bright colours, a puffy texture and extravagant decoration can all be signs of fake gelato. To avoid disappointment, take a moment to scope out the selection before handing over your cash: colours should look natural and muted (a good benchmark is pistachio which should be a sludgy, almost brownish green); the texture should be thick, dense and creamy, and the flavours, particularly the fruits, should mirror the seasons.

Fatamorgana

Coffee customs

Italians take their coffee very seriously and are very particular about what they like and how they like it. It is not uncommon to hear dozens of diverse orders shouted across the bar as locals specify everything from the temperature to the amount of froth to even what kind of cup it should be served in.

The staple order is a *caffè* (espresso) which may be *normale*, *lungo* (with a touch more water), *ristretto* (with less water), *macchiato* (with a little milk) or *decaffeinato* (decaf). After dinner you may hear the request for a *caffè corretto*, an espresso with the addition of a dash of alcohol (usually grappa or sambuca). *Caffè americano* is an espresso diluted with hot water and served in a larger cup either *con o senza latte* (with or without milk).

Milky beverages such as cappuccino and caffè latte are strictly for breakfast time. The digestion-obsessed Italians would never dream of consuming warm milk after lunch so expect some stares if ordering after 11am.

In the warmer months the Romans stick to *caffè freddo* (cold espresso) or *caffè shakerato* (espresso shaken with ice cubes in a cocktail shaker or whizzed in a blender).

Via dei Condotti

Shopping

Until not that long ago, shopping in Rome was a rather refreshing, old-fashioned experience with mainly independent, family-run establishments offering personal service and quality products. Huge department stores were rare and high street chains were largely absent. But these days the city's historic shops struggle to cling on in the harsh economic climate as rents rise and consumers become more willing to sacrifice service and quality for bargain prices.

However, the old-fashioned world hasn't disappeared completely – there are still plenty of unique gems buried among the now-ubiquitous international brands.

Look carefully and Rome's shopping scene can satisfy almost every need. While the Tridente's via del Corso is the closest thing that Rome has to a high street, just a short wander off the main drag into the narrow surrounding streets, or a trip to the smaller, up-and-coming neighbourhoods of Monti, Trastevere and Testaccio will reward you with one-off boutiques by emerging designers, quaint family-run delis and artisanal artists and craftsmen. Rome's markets, from the daily neighbourhood produce markets to the weekly flea markets, remain one of the most authentic ways to both shop and experience a slice of local life, while a stroll down the exclusive via dei Condotti will take you to the heart of the capital's high-fashion aristocracy.

Clothes & shoes

To splash the cash head to **via dei Condotti** (Tridente) where the major Italian labels such as Gucci, Prada and Dolce e Gabbana are interspersed with international names including Louis Vuitton, Jimmy Choo and Burberry. The surrounding streets in the Spanish Steps part of the Tridente are home to some smaller, but no-less exclusive, high-end boutiques. For more wallet-friendly options, **via del Corso** (Tridente) is lined with well-known chains, including Zara, H&M and Mango, as well as large sports brands; similar mid-range shops can also be found on **via Nazionale** in the Quirinale. Over in the Prati district, **via Cola di Rienzo** is a less-crowded, slightly higher-end version of via del Corso, with the addition of the glamorous **COIN Excelsior** department store.

Jewellery & watches

The big names in glitter production, like Bulgari and Cartier, cluster around piazza di Spagna in the Tridente area. Even if you don't plan to purchase, it's worth straying along diamond lane for a look at enviable and original baubles.

Abito - Le Gallinelle

Food & drink

Supermarket chains can be found throughout the city but for higher-quality cured meats, cheese and bread visit the *alimentari* (delicatessen) or *forno* (bakery) where food is sold by the *etto* (100 grams). **Beppe e I suoi Formaggi** (*see p93*) in the Ghetto is one of the best in town. Most neighbourhoods have a fresh produce market which takes place in the mornings from Monday to Saturday. For an authentic experience head to the newly renovated **Mercato Testaccio** or the

Mercato Testaccio

Nuovo Mercato Esquilino, with its diverse produce (*see p120*). Wine and liquor are sold at the *enoteca* (off-licences) which sometimes also have a bar for downing a glass or two, try **Les Vignerons** (*see p158*) in Trastevere or **Trimani** (*see p122*) in Esquilino.

Cosmetics & perfumes

Beauty superstores Sephora, Limoni and Beauty Point stock big-name ranges plus basic toiletries at non-rip-off prices at many central locations. Popular Italian cosmetics chain Kiko has stores in every corner of the city selling bright, fun products at great prices. For a more refined experience, follow your nose to one of the city's elegant *profumerie* such as **L'Olfattorio** (*see p114*) in the Tridente.

Antiques & homewares

Among the best areas for antiques are **via del Babuino** (Tridente), **via Giulia** (campo de' Fiori) and **via dei Coronari** (piazza Navona). Dealers/restorers thronging **via del Pellegrino** near campo de' Fiori may be cheaper, but quality dips too. For homeware **via delle Botteghe Oscure** and **via Arenula** located between campo de' Fiori and the Ghetto are full of shops that sell linen, fabric, laces and curtain ribbons.

Life's essentials

Most traveller essentials – including bus tickets, stamps and maps – can be found at the *tabacchi* (tobacconists). Identifiable by a large white T on a blue or black background, they not only sell tobacco products but often carry stationery, games and souvenirs. Many also have a postbox outside.

Rome's *edicole* (newsstands) are cute green kiosks which, aside from selling newspapers and magazines, also dispense transport tickets. They are also handy for directions and exchanging large notes for small change. The larger *edicole* will usually sell a selection of international newspapers and magazines.

Opening times

Opening hours aren't as traditional as they once were and now most central-Rome shops operate '*no-stop*'

Fresh market produce

opening hours, from 9.30-10am to 7.30-8pm every day. The occasional independent still clings to the traditional 1-4pm shutdown but will then reopen until 8-8.30pm, and in smaller neighbourhoods family-run businesses will generally close on Sundays.

The majority of clothing shops are closed, or open later, on Monday mornings. Some smaller shops shut down for at least two weeks each summer (generally in August) and almost all are shut for two or three days around the 15 August public holiday. If you're shopping with something particular in mind and you want to avoid finding a particular shop *chiuso per ferie* (closed for holidays), be sure to ring ahead.

Shopping practicalities

Non-EU residents are entitled to a sales tax (IVA) rebate on purchases of goods over €155, providing they are exported unused and bought from a shop with the 'Europe Tax Free' sticker. The shop will give you a receipt and a 'Tax Free Shopping Cheque', which should be stamped by customs before leaving Italy.

When you purchase anything, you should be given a *scontrino* (receipt). If you aren't, ask for it: by law, shops are required to provide one, and they and you are liable for a fine in the (wildly unlikely) event of your being caught without it. Major credit cards are accepted just about everywhere, although it's worth checking before queuing.

The rules on returning items are infuriatingly vague. Faulty goods, obviously, must be refunded or replaced. Most shops will also accept unwanted goods that are returned unused with a receipt within seven days of purchase, though this is not obligatory.

Centro storico

38

Entertainment

The turn of the millennium saw a growing cultural, artistic and musical vibrancy that began to turn the once sleepy Eternal City into a lively European capital. Rome is now back on the music-lover's map after more than a century of neglect. This is thanks, mainly, to the activity and eclectic programming of the Auditorium-Parco della Musica.

Of course, the Auditorium is not the only venue in Rome for music. Many of the more traditional concert halls and locations have also benefited from the surge of energy its development generated, and many boast high-quality programmes with resident and visiting artists. If the nocturnal scene has shown signs of slowing down recently, there's still plenty out there to keep night owls busy. International DJs still pass through Rome's clubs, and some interesting bands can be heard in a host of small clubs and venues. You will, however, need some inside information to avoid the Eurotrash played by the plethora of commercial venues.

Classical music & opera

The **Accademia Nazionale di Santa Cecilia** (www. santacecilia.it) is Italy's national music academy, and plays out its season at the much-admired Auditorium-Parco della Musica (*see p43*).

Many other institutions of all sizes make their voices heard. The **Accademia Filarmonica Romana** (www. filarmonicaromana.org) was founded in 1821 and boasts an illustrious history, with such composers as Rossini, Donizetti, Paganini and Verdi among its founders. It offers a varied programme of chamber music, ancient music, ballet and chamber opera. Another major concert provider is the **Istituzione Universitaria dei Concerti** (IUC, www.concertiiuc.it), founded after World War II to inject some life into Rome's university campus.

The 16th-century **Oratorio del Gonfalone** (*see p94*) hosts a chamber music season. Every concert and recital on the programme, which runs from December to May, seems to have been lovingly chosen to fit the beautiful frescoed surroundings, and to show off the Oratorio's magnificent 18th-century organ.

Rome offers the occasional concert in extraordinary settings. **Roma OperaOmnia** (www.romaoperaomnia.com) organises early music events inside historic sites like the Museo e Cripta dei Cappuccini (*see p107*) and Palazzo Doria Pamphilj (*see p81*). The Quirinale palace (*see p97*) also opens its doors to the public on Sunday mornings for a cycle of chamber music concerts and recitals in the Cappella Paolina.

Rome's opera scene is great for fine settings but not always so consistent where quality is concerned. In summer the breathtaking majesty of the **Terme di Caracalla** (*see p59*) is a unique backdrop and setting for lyrical productions.

Clubbing

Testaccio is one of Rome's liveliest quarters, with nightlife action concentrated around Monte Testaccio: you will be spoilt for choice. Fashionistas head for the *centro storico*: join them in the triangolo della Pace to be part of trendy Roman life. San Lorenzo is less pretentious: drinks are cheaper, and there's always something new going on. Trastevere has lovely alleys packed with friendly, crowded bars. North of the city, the Pigneto district has over the past few years achieved that critical mass of bars, restaurants and trendsters that turns a below-the-radar zone hip.

In the know
Kick-out time

By-laws forcing *centro storico* bars to shut at 2am have been lifted, to the great horror of residents and joy of clubbers. Discos and live venues stay open until the small hours. In Rome, evenings tend to start late and end early. Concerts rarely kick off before 10.30pm and most clubs close after 4am, even on weekdays.

Clubs and discobars generally charge an entrance fee at weekends but not on weekdays; you often have to pay for a *tessera* (membership card) on top of, or sometimes instead of, the entrance fee. At many clubs it pays to check out the venue's website before going along: some events are cheaper – or indeed only accessible – if you put yourself on the list prior to your arrival.

When picking a club, bear in mind that many mainstream clubs serve up commercial house or retro 1980s tunes on Fridays and Saturdays. Established venues like **Goa** (*see p144*) can always be relied upon to offer quality DJ sets.

Film

Rome's legendary film studio, **Cinecittà**, opened with Fascist pomp in 1937 on 99 acres of former farmland south-east of the city. *Roman Holiday* (1953) brought Gregory Peck and Audrey Hepburn, and *The Barefoot Contessa* (1954) drew Ava Gardner and Humphrey Bogart. Meanwhile, Federico Fellini was consecrating his elaborate visions in Teatro 5, the largest of Cinecittà's studio sheds, sandwiching *La Dolce Vita* (1960) between two US blockbusters, *Ben-Hur* (1959) and *Cleopatra* (1963). After its *dolce vita* heyday, however, the studio would mostly churn out TV variety shows and commercials.

Launched over a decade ago, the **Festival Internazionale del Film di Roma** (*see p60*) remains in the second division of international movie meets, but the enthusiasm it creates locally is palpable.

Romans, like most Italians, are keen filmgoers; and though most still like their movies dubbed, there's a growing roster of original-language (*versione originale* – VO) offerings. Arthouse fans are well served by the **Circuito Cinema** chain (www.circuitocinema.com), which controls several first-run outlets, and by the first-run independent **Nuovo Sacher** (*see p158*).

💙 Auditorium-Parco della Musica

Via P de Coubertin 15, Flaminio (06 80241281, www.auditorium. com). Bus 53, 217, 223, 910, M/tram 2. **Box office** *11am-8pm Mon-Sat; 10am-8pm Sun.*

Fifteen years after its much-trumpeted opening, Rome's stunning Auditorium-Parco della Musica continues to take centre stage in the city's cultural life. For anyone who wishes to establish their cultural credentials, it's quite the chic-est place to be seen – once you get there. Strap-hang on the rattly no.2 tram to the leafy residential area north of piazza del Popolo where the lead roofs of the three giant scarab-shaped concert halls rise.

Its programme – which ranges from symphonies to soul, and from jazz to jugglers – has cast its spell over Roman citizens, many of whom have never set foot in a classical-music venue in their lives. All kinds of music – especially jazz – are taken seriously here, as well as poetry and debate, contemporary art, the sciences and cinema. The acoustics – and the catering, of course (this is Italy!) – are beyond reproach.

Each day is packed with events. Sunday is family day, when the Auditorium's genial director Antonio Pappano (when he's not conducting at Covent Garden) can often be found explaining to rapt youngsters what exactly a bassoon is. On select weekend mornings there's a farmers' market.

The Auditorium even has its own Roman villa nestling between starchitect Renzo Piano's trio of cherry-wood halls. If Rome's Auditorium experiment has proved one thing, it's that if you provide a constant diet of excellence, you will never be short of an audience.

The best source of information for what's on, including summer venues, is the local section of daily newspaper *La Repubblica*, while the paper's website hosts www.trovacinema.it with programme details for first-run cinemas all over Italy. Programmes generally change on Fridays.

Live music

To a large extent, the recent rise in the popularity of concert-going in Rome is due to the multifunctional **Auditorium-Parco della Musica** (*see p43*). Rome's vocation for live music is also being prodded along by a string of smallish live clubs, and by the daring programme of goodies on offer at the cool **Teatro Palladium** (*see p144*). Moreover, city hall continues to fund the exciting **RomaEuropa Festival** (*see p60*) and the occasional free mega-concert.

In the summer, don't miss the most atmospheric and relaxing of the summer festivals: **Roma Incontra Il Mondo** (*see p58*), where musicians from around the world play on a lakeside stage beneath the venerable trees of the Villa Ada park. Music ranges from reggae to jazz, in a spectacular yet laidback setting. Beyond music, the festival also showcases political debates, art exhibitions, book readings and workshops.

Theatre & dance

The Roman theatregoing public is becoming ever more sophisticated, its standards raised mainly thanks to some excellent seasonal festivals (in particular the **RomaEuropa Festival**; *see p60*) that bring the best national and international fare to the city's excitement-starved stages. Rome has no lack of performing arts venues: there are some 100 theatres in the city. However, chronic underfunding of theatres has bred turmoil in recent years, from protests to privatisations and closures.

LGBT Rome

A varied but dispersed scene awaits

Italy started recognising same-sex civil unions in 2016, becoming the last major Western country in Europe to do so and overcoming strong opposition from the Catholic Church. Don't expect to find one main gay area or gaybourhood: the scene is pretty scattered throughout the city. A historic gathering point is the so-called 'Gay Street' behind the Colosseum, a 300-metre stretch in via di San Giovanni in Laterano, dotted with gay and gay-friendly bars, restaurants and shops. Chief among them is **Coming Out** (*see p130*), Rome's oldest openly gay bar.

A diverse gay market continues to cater for distinct clienteles, with restaurants, pubs, clubs and bars attracting punters of all ages. Mixed one-nighters allow men and women to have fun under the same roof – and, for that matter, in the open air. The summer event **Gay Village** (*see p57*) has been all the rage since it launched in the early 2000s. The most popular and awaited event of

the year is the **Gay Pride Parade** (www.romapride.it), usually held on the second weekend of June.

Rome has yet to host a permanent lesbian club, but most gay venues and events are also popular with women. The **Venus Rising** (www.facebook.com/venusrisingroma) is the only women-only one-nighter in the capital. It's changed location several times, from Goa, to Planet, to Alibi.

Admission prices to Rome's gay bars and clubs can be confusing. Some places may charge no entrance fee, but will instead oblige you to buy a drink, while others include the first of your drinks in the admission price.

Many venues also ask for a membership card: the Arcigay/Arcilesbica card costs €15, and the Anddos card costs €17 for annual membership (or €10 if you just go to one club). Both cards can be bought at any venue that requires it (you'll need photo ID) and is valid throughout Italy.

Dance has always been the Cinderella of the arts in Italy, notwithstanding a string of influential Italian dancers and choreographers, such as Maria Taglioni and Enrico Cecchetti. An ever-inadequate arts funding package means that many excellent young Italian dancers find fame and fortune abroad, then drop in here occasionally to star as guest artists in Italian corps de ballet. Dance fans should keep an eye on the programme at the **Teatro Olimpico** (www.teatroolimpico.it), which hosts visiting international companies. The **Teatro dell'Opera** (*see p122*) is where the Opera's corps de ballet stretches its limbs. Its seasonal programme invariably includes two or three classics and a handful of contemporary works.

💙 A match at the Stadio Olimpico

Viale dello Stadio Olimpico, Flaminio (06 323 7333). Bus 32, 48, 53, 168, 186, 224, 271, 280, 690, 910, 911, C2, C3/tram 2. **Tickets** *€11-€115. No cards.*

Rome has two first-class football clubs – AS Roma (www.asromacalcio.it) and SS Lazio (www.sslazio.it) – which share the Stadio Olimpico. Set in the Fascist-era Foro Italico, it was originally built for the 1960 Olympic Games before being rebuilt for the 1990 World Cup, and it's definitely showing its age.

When Roma and Lazio play each other tension is thick across the city: derbies are an excuse for *romanisti* and *laziali* to attempt to out-do each other with the wittiest banners, the rudest chants and the most impressive displays of team-colour pyrotechnics. Lazio was founded in 1900, the younger Roma in 1927. Both teams are a solid presence in Serie A. While only the most intrepid visitor may want to attend a Roma-Lazio game, a trip to the stadium is an interesting addition to a trip to Rome for football fanatics: a spectacle of flares and chanting and a touch of atmospheric drama a million miles away from the elegant *bella figura* of the *centro storico*. For some of the atmosphere without the possibility of too much hooliganism, skip the derbies and choose another meet.

As part of measures to curb stadium violence, tickets can no longer be purchased directly from the Stadio Olimpico box office. Get them online from www.listicket.it, or from registered ticket sellers through the team websites; other sites are not always reliable. Tickets are personal and non-transferable. You can buy tickets for a limited number of other people but you will need a photo-ID document (some outlets will accept photocopies) for each ticket-holder. Each must then present photo ID (corresponding, obviously, with the name on the ticket) at the turnstiles when they get to the stadium. Important matches sell out quickly. All seats have a decent view but bear in mind the cheap seats in the Curva are favoured by the 'Ultras' and can be extremely rowdy.

It's not possible to visit the stadium outside games, but a stroll around the arena is still a worthwhile trip.

Roma fans

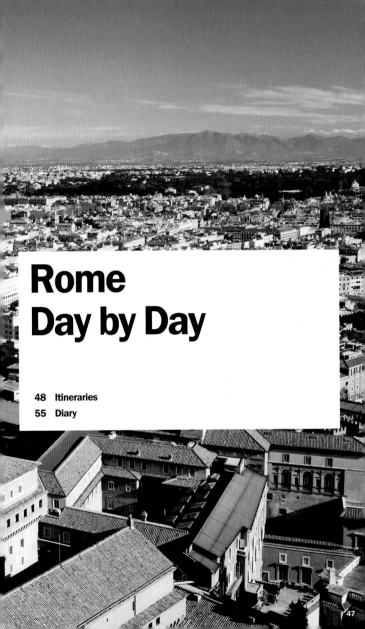

Rome
Day by Day

Itineraries

Whether you're here for a quick weekend break or planning a serious museum marathon, these itineraries will help you to make the most of your visit. However, be prepared for your carefully hatched plans to go awry; time may pass all too quickly as you people-watch with a *caffé* at a pavement table, or dawdle over dinner in a traditional trattoria.

▶ *Budgets include transport, meals and admission prices, but not accommodation and shopping.*

ESSENTIAL WEEKEND

Rome in two days
Budget €400 for two
Getting around Walking

DAY 1

Morning

Ancient Rome permeates the modern city in many ways, and getting to grips with the very old will help you appreciate the many layers added through ensuing centuries to make the glorious jumble that greets you today.

An overview shows the extent to which the hub of the ancient city is still with us. Climb the steep steps up to the forecourt of **Santa Maria in Aracoeli** (*see p74*), from where you can take a lift to the very top of the white **Vittoriano** monument in piazza Venezia (*see p73*). If it's a clear day, you'll feel you can see forever.

Cross to the south-east side of the Michelangelo-designed piazza del Campidoglio and enjoy the view over the **Foro Romano** (*see p68*) as you make your way to its entrance: queues here are generally less daunting than at the Colosseum (one ticket covers both). You'll have your work cut out for you to see the whole site before lunch. But it's worth slogging up the **Palatine hill** (also included on the ticket) for another wild view over Rome – not to mention a little welcome shade – at the verdant **Horti Farnesiani** gardens.

Afternoon

At the piazza Venezia end of the Imperial Fora, **Terre e Domus** (*see p74*) serves produce and wine from Rome's surrounding Lazio region; try to get a table overlooking Trajan's marvellous column.

If you've been very efficient – and if you've pre-booked – you may make the 2pm or 2.30pm visit in English of the fascinating **Domus Romane** (*see p65*). If not, press on.

Stroll up past **Mercati di Traiano** (*see p69*), then down salita del Grillo and pretty via degli Ibernesi for an unexpectedly quiet glimpse of Rome's medieval heart in the Monti district. You might want to tack along via della Madonna dei Monti to grab a gelato at **Fatamorgana** (*see p125*) to keep energy levels up before tackling the **Colosseum** (*see p70*).

Evening

Ready for *aperitivi*? Head back into the warren of streets in Monti to join tipplers at one of the innumerable wine bars, such as **Ai Tre Scalini** (*see p125*). If you've got the energy, head to the outskirts of town to the stunning **Auditorium-Parco della Musica** (*see p43*) for a cultural feast, whatever your music taste.

DAY 2

Morning

The complicated geography of Rome's *centro storico* reflects the city's history. Roman foundations were used for medieval re-building; urban planning sprees by Renaissance popes remain intact; baroque *piazze* follow the lines of ancient constructions. The *centro* is conveniently compact and walkable.

The **Spanish Steps** (*see p110*) are a grandiose monument, especially after a recent restoration. At the foot of the steps, the **Keats-Shelley Memorial House** (*see p108*) will be of interest to lovers of Romantic poetry.

Via del Babuino is lined with chic antique and furnishing shops; running parallel to the east and far less trafficked, via Margutta was once full of artists' studios, one of which featured as Gregory Peck's bachelor pad in the movie classic *Roman Holiday*, and is now occupied by chi-chi galleries and high-rent pieds-à-terre. Via del Babuino emerges in piazza del Popolo with its obelisk, magnificent gate in the Roman wall and the Caravaggio-filled church of **Santa Maria del Popolo** (*see p110*).

With some art under your belt, you deserve a coffee. Elegant café **Rosati** (*see p113*) is a Roman classic.

Via Ripetta leads out of the square and along to the **Museo dell'Ara Pacis** (*see p109*). Besides the beautiful Altar of Peace, this museum has exhibits explaining the layout of the ancient city.

Fontana dei Quattro Fiumi
(Gian Lorenzo Bernini, 1651)

Afternoon

Head down via della Croce for a cheap and cheerful – and very tasty – pasta lunch at **Pastificio Guerra** (*see p111*). Continue back along via Ripetta, which becomes via della Scrofa. In piazza **Sant'Agostino**, the church (*see p77*) of the same name contains another superb Caravaggio. And if you still have an appetite for this bad boy of the baroque, his St Matthew series in the nearby church of **San Luigi dei Francesi** (*see p83*) is a must.

Piazza Navona (*see p80*), which follows the lines of Emperor Domitian's great stadium, merits a saunter; Gianlorenzo Bernini's **Fontana dei Quattro Fiumi** dominates the space.

Evening

Join the crowd at **Il Vinaietto** (*see p92*) in campo de' Fiori – a fantastic place for an *aperitivo*. **Armando al Pantheon** (*see p82*) is a lively place for dinner. Skip over to the nearby **Shari Vari Playhouse** (*see p86*) to dance the night away.

FAMILY DAY OUT

Keeping the kids amused
Budget €130 for two adults, two children
Getting around Walking, bus

Morning

Rome doesn't go out of its way to entertain your children. There's a zoo but it's nothing to write home about. What it does offer is endless curiosities and hidden surprises, each of which has a fascinating tale behind it. Then, when even those fail... there are parks and ice-creams (*see p31* Gelato).

Begin in **piazza Navona** (*see p80*) – a magnificent space with splashing fountains, street 'artists' and tales of artistic rivalry. Remind kids that summer entertainment until the mid 19th century included flooding this square so overheated Romans could cool their feet off. If you're here over the Christmas period, it will be full of stalls and merry-go-rounds.

A short walk eastwards, the **Pantheon** (*see p80*) is that rare thing: an ancient Roman building in its gob-smacking entirety. Yes, that hole in the roof is open: come during a storm if you have any doubts. In neighbouring piazza della Maddalena is a handy branch of **Il Gelato di San Crispino** (*see p98*), Rome's original gourmet ice-cream maker.

It's worth tacking south here for a look at a most unexpected bit of the ancient world. Where via del Gesù meets via Pie di Marmo there's a massive sandal-clad marble foot. Occasionally pranksters paint its toenails bright colours.

Not far away, the church of **Sant'Ignazio di Loyola** (*see 82*) was built without a dome when neighbours complained that a cupola would ruin their view. So a fake one was painted on the ceiling. The optical illusion only works from one (marked) spot though: stand on it and the pretend-dome goes from distressingly wonky to perfect.

Pantheon

Tempio di Esculapio, Villa Borghese

Afternoon

Cross busy via del Corso to via di San Marcello. The **Antica Birreria Peroni** (*see p98*) is a big, noisy, inexpensive place to refuel for an afternoon's exploring. And it's a short stroll from the **Fontana di Trevi** (Trevi Fountain, *see p95*) where throwing three coins into the water guarantees a return to the city... if you can make it to the fountain's edge through the crowds.

You might want to hop on one of the buses plying via del Tritone to the next stop on this itinerary: the **Cripta dei Cappuccini** (*see p107*) – not the frothy coffee but the Capuchine friars' church and museum. Note that this is not for the over-sensitive. After an exhibition glorifying the deeds of this minor Franciscan order, visitors reach the crypt – a burial-ground with limited space where older bones have been dug up over the centuries and arranged in curlicues around the walls.

After which you'll be ready for the leafy spaces of the **Villa Borghese** gardens (*see p100*). Walk (or take a bus) to the park's entrance at the top of via Veneto. Once there, you'll find bikes for hire, swings, a lake with rowing boats and acres of room for letting off steam.

BUDGET BREAK

For the euro-conscious visitor
Budget €70 for two
Getting around Walking

Morning

So many of Rome's wonders are out there in the open for all to see that it's easy to feel you've 'done' the city without spending a *centesimo*. There's no charge to enter even the most masterpiece-packed churches. And the *centro* is sufficiently compact to navigate without much recourse to (its admittedly really very inexpensive) public transport.

Begin in piazza Santa Maria in Trastevere, admiring the 13th-century mosaics in the **church** (*see p151*). A couple of blocks to the south of here, the morning **market** in piazza di San Cosimato is the perfect place for grabbing some picnic lunch ingredients and lots of Roman atmosphere.

Across thundering viale di Trastevere, the church of **San Francesco a Ripa** (*see p149*) has one of Bernini's most sensuous statues (*see p156* Bernini's Babes) and the cell where St Francis stayed on a visit in 1229. **Santa Cecilia in Trastevere** (*see p152*) conceals a spectacular fresco by Pietro Cavallini (open until 12.30pm): well worth paying €2.50 to see.

Santa Maria in Trastevere

Santa Maria in Trastevere

Afternoon

A wander through the maze of streets will lead you to the **Tiber Island** (*see p86*): down on the water-level promenade, the din of rushing water replaces traffic sounds, making it a fine place for your picnic.

North of the island, descend from the end of via del Portico d'Ottavia for a close-up look at the **Teatro di Marcello** (*see p89*) from the rather neglected, rather pretty archaeological area that skirts it.

Via Petroselli descends to **Santa Maria in Cosmedin** (*see p90)*, with its hand-munching 'mouth of truth' and gorgeous Romanesque interior.

From here, continue south, taking time to stop and admire the vast proportions of the **Circo Massimo** (*see p64*). Climb the well-heeled residential **Aventine hill** by which time a sit-down in orange tree-filled **Parco Savello**, with its glorious view over the city, will be most welcome. Right next door, starkly beautiful **Santa Sabina** (*see p134*) is well worth a visit. And don't forget to peer through the keyhole in piazza dei Cavalieri di Malta.

Back down the hill, still further south, lies the Testaccio district where the *aperitivo* spread at **L'Oasi della Birra** (*see p140*) on central piazza Testaccio is remarkably generous. If that doesn't satisfy your hunger, the pizzas at nearby **Da Remo** (*see p138*) are as good as they are cheap. On a Sunday evening, Testaccio's salsa club **Caruso Café de Oriente** (*see p143*), offers free entry and a friendly atmosphere.

Tiber Island

Diary

The Romans, perennial fun-seekers, have never needed much of an excuse for a knees-up; in ancient times a whopping 150 days were set aside every year for R&R. Important religious holidays have different effects on the city (the Assumption on 15 August shuts it down; Easter brings hordes of pilgrims). Districts of Rome hold smaller-scale celebrations of their own patron saints in their own way, from calorific blowouts to extravagant firework displays. Occasional large-scale city-run events make ample use of Rome's endless supply of photogenic venues.

Spring

Spring in Rome can be dreamily warm. Or it can be weirdly wintery. Usually it's a bit of both. With glorious wisteria flowers cascading over walls and pergolas, and the Judas trees in bloom, the city is at its lushest. You might find the *centro* completely car-free for the Rome Marathon, or with a host of normally shuttered *palazzi* and churches open for the Giornate FAI. Easter brings throngs for religious festivities, including the pope's Stations of the Cross in the Colosseum during Settimana Santa on Good Friday.

8 Mar Festa della Donne

Rome celebrates International Women's Day by offering women free entry to the state-run museums and attractions.

9 Mar Festa di Santa Francesca Romana

This feast day is a rare opportunity to visit this medieval nunnery; Romans have cars blessed at the church of Santa Francesca Romana in the Roman Forum.

16 Mar Palazzo Massimo alle Colonne

Once-a-year opening of the patrician Massimi family's fabulous palace (Corso Vittorio Emanuele 141, 8am-1pm), on the feast of San Filippo Neri.

❤ Late Mar Maratona della Città di Roma

www.maratonadiroma.it
The annual Maratona della Città di Roma attracts some big-name runners, hordes of amateur pavement-pounders and flocks of locals and visitors just happy to observe the sporting activity along city streets marvellously empty of motor vehicles. A party atmosphere prevails as runners set off jubilantly south... then limp back through the

Natale di Roma

centro storico to the finishing line. The serious race begins and ends in via dei Fori Imperiali.

Late Mar Giornate FAI

www.giornatefai.it
For one weekend each spring, private and institutional owners of interesting historic properties throw open their spectacular interiors and gardens to the public.

❤ Late Mar-early Apr Settimana Santa & Pasqua

www.vatican.va
Tourists and pilgrims flood into the city on the Saturday before Palm Sunday, cramming inside St Peter's square for the open-air Mass. The non-stop services of Holy Week peak in the pope's Stations of the Cross (*via Crucis*) and Mass at the Colosseum late on the evening of Good Friday. On *Pasquetta* (Easter Monday) Romans feast upon specialities such as *torta pasqualina* (cheesy bread, with salami and hard-boiled eggs) and *fave e pecorino* (broad beans and cheese).

Late Mar/early Apr Mostra delle Azalee

Spring arrives early in Rome, bringing masses of blooms. Some 3,000 vases of vividly hued azaleas decorate the Spanish Steps.

❤ 21 Apr Natale di Roma

www.natalidiroma.it
Not all cities celebrate their birthday... but Rome, 'born' in 753 BC, is no ordinary city. The bulk of the festivities take place around the ancient sites with costumed processions, gladiator fighting, historical re-enactments and enormous amounts of fireworks.

25 Apr Festa della Liberazione

This public holiday commemorates the liberation of Italy by Allied forces at the end of World War II.

Apr/May Settimana della Cultura

www.beniculturali.it
For Cultural Heritage Week, state-owned museums and monuments open to the public without charge.

1 May Primo Maggio

www.primomaggio.net
Trades unions organise a huge, free rock concert for May Day, which is traditionally held in front of San Giovanni in Laterano.

Early May Campionato Internazionale di Tennis

www.internazionalibnlditalia.it
The Italian Open tennis tournament takes place at the Foro Italico, next-door to the Olympic Stadium.

Late May Concorso Ippico Internazionale di Piazza di Siena

www.piazzadisiena.com
The city's ultra-smart four-day show-jumping event in piazza di Siena, Villa Borghese.

Late May/early June Pentecoste

Exactly 50 days after Easter, the Pentecost mass at the Pantheon spectacularly concludes with tens of thousands of red rose petals scattered through the oculus in the dome upon the heads of attendees.

Late May-Sept Art City

www.art-city.it
A circuit of events to promote art, architecture, performing arts and literature.

Summer

July and August in Rome will test the tolerance of the greatest heat-lover, but there's respite to be found in the city's leafy parks and in a fantastic series of outdoor evening concerts. A vast choice of goodies in lovely venues around Rome comes under the Estate Romana summer entertainment umbrella.

June-July Festival delle Letterature

www.festivaldelleletterature.it
The floodlit basilica of Maxentius in the Roman Forum provides a theatrical backdrop to readings by some of the most important names in contemporary literature.

2 June Festa della Repubblica

The date on which Italy became a republic in 1946 is celebrated with appropriate pomp and circumstance by a military parade along via dei Fori Imperiali.

Early June-early Sept Gay Village

www.gayvillage.it
An all-summer open-air bonanza with bars, restaurants, live acts, discos and cinema, for boys and girls.

Early June-end Sept Estate Romana
*www.estateromana.
comune.roma.it*
The city comes alive with music
from local bands, films are shown
on outdoor screens late into the
night, and cultural events take
place in venues around town.

❤ Mid June-early Aug Roma Incontra il Mondo
www.villaada.org
Musicians from around the world
play on a lakeside stage beneath
the venerable trees of the Villa
Ada park. This multicultural series
of events is an institution of the
Roman summer. Music ranges from
reggae to jazz, in a spectacular yet
laidback setting. Beyond music,
the festival also showcases political
debates, art exhibitions, book
readings and workshops.

Mid June-early Sept Just Music Festival
www.justmusicfestival.it
Started in 2015, and already a
smash due to A-list headliners such
as Björk, Massive Attack, Public
Enemy, Burt Bacharach, Pet Shop
Boys and Fatboy Slim.

29 June Santi Pietro e Paolo
Street fair outside St Paul's basilica
and mass at St Peter's for the feast
day of Rome's patron saints.

❤ Mid July Festa de' Noantri
www.festadenoantri.it
Trastevere's residents celebrate
its humble working-class origins
with gusto during the Festa
de' Noantri. Two weeks of arts
events and street performances
culminate with fireworks on the
closing night.

Mid July-mid Aug International Chamber Ensemble
icensemble.it
Chamber and symphonic music,
as well as opera, takes place in a
splendid example of Renaissance
architecture: the courtyard of
Sant'Ivo alla Sapienza.

1 Aug Festa delle Catene
The chains that are said to have
bound St Peter are displayed in
a special mass at San Pietro in
Vincoli dedicated to him.

5 Aug Festa della Madonna della Neve
A blizzard of rose petals flutters
down on festive mass-goers
at Santa Maria Maggiore to
commemorate a miraculous
snowfall on this day in AD 358.

10 Aug Notte di San Lorenzo
Nuns distribute bread and candles
on this, the night of shooting stars,
in San Lorenzo in Panisperna.

15 Aug Ferragosto
Rome closes down for the feast of
the Assumption. Many locals head
to the coast for the long weekend.

Autumn
November is tops for average
monthly rainfall in the Eternal
City, but occasional stolen days of
summery warmth and sunshine
make up for the damp. Visiting
crowds begin to thin at this
time of year. But there are still
outstanding offerings, including
the RomaEuropa Festival with its
programme of world-class avant-
garde theatre and dance.

Sept Taste of Rome
www.tasteofroma.it
The city's top chefs unite in the
gardens of the Auditorium-Parco
della Musica for this gastronomic
festival where visitors can
participate in courses and demos
by Rome's culinary stars.

💜 Opera at Terme di Caracalla

*Terme di Caracalla (see p135 M15, 06 3996 7700, www.ticketone.it). **Box office** at Teatro Costanzi (see p122) or 1hr30mins before show start. **Tickets** €25-€100.*

Born as a cultural policy experiment in 1937, the Opera di Roma's season at the Baths of Caracalla is now a highlight of the Roman summer, staging world-class performances amid colossal ancient ruins and cool evening breezes.

The programme starts in mid to late June and ends in early August, and packs in over 20 opera shows, between opening nights and encore performances.

The atmosphere and the dress code are less formal than a traditional theatre setting, which, together with the crowd-pleasing calendar, have helped promote these initiatives among a wider and younger audience.

The opera most intrinsically associated with the site (and most represented) is Giuseppe Verdi's *Aida*: its triumphal marches, with horses and camels, perfectly fit the monumentality of the stage and its surroundings.

The stage is placed in front of the caldarium, slightly removed from the ruins which serve as a dramatic backdrop with cinematic lighting. On each side, two screens project subtitles both in Italian and English, while the orchestra plays live from the pit in front of it.

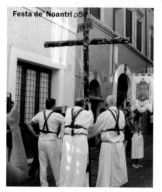
Festa de' Noantri *p58*

Sept-Nov RomaEuropa Festival
www.romaeuropa.net
Rome's cutting-edge performing arts festival offers music, dance and theatre, with an eclectic mix of international acts and emerging young local talent.

Oct-Nov Festival Internazionale del Film di Roma
www.romacinemafest.it
Ten days of screenings and movie-related happenings at Rome's international film festival, held at the Auditorium-Parco della Musica.

1-2 Nov Ognissanti/Giornata dei Defunti
Otherwise known as Tutti santi, All Saints' Day (*Ognissanti*) is followed by *La commemorazioni dei defunti* (or *Tutti i morti*), when the pope celebrates Mass at Verano Cemetery in the San Lorenzo district.

Winter
When the northerly *tramontana* wind whips down from snow-covered mountains, Rome can be icy. It can also be brilliantly blue: if you can take the cold, the view from the top of the Vittoriano on a crystal winter's day is unbeatable.

So wrap up warm if you're coming to enjoy the Christmas celebrations, or, later in the season, the Carnevale fun (though it should be said, this is a minor event here compared to Viareggio and Venice). Until the Easter rush brings new-season crowds, a relatively quiet Rome may seem very intimate.

8 Dec Immacolata Concezione
In Piazza di Spagna the pope blesses a wreath and sends a fireman up his ladder to hang it on the statue of Mary for the feast of the Immaculate Conception.

25-26 Dec Natale & Santo Stefano
Nativity scenes in churches; Christmas fair in piazza Navona.

31 Dec San Silvestro
New Year's Eve events around the city often include free concerts (check www.comune.roma.it for details), much street partying and fireworks.

1 Jan Capodanno
New Year's Day.

6 Jan Epifania – La Befana
Tradition has it that on the eve of Epiphany Italian children receive a visit from an old witch (*la befana*). Piazza Navona hosts a Christmas fair, with market stalls peddling sweets and cheap tat.

17 Jan Festa di Sant'Antonio Abate
Romans commemorate the feast of the protector of animals, Sant'Antonio Abate, in the church of Sant'Eusebio... and get their pets blessed.

Feb/Mar Carnevale
In the Middle Ages, this riotous last fling before the rigours of Lent was celebrated with wild abandon on Monte Testaccio. Nowadays, kids dress up and throw confetti.

Julius Caesar, Via dei Fori Imperiali

Rome
by Area

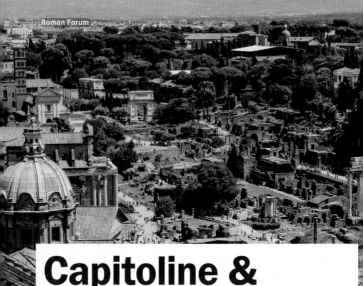

Capitoline & Palatine

In the eighth century BC, a collection of grass huts was built on a hill overlooking the marshy flood plain of a tributary of the River Tiber. In the following century, the land was drained and the settlement expanded down the slopes into what would become the Roman Forum. A thousand years of expansion later, this had become the heart of the ancient world's most powerful city, the capital of an empire that stretched from Scotland to the Sahara. The huts were replaced with splendid Imperial palaces (the Palatine); great temples were constructed on the neighbouring hill (the Capitoline), and emperors kept public discontent to a minimum with gory entertainment in the Colosseum.

The Capitoline (Campidoglio) was the site of two major temples: to Jupiter Capitolinus – chunks of which are visible inside the **Musei Capitolini** – and to Juno Moneta, 'giver of advice', where the church of **Santa Maria in Aracoeli** now stands. The splendid piazza that today tops the Capitoline was designed in the 1530s by Michelangelo; the best approach is via the steps called the *cordonata*, also by Michelangelo, with two Roman statues of the mythical twins Castor and Pollux at the top. The building directly opposite is Rome's city hall; on either side are the *palazzi* housing the Capitoline Museums. The equestrian statue of Marcus Aurelius that stands in the centre is a computer-generated replica; the second-century gilded bronze original is inside the museum.

At the bottom of the *cordonata* is **piazza Venezia**, a dizzying roundabout dominated by the **Vittoriano** (*see p73*), a vast piece of nationalistic bombast. Across the piazza, the high-tech display on genteel ancient living in the **Domus Romane** – a Roman house excavated below the provincial government HQ Palazzo Valentini – is excellent (*see p65*). On the west side, **Palazzo Venezia** (via del Plebiscito 118, www.museopalazzovenezia. beniculturali.it) houses a hotchpotch of artefacts, from

➔ **Getting around**

This area is very walkable and densely packed with some of Rome's most celebrated sites. From piazza Venezia make your way south-west to visit the Forum and continue to the Palatine and Colosseum. Alternatively, take metro line B to Colosseo and start at the Colosseum before walking the short distance to the entrance to the Palatine/Forum site on via di San Gregorio.

terracotta models by Bernini to medieval decorative art. Next to it is **San Marco**, a church with a noticeable Venetian flavour, founded in the fourth century but remodelled in the 15th century for Pope Paul II.

South from the Capitoline hill, meanwhile, lies what is arguably the world's most extraordinary concentration of archaeological riches, around the **Palatino** and **Foro Romano** (Roman Forum) below. It was from here that the Republic – and later the Empire – was run and justice administered, in grandiose buildings around richly decorated public squares. Flanking the Roman Forum, the **Imperial Fora** were developed in the following centuries by successive emperors, as they strove to assert their own importance and munificence. These rulers kept public discontent at bay with gory diversions and heart-stopping sports at the **Colosseo** (*see p70*) and the **Circo Massimo**.

Sights & museums

Carcere Mamertino

Clivio Argentario 1 (06 698 961, www.tullianum.org). See p63 Getting around. **Open** *Oct-Mar 8.30am-3.30pm daily. Apr-Sept 9am-6pm daily.* **Admission** *€10; free under-10s.* **Map** *p66 K10.*
Just off the steps leading from the Capitoline hill down to the Roman Forum is the Mamertine Prison (aka Carcer Tullianum). Into this prison went anyone thought to pose a threat to the security of the ancient Roman state. A dank, dark, tiny underground dungeon, its lower level (built in the fourth century BC) was once only accessible through a hole in the floor. Innumerable prisoners starved to death here, or drowned when the water table rose and flooded the cell. The most famous of the prison's residents, according to legend, were Saints Peter and Paul. Peter caused a miraculous well to bubble up downstairs in order to baptise his prison guards, whom he converted. Once an atmospheric minor stopover, the prison has now become a rather tawdry 'audio-visual experience' which takes about an hour.

Circo Massimo

Via del Circo Massimo. Metro Circo Massimo/bus 75, 80, 81, 118, 160, 628, 673,715/tram 3. **Map** *p66 K13.*
The oldest and largest of Rome's ancient arenas, the Circus Maximus hosted chariot races from at least the fourth century BC. It was rebuilt by Julius Caesar to hold as many as 300,000 people. Races involved up to 12 rigs of four horses each; the first charioteer to complete the seven treacherous, sabotage-ridden laps around the *spina* (ridge in the centre) won a hefty prize and the adoration of the populace. The circus was also used for the ever-popular fights with wild animals, and the occasional large-scale execution.

❤ Domus Romane

*Piazza Foro Traiano 85 (06 32 810, www.palazzovalentini.it). See p63 Getting around. **Open** 9am-6.30pm Mon, Wed-Sun. **Admission** €12; €8 reductions (plus €1.50 booking fee). Pre-booking obligatory. **Map** p66 K9.*

Discovered beneath the offices of the government of the Metropolitan City of Rome (formerly the Province of Rome until recent modifications to local government), the excavations of the Domus Romane offer a glimpse into the richly decorated houses of well-heeled citizens of the Roman Empire.

Since the inauguration in 2010, modern technology has been used with great success to bring back to life the domestic surroundings and lifestyles of the movers and shakers of ancient Rome, a stone's throw from their public lives in the Forum. Beneath the street level, surviving traces of mosaics, multi-coloured marble floors, and wall paintings provide the point of departure for projected reconstructions, detailing the various periods of the buildings' histories.

The visit also includes a great view and virtual reconstruction of Trajan's Forum, including his column, libraries, and the Basilica Ulpia (law court). The column is a spectacular monument of triumph carved with a relief that records Trajan's conquest of Dacia (modern-day Romania), culminating in the death of King Decebalus.

The site is definitely the best that central Rome offers for putting the ancient world in context – a veritable time machine.

Visits in English begin at 9.30am, 1.30pm, 2pm, and 2.30pm and advance booking is essential. Any disabled visitors or those with mobility difficulties should make this known when booking as there is provision for assistance.

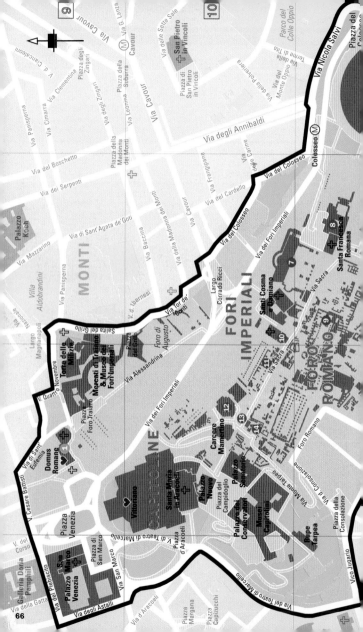

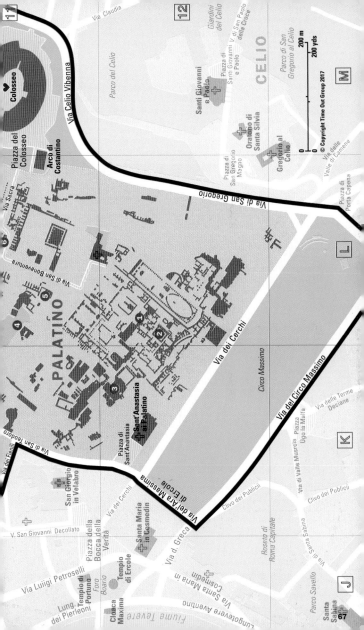

❤ Foro Romano & Palatino

*Via di San Gregorio 30/Largo della Salaria Vecchia 5/6 (06 3996 7700, archeoroma.beniculturali.it). Metro Colosseo/bus 53, 75, 80, 81, 85, 87, 117, 673, 810/tram 3. **Open** daily, see p70 Colosseo. **Admission** (incl Forum & Palatine) €12; €7.50 reductions; free under-18s. **Map** p66 K11.*

Numbers (❶) refer to the map on p66.

Palatino

Legend relates that a basket holding twin babes Romulus and Remus was found in the swampy area near the Tiber to the west of here, and that the twins had been suckled by a she-wolf in a cave. In 753 BC, having murdered his brother, Romulus scaled the Palatine hill and founded Rome. Archaeological evidence shows that proto-Romans had settled on il Palatino a century or more before that.

> **In the know**
> **Ticket advice**
>
> The Forum, Palatine and Colosseum are visited on the same ticket: one entrance to the Palatine and Forum (counted as a single site), and one to the Colosseum over a two-day period. Save yourself a wait and buy tickets at the quieter via di San Gregorio Forum & Palatine entrance. Alternatively, pre-purchase your ticket (€14 including booking fee) from www.coopculture.it.
>
> If you already have a ticket, enter on via di San Gregorio or by the Mamertine Prison on the Capitoline hill. On entering, queues for security are divided between ticket holders and non, but can be equally long, especially at weekends and in high summer. The best advice is to pre-buy tickets and arrive between 8.45 and 9.30am, or in the last hour or two before closing.

Later, the Palatine became the Beverly Hills of the ancient city, where movers and shakers built palaces. On the southern side of the Palatine are the remains of vast Imperial dwellings, including Emperor Domitian's *Domus augustana* ❶, with what may have been a private stadium in the garden. Next door, the Museo Palatino ❷ charts the history of the Palatine from the eighth century BC.

Immediately west of here is the House of Augustus (Domus augusti ❸) where you can visit four of its spectacularly frescoed rooms.

With Rome's decline, the Palatine became a rural backwater; in the 1540s, much of the hill was bought by Cardinal Alessandro Farnese, who created a pleasure villa. His gardens, the Horti Farnesiani ❹, are still a lovely, leafy – if unkempt – place to wander on a hot day. Beneath the gardens, the *cryptoporticus* ❺ is a semi-subterranean tunnel built by Emperor Nero.

Foro Romano

During the early years of the Republic, this was an open space with shops and a few temples, and it sufficed; but by the second century BC, ever-conquering Rome needed to convey authority and wealth. Out went the food stalls; in came law courts, offices and immense public buildings with grandiose decorations. The Foro Romano was the symbolic heart of the Empire.

Seen as one descends from the Palatine, the Forum is framed by the Arch of Titus (AD 81; ❻), built to celebrate the sack of Jerusalem. To the right are the towering ruins of the Basilica of Maxentius ❼, completed in AD 312. Beyond this, towards the Colosseum, is the massive second-century Temple of Venus and Roma ❽.

Backtracking, on the left is the house of the Vestal Virgins ❾. Along the via Sacra, the Forum's high street, are (right) the great columns of the Temple of Antoninus and Faustina ❿; the giant Basilica Emilia (right; ⓫) – once a bustling place for administration, courts and business; the Curia ⓬, the home of the Senate, begun in 45 BC by Julius Caesar; and the Arch of Septimius Severus ⓭, built in AD 203. Beside the arch are the remains of an Imperial rostrum ⓮, from where Mark Antony supposedly asked Romans to lend him their ears.

❤ Mercati di Traiano & Museo dei Fori Imperiali

Via IV Novembre 94 (06 6992 3521, www.mercatiditraiano.it).
Bus 40, 60, 64, 70, 117, 170, H.
Open *9.30am-7.30pm Tue-Sun.*
Admission *€13; €11 reductions.*
Map *p66 K9.*

When the Roman Forum became too small to cope with the ever-growing city, emperors combined philanthropy with propaganda and created new *fora* of their own in what is now known collectively as the Fori imperiali (Imperial Fora). Along the via dei Fori Imperiali (sliced cavalierly through the ruins in the early 20th century) are five separate fora – each one built by a different emperor.

Excavations in the 1990s unearthed great swathes of this archaeological space. It's not easy to interpret the ruins, most of which are visible from street level, but a pre-emptive visit to the scale model of the *fori* at the visitors' centre will help.

The best-preserved and unquestionably most impressive part of the complex is Trajan's Forum and the towering remains of Trajan's markets behind. Two years of restoration work gave Trajan's markets a gloriously cleaned-up interior, a beautifully lit collection of marble artefacts and a new name: the Museo dei Fori Imperiali. Moreover, it opened up atmospheric stretches of the ancient streets and medieval buildings surrounding the market itself.

Entering Trajan's markets from via IV Novembre, the first room is the Great Hall, a large space possibly used for the corn dole in antiquity and often hosting exhibitions today. To the south of the Great Hall are the open-air terraces at the top of the spectacular Great Hemicycle, built in AD 107. To the east of the Great Hall, stairs lead down to the so-called via Biberatica, an ancient street flanked by remarkably well-preserved shops. More stairs lead down through the various layers of the Great Hemicycle, where most of the 150 shops or offices are still in perfect condition, many with door jambs still showing the grooves of the shutters.

Below the markets, at the piazza Venezia end of via dei Fori Imperiali, is Trajan's Forum, laid out in the early second century AD. It's dominated by Trajan's Column (AD 113), with detailed spiralling reliefs showing victories over Dacia (modern-day Romania). The rectangular foundation to the south of Trajan's column, where several imposing granite columns still stand, was the basilica Ulpia, an administrative building.

Across the road from Trajan's Forum, Caesar's Forum was the earliest of the Fori Imperiali, built in 51 BC by Julius Caesar. Three columns of the Venus generatrix temple have been rebuilt. Back on the same side as Trajan's Forum, Augustus's Forum was inaugurated in 2 BC. Three columns from the Temple of Mars Ultor still stand, as does the towering wall separating the forum

❤ **Colosseo**

Piazza del Colosseo (06 0608/06 3996 7700, www.coopculture.it). Metro Colosseo/bus 53, 75, 80, 81, 85, 87, 117, 673, 810/tram 3. **Open** *late Oct-mid Feb 8.30am-4.30pm. Mid Feb-mid Mar 8.30am-5pm. Mid Mar-end Mar 8.30am-5.30pm. End Mar-Aug 8.30am-7.15pm. Sept 8.30am-7pm. Oct 8.30am-6.30pm daily. Last entry 1hr before close.* **Admission** *(incl Forum & Palatine) €12; €7.50 reductions; free under-18s.* **Map** *p66 M11.*

Vespasian began building the Colosseum in AD 72 on the site of a newly drained lake in the grounds of Nero's Domus Aurea. Properly called the Amphitheatrum Flavium (Flavian amphitheatre), the building was later known as the Colosseum not because it was big, but because of a gold-plated colossal statue, now lost, that stood alongside. The arena was about 500 metres (a third of a mile) in circumference, could seat over 50,000 people – some scholars estimate capacity crowds numbered as many as 87,000 – and could be filled or emptied in ten minutes through a network of *vomitoria* (exits) that remains the basic model for stadium design today.

Nowhere in the world was there a larger or more glorious setting for mass slaughter. If costly, highly trained professional gladiators were often spared at the end of their bloody bouts, not so the slaves, criminals and assorted unfortunates roped in to do battle against them. And just to make sure there was no cheating, when the combat was over, corpses

were prodded with red-hot pokers to ensure no one tried to elude fate by playing dead.

It was not only human life that was sacrificed to Roman blood-lust: wildlife, too, was legitimate fodder. Animals fought animals; people fought animals. On occasion, however, the tables turned and the animals got to kill the people: a common sentence in the Roman criminal justice system was *damnatio ad bestias*, when thieves and other miscreants were turned loose, unarmed, into the arena, where hungry beasts would be waiting for them.

Entrance to the Colosseum was free for all, although a rigid seating plan kept the sexes and social classes in their rightful places. The emperor and senators

occupied marble seats in the front rows; on benches higher up were the priests and magistrates, then above them the foreign diplomats. Women were confined to the upper reaches – all of them, that is, except the pampered Vestal Virgins, who had privileged seats right near the emperor.

By the sixth century, with the fall of the Roman Empire, bloodsports in the Colosseum were less impressive: chickens pecked each other to death here. The Roman authorities discontinued the games and the Colosseum became little more than a quarry for the stone and marble used to build and decorate Roman *palazzi*. This irreverence toward the Colosseum was not halted until the mid 18th century, when Pope Benedict XIV consecrated it as a church. For another century it was left to its own devices, becoming home to hundreds of species of flowers and plants, as well as to a fair number of Roman homeless. After Unification in 1870 the flora was yanked up and the squatters kicked out.

The hypogeum (underground cells), where animals were held and combatants warmed up, and the upper tier of the stalls in the Colosseum can now be visited on guided tours, including night-time tours affording fantastic views over the lights of the city from the top of the arena. Guided tours cost €9 (under-12s free) and must be booked in advance (through the website above).

Marforio (Oceanus), Musei Capitolini

from what was the sprawling Suburra slum. Nerva's Forum (AD 97) lies mainly beneath via dei Fori Imperiali. On the south side of the road, Vespasian's Forum (AD 75) was home to the Temple of Pax (Peace), part of which is now incorporated into the church of Santi Cosma e Damiano. Maps put up on a wall here by Mussolini show how Rome ruled the world.

❤ Musei Capitolini

Piazza del Campidoglio 1 (06 0608, www.museicapitolini.org). See p63 Getting around. **Open** *9am-7.30pm Tue-Sun.* **Admission** *€15; €13 reductions.* **Map** *p66 K10.*
Housed in two *palazzi* facing each other on Michelangelo's piazza del Campidoglio, the Capitoline Museums (Musei Capitolini) are the oldest museums in the world, opened to the public in 1734, though the collection was begun in 1471

by Pope Sixtus IV. His successors continued to add ancient sculptures and, later, paintings.

Entry is through the Palazzo dei Conservatori (to the right at the top of the steps). The courtyard contains parts of a colossal statue of Emperor Constantine that originally stood in the Basilica of Maxentius in the Roman Forum. Inside, ancient works are mixed with statues by the Baroque genius Gian Lorenzo Bernini. In room 7 (Sala della Lupa) is the much-reproduced statue of the she-wolf suckling twins Romulus and Remus.

In a smart section on the first floor, the second-century AD statue of Emperor Marcus Aurelius has been given a suitably grand space. Also here are chunks of the Temple of Jupiter.

The second-floor gallery contains paintings by greats

💜 Vittoriano

Piazza Venezia/via di San Pietro in Carcere/piazza Aracoeli (06 678 3587, www.ilvittoriano. com). See p63 Getting around. **Monument, lift & Museo del Risorgimento** *9.30am-6.45pm daily.* **Sacrario delle Bandiere** *9.30am-3pm Tue-Sun.* **Ala Brasini** *(06 678 0664, open during exhibitions only) 9.30am-7.30pm Mon-Thur; 9.30am-10pm Fri, Sat; 9.30am-8.30pm Sun.* **Admission** *Monument, Sacrario free; Museo del Risorgimento €5; €2.50 reductions. Lift €7; €3.50 reductions. Ala Brasini varies.* **Map** *p66 K10.*

It's worth climbing to the top of this monument, not only to appreciate the enormity of the thing, but also to see the Art Nouveau mosaics in the colonnade and – most importantly – to enjoy the view from the only place where you can see the whole city centre without the panorama being disturbed by the bulk of the Vittoriano itself.

Even more impressive than the view after a hike up the steps is the panorama from the very top level of the monument, reached by a glass elevator accessed from behind the monument, by the side of the Aracoeli church (*see p74*). Choose a clear day: extending over the whole city and out to countryside and hills beyond, the panorama is simply breathtaking.

The building also contains various exhibition spaces: on the south-east side of the monument the **Museo Centrale del Risorgimento** (www. risorgimento.it, entrance on via

San Pietro in Carcere) has all kinds of exhibits on the 19th-century struggle to unify Italy, including the rather fancy boot worn by Giuseppe Garibaldi when he was shot in the foot in 1862, and panels (in English) explaining the key figures and events of the period. The museum also often hosts modern art exhibitions in the **Ala Brasini**. (Any exhibition advertised as held at the Complesso del Vittoriano will be here.)

The **Sacrario delle Bandiere** (entrance in via dei Fori Imperiali) contains standards from many Italian navy vessels. It also has a couple of torpedo boats, including a manned *Maiale* (Pig) torpedo.

such as Titian, Tintoretto and Caravaggio. Across the piazza (or through the underground Tabularium, the ancient Capitoline archive building), the Palazzo Nuovo houses one of Europe's greatest collections of ancient sculpture, including the coy *Capitoline Venus*, the *Dying Gaul* and countless portrait busts of emperors and their families.

The top-floor café and restaurant (which are accessible without paying the museum entrance fee) are rather overpriced, but offer a magnificent view over the city.

San Marco

Piazza San Marco 48 (06 679 5205). See p179 Getting around. **Open** *8.30am-12.30pm, 4-7pm Tue-Sun.* **Map** *p66 J9.*

There's a strong Venetian flavour to this church, which, according to local lore, was founded in 336 on the site of the house where St Mark the Evangelist – the patron saint of Venice – stayed. There are medieval lions, the symbol of St Mark, by the main entrance door; inside are graves of Venetians and paintings of Venetian saints. Rebuilt during the fifth century, the church was further reorganised by Pope Paul II in the 15th century when the neighbouring Palazzo Venezia was built. San Marco was given its Baroque look in the mid 18th century. Remaining from its earlier manifestations are the 11th-century bell tower, a portico attributed to Leon Battista Alberti, the 15th-century ceiling with Paul II's coat of arms, and the ninth-century mosaic of Christ in the apse.

Santa Maria in Aracoeli

Piazza del Campidoglio 4 (06 6976 3839). See p63 Getting around. **Open** *May-Sept 9am-7pm daily. Oct-Apr 9.30am-5.30pm daily.* **Map** *p66 K10.*

At the head of a daunting flight of 120 marble steps, the Romanesque Aracoeli ('altar of heaven') stands on the site of an ancient temple to Juno Moneta.The first record of a Christian church here was in the sixth century. The current basilica-form church was designed (and reoriented to face St Peter's) for the Franciscan order in the late 13th century, perhaps by Arnolfo di Cambio.

Dividing the church into a nave and two aisles are 22 columns purloined from Roman buildings. There's a cosmatesque floor punctuated by marble gravestones and a richly gilded ceiling commemorating the Christian victory over the Turks at the Battle of Lepanto in 1571. The two stone pulpits in front of the altar have intricate cosmatesque mosaic work.

Restaurants

Terre e Domus Enoteca della Provincia di Romana €€

Largo del Foro Traiano 84 (06 6994 0273, www.palazzovalentini. it/terre-domus). See p63 Getting around. **Open** *12.30-3pm, 7.30-11pm daily.* **Map** *p66 K9* ❶

Enoteca

Buried round the back of the Rome provincial government offices, overlooking Trajan's Column, this local-government-sponsored wine bar and restaurant is located inside Palazzo Valentini, which also houses the Domus Romane (*see p65*). This *enoteca* serves wines and produce exclusively from the area immediately surrounding the capital. The atmosphere is warmly cordial; the small blackboard menu changes regularly to focus on traditional, seasonal food with fresh vegetables coming from the garden of the city's Rebibbia prison, while the wine menu (with large by-the-glass choice) is full of pleasant surprises. Book ahead for a table.

Pantheon, Ghetto & Quirinale

From the earliest of ancient times, the area in the great loop of the River Tiber was the *campus martius* (field of war), where Roman males did physical jerks to stay fighting fit. As time went on, it became packed with theatres providing lowbrow fun. After barbarian hordes rampaged through Rome in the fifth and sixth centuries, the area fell into ruin. By the late Middle Ages, it was densely populated and insalubrious.

The *campus martius* saw its fortunes improve when the pope made the Vatican – across the river – his main residence in the mid 15th century, bringing pilgrims and prosperity to the surrounding neighbourhoods. In 1574 the Palazzo del Quirinale was built on the Quirinale hill, to the east of the city – a bid by Pope Gregory XIII to escape the malarial heat of the marshy river valley. Over the following decades, the surrounding district became the centre of papal bureaucracy. The Quirinale palace served as Pope Pius IX's last hiding place, following the collapse of the Papal States in 1870, and is now home to the Italian president. Close by, if you follow the tangle of medieval streets, you will find the Baroque tourist trap, the Fontana di Trevi.

This area of the *centro storico* is characterised by tightly wedged buildings, cobbled alleys, graceful Renaissance columns and chunky blocks of ancient travertine, all of which form the perfect backdrop to Roman streetlife.

→ **Getting around**
This area is densely packed with cobbled streets and ancient ruins. The best way to explore the narrow and winding streets is most definitely on foot.

Pantheon & piazza Navona

After the fall of the Roman Empire, this area of the *campus martius* in the loop of the river north of corso Vittorio Emanuele became prime construction territory, with great marble palazzi scattered among the modest homes of ordinary folk. Today, this picturesque section of the *centro storico* retains its historical mix of the very grand and the very humble. After dark, hip bars, smart restaurants and, increasingly, tourist-trap rip-offs, fill to bursting, especially around **Santa Maria della Pace**. Don't miss the **Chiostro del Bramante**, attached to Santa Maria, with its beautiful early 16th-century cloister designed by Donato Bramante.

Two squares – both living links to ancient Rome – dominate the district: **piazza della Rotonda** – home to the **Pantheon** – and magnificent **piazza Navona**, with Bernini's fountains, Borromini's church of **Sant'Agnese in Agone** (www.santagneseinagone.org) and picturesque pavement cafés.

Just north of piazza Navona are **Palazzo Altemps**, with its spectacular collection of antique statuary; **Sant'Agostino** (on the piazza of the same name), which contains a Caravaggio masterpiece; and the **Museo Napoleonico** (piazza di Ponte Umberto I, www.museonapoleonico.it). Between the piazza and the Pantheon are **Palazzo Madama** (corso Rinascimento, www. senato.it); the church of **San Luigi dei Francesi**, with yet more Caravaggios (*see p83*); and Borromini's breathtaking **Sant'Ivo alla Sapienza** (corso Rinascimento 40).

To the east of the Pantheon, the **Galleria Doria Pamphilj** (*see p81*) contains one of Rome's finest art collections, while the charmingly rococo **piazza Sant'Ignazio** looks like a stage set. South of the Pantheon, central Rome's only Gothic church, **Santa Maria sopra Minerva** (www. basilicaminerva.it), stands in piazza della Minerva.

Sights & museums

Palazzo Altemps

Piazza Sant'Apollinare 46 (06 3996 7700). Bus 30Exp, 70, 81, 87, 492, 628. **Open** *9am-7.45pm Tue-Sun.* **Admission** *€7; €3.50 reductions. Exhibition price varies.* **Map** *p78 G8.*
The 15th- to 16th-century Palazzo Altemps has been beautifully restored to house part of the state-owned Museo Nazionale Romano stock of Roman treasures (*see p121 In the know*). Here, in perfectly lit salons, loggias and courtyards, you can admire gems of classical statuary from the formerly private Boncompagni-Ludovisi, Altemps and Mattei collections.

The Ludovisis were big on 'fixing' statues broken over the ages or which simply didn't appeal to the tastes of the day.

Four newly opened rooms contain more of the Mattei collection plus some remarkable Egyptian artefacts from ancient sites in and around Rome, including the recently discovered Artemis of Ephesus statue, displayed for the first time. These rooms can be seen on guided tours at 11am, noon, 4pm and 5pm from Tuesday to Saturday, and all day Sunday.

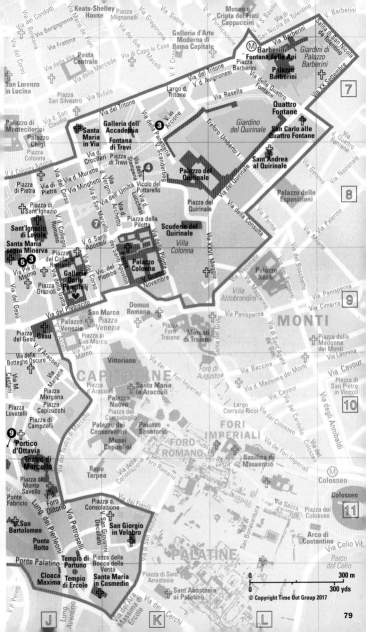

❤ Pantheon

Piazza della Rotonda (06 6830 0230). Bus 30Exp, 40Exp, 46, 53, 62, 63, 64, 70, 81, 85, 87, 117, 160, 492, 571, 628, 810, 916/ tram 8. **Open** *8.30am-7.15pm Mon-Sat; 8.30am-5.45pm Sun; 8.30am-12.45pm public hols.* **Admission** *free.* **Map** *p78 H8.*

The Pantheon is the best-preserved ancient building in Rome. It was built (and possibly designed) by Hadrian in AD 119-128 as a temple to the 12 most important classical deities; the inscription on the pediment records an earlier Pantheon built a hundred years earlier by Augustus' general Marcus Agrippa (which confused historians for centuries). Its fine state of preservation is due to the building's conversion to a Christian church in 608, when it was presented to the pope by the Byzantine Emperor Phocas. The Pantheon has nevertheless suffered over the years – notably when bronze cladding was stripped from the roof in 667, and when Pope Urban VIII allowed Bernini to remove the remaining bronze from the beams in the portico to melt down for his *baldacchino* in St Peter's in 1628. The simplicity of the building's exterior remains largely unchanged, and it retains its original Roman bronze doors. Inside, the Pantheon's real glory lies in the dimensions, which follow the rules set down by top Roman architect Vitruvius. The diameter of the hemispherical dome is exactly equal to the height of the whole building; it could potentially accommodate a perfect sphere. At the exact centre of the dome is the oculus, a circular hole 9 metres (30 feet) in diameter, the only source of light and a symbolic link between the temple and the heavens. The building is still officially a church, and contains the tombs of eminent Italians, including the artist Raphael and united Italy's first king, Vittorio Emanuele II. Until the 18th century the portico was used as a market: supports for the stalls were inserted into the notches still visible in the columns.

❤ Piazza Navona

Bus 30Exp, 40Exp, 46, 62, 64, 70, 81, 168, 492, 628, 916. **Map** *p78 G8.*

This tremendous theatrical space, centred on the gleaming marble composition of Bernini's Fontana dei Quattro Fiumi (Fountain of the Four Rivers), is the hub of the *centro storico*. The piazza owes its shape to an ancient athletics stadium, built in AD 86 by Emperor Domitian, which was the scene of sporting events, and at least one martyrdom.

The piazza acquired its current form in the mid 17th century under Pope Innocent X of the Pamphilj family. Its western side is dominated by Borromini's façade for the church of **Sant'Agnese in Agone** and the adjacent **Palazzo Pamphilj** (now the Brazilian embassy), built in 1644-50. The central fountain, finished in 1651, is one of the most extravagant masterpieces designed – though only partly sculpted – by Bernini. Its main figures represent the longest rivers of the four continents known at the time: the Ganges of Asia, Nile of Africa, Danube of Europe and Plata of the Americas, surrounded by geographically appropriate flora and fauna. The figure of the Nile is veiled, because its source was unknown. For centuries, the story went that Bernini designed it that way to show the river god recoiling in horror from the façade of Sant'Agnese, designed by his arch-rival Borromini; in fact, the church was built after the fountain was finished. The obelisk at the fountain's centre, moved

💜 Galleria Doria Pamphilj

*Via del Corso 305 (06 679 7323, www.dopart.it). Bus 53, 62, 63, 80, 81, 83, 85, 117, 492, 628. **Open** 10am-7pm daily. **Admission** €12; €8 reductions. **Map** p78 J9.*

The collection of one of the great families of Rome's aristocracy (spelled either Pamphili or Pamphilj), now headed by two half-British siblings, is a very personal one: hung according to an inventory of 1760, some extraordinarily good paintings are packed in with the occasional bad copy to give a unique view of the tastes of late 18th-century Rome.

The entrance is through the state apartments planned by Camillo Pamphilj in the mid 16th century. The nephew of Pope Innocent X, Camillo escaped the College of Cardinals to marry fabulously wealthy Olimpia Aldobrandini, to whom the oldest part of the palace belonged, and who had already been left a widow by a member of the Borghese family. The family chapel was designed in 1689 by Carlo Fontana but heavily altered in the 18th and 19th centuries when the trompe l'oeil ceiling was added. The star turns are the corpses of two martyrs: St Justin, under the altar, and St Theodora, visible to the right of the door. The main galleries are on all four sides of the central courtyard. Hard-nosed Olimpia is shown in Algardi's stylised portrait bust by the windows in the first gallery.

Velázquez's portrait of a no-nonsense Pope Innocent X is the highlight of the collection. With Bernini's splendid bust next to it, it's difficult to see how the vital presence of Innocent X could be bettered. Other highlights include two paintings attributed to Caravaggio: *Rest on the Flight into Egypt* (1597) and *Penitent Magdalene* (c1595), shown alongside the *Portrait of Two Men* by Raphael (c1516) in the Aldobrandini room (at the end of the third gallery, down a few steps and home also to ancient sculpture). This leads onto a dark room that contains a beautifully tragic *Deposition* by Hans Memling (c1485-90). On the way, keep an eye out for Guercino's *St Agnes* (1652).

here from the Circus of Maxentius on the Appian Way, was carved in Egypt under the orders of Domitian (the hieroglyphics are a Roman addition describing him as 'eternal pharaoh'). The less-spectacular Fontana del Moro is at the southern end of the piazza. The central figure of the Moor was designed by Bernini in 1653, and executed by Antonio Mari.

Sant'Ignazio di Loyola

*Piazza Sant'Ignazio (06 679 4406). Bus 53, 62, 63, 80, 81, 83, 85, 117, 160, 492, 628, C3. **Open** 7.30am-7pm Mon-Sat; 9am-7pm Sun. **Map** p78 J8.*

Sant'Ignazio was begun in 1626 to commemorate the canonisation of St Ignatius, founder of the Jesuit order. Trompe l'oeil columns soar above the nave, and architraves by Andrea Pozzo open to a cloudy heaven. Trickery was also involved in creating the dome: the monks next door claimed that a real dome would rob them of light, so Pozzo simply painted a dome on the inside of the roof. The illusion is fairly convincing if you stand on the disc set in the floor of the nave. Walk away, however, and it dissolves.

Santa Maria della Pace

*Vicolo del Arco della Pace 5. Bus 30Exp, 70, 81, 87, 116, 130, 186, 492, 628, C3. **Open** 9am-noon Mon-Wed, Sat. Mass 11am Sun. **Map** p78 G8.*

Built in 1482 for Pope Sixtus IV, Santa Maria della Pace was given its theatrical Baroque façade by Pietro da Cortona in 1656. The church's most famous artwork is just inside the door: Raphael's *Sibyls*, painted in 1514 for Agostino Chigi, the playboy banker and first owner of the **Villa Farnesina** (*see p151*). Even if the church is closed, you can visit the beautifully harmonious cloister by Bramante, his first work after arriving in Rome in the early 16th century. **Note** that opening hours

depend on the presence of the custodian, but the church is always open for Mass on Sundays from 11am to 12.30pm.

Restaurants

❤ Armando al Pantheon €€

*Salita de' Crescenzi 31 (06 6880 3034, www.armandoalpantheon. it). Bus 30, 40, 46, 62, 63, 64, 70, 81, 87, 492, 628, 810, 916, H/tram 8. **Open** 12.30-3pm, 7.15-11pm Mon-Fri; 12.30-3pm Sat. Closed Sat, Sun in July, Aug. **Map** p78 H8* ❶ *Trattoria*

Armando is a no-frills trattoria of the kind that once was common in Rome but now is like gold dust, especially when its location is taken into account – just a few yards from an A-league attraction. A recent renovation has spruced up the interior but all the hallmarks of authenticity remain, including indifferent artworks and wonderfully friendly service from the family that has run it since 1961. The menu sticks with tried-and-tested Roman pasta and meat classics executed with love by smiley chef Claudio Gargioli. Unusually attentive to special dietary requirements, they will gladly substitute in gluten-free pasta.

Coromandel €€

*Via di Monte Giordano 60-61 (06 68802461, www.coromandel.it). Bus 40, 46, 62, 64, 628, 916. **Open** 8.15am-3pm, 8-11pm Tue-Sat. Closed 2wks Aug. **Map** p78 G8* ❷ *International*

The brunch menu at Coromandel has earned it a loyal following among foreign expats needing an occasional change from the ubiquitous Italian breakfast pastries, thanks to its pancakes, waffles, bagels and eggs Benedict as well as a good choice of teas and fresh juices. There is also a daily

❤ San Luigi dei Francesi

Piazza San Luigi dei Francesi (06 688 271, www.saintlouis-rome.net). Bus 30Exp, 70, 81, 87, 492, 628. **Open** *9.30am-12.45pm Mon-Fri; 9.30am-12.15pm Sat; 11.30am-12.45pm Sun.* **Map** *p78 H8.*

Completed in 1589, San Luigi (St Louis) is the church of Rome's French community. Most visitors ignore the gaudily lavish interior, and make a beeline for Caravaggio's spectacular scenes from the life of St Matthew in the last chapel on the left, the funerary chapel of Matheiu Cointrel. Italianised as the Contarelli Chapel, it was the first of Caravaggio's major church commissions. He was awarded the contract thanks to the intervention of his patron, the Cardinal del Monte, a retainer of

the Medici whose Rome palace, the Palazzo Madama (now the Italian Senate), was next to the French church.

Painted in 1600-02, the scenes depict Christ singling out a very reluctant Matthew in a contemporary tavern setting (left), Matthew attacked by his assassins, clearly reluctant to succumb to martyrdom (right) and an angel briefing the evangelist about what he should write in his gospel (over the altar).

Don't let Caravaggio's brooding brilliance and dramatic effects of light and shade blind you to the lovely frescoes of scenes from the life of St Cecilia by Domenichino (1615-17), which are in the second chapel on the right. Take a few coins for instant meter-operated illumination.

Contarelli Chapel, San Luigi dei Francesi

lunch blackboard and a full à la carte selection for dinner, all served in the cosy dining room on pretty mismatched china.

💙 Da Simo Pane e Vino €
Via di Parione 34 (06 8670 9955, www.facebook.com/ dasimopaneevino). Bus 40, 46, 62, 64, 916. **Open** *noon-11pm daily.* **Map** *p78 G8* ❸ *Sandwich bar*

This tiny place cooks up hearty Roman casseroles and salads which are generously stuffed into panini and served on the ramshackle outside tables. The selection changes daily but there are always at least 8-10 choices from traditional *trippa alla romana* (tripe in tomato sauce) and *coda alla vaccinara* (oxtail stew) to aubergine parmigiana and owner Simona's grandmother's recipe of sausage stew with grapes. The exuberant staff and extremely affordable prices (panini start at €4.50 and bottles of beer are just €1) make Da Simo a hidden gem in one of the most touristy parts of town.

Le Tartarughe p86

Cafés, bars & pubs

Bar del Fico
Piazza del Fico 26-28 (06 6889 1373, www.bardelfico.com). Bus 40, 46, 62, 64, 916. **Open** *8.30am-2.30am daily.* **No cards.** **Map** *p78 G8* ❶ *Bistro*

This long-established *centro storico* fixture – named after the ancient fig tree (*fico*) outside – underwent a refurbishment a few years back and transformed from an old-school local bar to a vintagey French-style bistro with a laid-back boho ambience. Not that this has deterred the regulars however, and the old blokes can still be found playing chess outside. Open from breakfast until the small hours, it is the perfect central meeting place.

💙 Caffè Sant'Eustachio
Piazza Sant'Eustachio 82 (06 6880 2048, www.santeustachioilcaffe. it). Bus 30, 40, 46, 62, 63, 64, 70, 81, 87, 190, 492, 628, 810, 916, H. **Open** *7.30am-1am Mon-Thur, Sun; 7.30am-1.30am Fri; 7.30am-2am Sat.* **No cards.** **Map** *p78 H9* ❷ *Coffee shop*

This is one of the city's most famous coffee bars, and its walls are plastered with celebrity testimonials. The coffee is quite extraordinary, if pricier than elsewhere; the barmen turn their backs while whipping up a cup so as not to let their secret out (though a pinch of bicarbonate of soda is rumoured to give it its froth). Try the *gran caffè*: the *schiuma* (froth) can be slurped out with a spoon or finger afterwards. Unless you specify (*amaro* means 'no sugar'; *poco zucchero* means 'a little sugar'), it comes very sweet.

Cul de Sac
Piazza Pasquino 73 (06 6880 1094, www.enotecaculdesacroma.it). Bus 40, 46, 62, 64, 492, 628, 916. **Open** *noon-midnight daily.* **Map** *p78 G9* ❸ *Wine bar*

Rome's first ever wine bar, the Cul de Sac was founded in 1977. Looking very traditional nowadays, it's cramped inside and out, with long pine benches and tables, and is decidedly no-frills. But the location – just off piazza Navona, with a ringside view of the 'talking' statue of Pasquino – coupled with fairly reasonable prices and an encyclopaedic wine list, ensures full occupancy all the time. The food is standard wine-bar fare including a selection of home-made pâtés as well as generous sharing plates of cured meats and cheeses.

♥ Tazza d'Oro
Via degli Orfani 84 (06 678 9792, www.tazzadorocoffeeshop.com). Bus 52, 53, 62, 63, 71, 80, 83, 85, 117, 160, 492, 590. **Open** *7am-8pm Mon-Sat, 10.30am-7.30pm.* **Map** *p78 H8* ❹ *Coffee shop*
The powerful aroma wafting from this ancient *torrefazione* (coffee-roasters) overlooking the Pantheon is a siren call to coffee-lovers. The place is packed with coffee sacks, tourists and regulars, who flock for *granita di caffè* (coffee sorbet) in summer, and *cioccolata calda con panna* (hot chocolate with whipped cream) in winter. It sells speciality teas too.

Shops & services

♥ Borsalino
Via Campo Marzio 72/A (06 679 6120, www.borsalino.com). Bus 70, 81, 117, 301, 913, 628. **Open** *10am-7.30pm daily.* **Map** *p78 H7* ❶ *Hats*
Hat maker extraordinaire Giuseppe Borsalino created his brand in 1857 and since then the label's signature designs have donned the heads of such diverse names as Winston Churchill, Giuseppe Verdi, Audrey Hepburn and Leonardo di Caprio.

Still created using the original techniques, craftsmanship and quality at this level certainly doesn't come cheap.

Cartoleria Pantheon
Via della Rotonda 15 (06 687 5313, www.pantheon-roma.com). Bus 30, 40, 46, 62, 63, 64, 70, 81, 87, 492, 628, 780, 916, H/tram 8. **Open** *10.30am-8pm Mon-Sat; 1-8pm Sun.* **Map** *p78 H8* ❷ *Gifts & souvenirs*
Bring out your literary soul with leather-bound notebooks, hand-painted Florentine stationery and rare paper from Amalfi. Nearly everything for sale has been handcrafted. **Other locations** via della Maddalena 41 (06 679 5633); piazza Navona 42.

Moriondo & Gariglio
Via del Piè di Marmo 21 (06 699 0856). Bus 30, 40, 46, 53, 62, 63, 64, 70, 80, 81, 83, 85, 87, 117, 160, 190, 492, 628, 916. **Open** *9am-7.30pm Mon-Sat. Closed Aug.* **Map** *p78 J9* ❸ *Chocolatier*
This fairytale chocolate shop with beautiful gift-boxes is especially lovely at Christmas, when you'll have to fight to get your hands on the excellent *marrons glacés*. The prices are as extravagant as the packaging.

Il Papiro
Via del Pantheon 50 (06 679 5597, www.ilpapirofirenze.it). Bus 30, 40, 46, 62, 63, 64, 70, 81, 87, 492, 628, 780, 916, H/tram 8. **Open** *10am-7.30pm daily.* **Map** *p78 H8* ❹ *Gifts & souvenirs*
A great place to buy something for the writer in your life, at Il Papiro Florentine paper is incorporated into albums, notebooks and more. Don't ruin the effect with a biro: the shop also stocks quill pens and ink in a range of jazzy colours. **Other locations** Salita de' Crescenzi 28 (06 686 8463).

♥ **Le Tartarughe**

Via Pie' di Marmo 17 (06 679 2240, www.letartarughe.eu). Bus 30, 40, 46, 53, 62, 63, 64, 70, 80, 81, 83, 85, 87, 117, 160, 190, 492, 628, 916. **Open** *noon-7.30pm Mon; 10am-7.30pm Tue-Sat. Closed 2wks Aug.* **Map** *p78 J9* ❺ *Fashion*

Susanna Liso's sumptuous designs fill this chic boutique near the church of Santa Maria sopra Minerva. The lines of these eminently wearable garments – ranging from cocktail dresses to elegant workwear – are classic with a twist; the colours are eye-catching but never garish.

Entertainment

Shari Vari Playhouse

Via De' Nari 14 (06 6880 6936, sharivari.it). Bus 30, 46, 64, 492, 5N, 6N, 8N, H/tram 8. **Open** *10pm-4am Tue-Sat, 10pm-2am Sun. Closed Aug.* **Map** *p78 H9* ❶ *Nightlife*

Its central location – conveniently nestled between campo de' Fiori, the Pantheon, and piazza Navona – has made this restaurant and underground club a very popular destination. It's usually packed during the winter. Getting in is up to the stable of beefy bouncers at the door (best to avoid t-shirts and casual outfits). The music selection in the three dance rooms is very eclectic, from commercial and pop to electro, and from house to hip-hop, to revival.

Ghetto & campo de' Fiori

This area is one of contrasts: **campo de' Fiori** – with its lively morning market and livelier partying crowds at night – stands next to solemn, dignified piazza Farnese, with its grand **Palazzo Farnese**, partly designed by Michelangelo. Top-end antique

dealers in via Giulia rub along with craftsmen plying their trades in streets with names – via dei Leutari (lutemakers), via dei Cappellari (hatmakers) – that recall the jobs of their medieval ancestors.

To the north, on corso Vittorio Emanuele II (universally known as corso Vittorio), is the **Museo Barracco di Scultura Antica**; further east are the churches of **Sant'Andrea della Valle** (corso Vittorio 6), topped by Rome's second-tallest dome, and **Gesù**, mother church of the Jesuit order. Nearby, **largo Argentina** is a polluted transport hub with a chunk of ancient Rome at its heart: visible when you peer over the railings are columns, altars and foundations from four temples. View more of Rome's architectural accretions over the ages at the **Crypta Balbi**.

South of largo Argentina lies the Ghetto: its picture-postcard winding alleys mask a sorrowful Roman Jewish history that stretches back over 2,000 years. Via Portico d'Ottavia, an anarchic hotchpotch of ancient, medieval and Renaissance architecture leading to the **Portico d'Ottavia** itself, used to mark the boundary of the Ghetto, which was walled off from the rest of the city from 1556 until the 1870s. Visit the fascinating **Museo Ebraico**, in the Ghetto's synagogue, to learn more about the area. Nearby, a bridge crosses to the **Tiber Island**, dominated by the Fatebenefratelli hospital, just the latest incarnation of the island's long association with healing. Back on the east bank, **San Nicola in Carcere** (via del Teatro di Marcello 46) is built over three Roman temples and an Etruscan marketplace. There are two more temples to the south, plus **Santa Maria in Cosmedin**, with its 'bocca della verità' (mouth of truth).

Gesù p88

Sights & museums

❤ Crypta Balbi

*Via delle Botteghe Oscure 31
(06 678 0167, archeoroma.
beniculturali.it). Bus 30, 40, 46,
62, 63, 64, 70, 87, 190, 492, 780,
810, 916, H/tram 8.* **Open** *9am-7pm
Tue-Sun.* **Admission** *€7; €3.50
reductions. Exhibition price varies.*
Map *p78 J10.*

Part of the Museo Nazionale
Romana (*see p121* In the know),
the Crypta Balbi displays one of
Rome's more interesting recent
archaeological finds, and is packed
with displays, maps and models
that explain (in English) Rome's
evolution from its bellicose pre-
Imperial era, to early Christian
times and on through the dim
Middle Ages. The underground
ruins themselves – visible
occasionally through the day in a
tour – show the foundations of the
gigantic *crypta*, or theatre lobby,
constructed by Cornelius Balbus,
a Spaniard much in favour at the
court of Augustus. Excavations
continue, while upstairs is a display
of the minutiae of everyday life
in ancient Rome: plates, bowls,
glasses, amphorae, oil lamps
and artisans' tools. The upper
levels provide a fantastic view of
Roman rooftops.

♥ Gesù

Piazza del Gesù (06 697 00232, Loyola's rooms 06 697 001, www. chiesadelgesu.org). Bus 30Exp, 40Exp, 46, 62, 63, 64, 70, 81, 87, 492, 780, 810, 916, H. **Church** *7.30am-12.30pm, 4-7.45pm daily.* **Loyola's rooms** *4-6pm Mon-Sat; 10am-noon Sun.* **Admission** *free.* **Map** *p78 J9.*

The Jesuits were the richest Catholic order, founded by Basque soldier Ignatius Loyola in the 1530s. They were also the most energetic, sending teams of fired-up missionaries to the four corners of the (then) known world. This church is the flagship church of the Jesuits, their showcase, and Loyola's final resting place.

The Gesù (built 1568-84) was designed to involve the congregation as closely as possible in the proceedings, with a nave unobstructed by aisles, offering a clear view of the main altar. Giacomo della Porta added a façade that would be repeated *ad nauseam* on Jesuit churches across Italy (and the world) for decades afterwards. A large, bright fresco, *Triumph in the Name of Jesus*, by Il Baciccia (1676-79) – one of Rome's great Baroque masterpieces – decorates the gilded ceiling of the nave, which seems to dissolve on either side as stucco figures (by Antonio Raggi) and other painted images are sucked up into the dazzling light of the heavens. (The figures falling back to earth are presumably Protestants.)

On the left is another spectacular Baroque achievement: the chapel of Sant'Ignazio (1696-1700) by Andrea Pozzo, which is adorned with gold, silver and coloured marble; the statue of St Ignatius entering heaven is now covered the majority of the time with a canvas by Pozzo, but is uncovered at 5.30pm every afternoon in a marvellous piece of baroque theatre (*see right* In

the know). Towering above the altar is what was long believed to be the biggest lump of lapis lazuli in the entire world... in fact, the piece is merely covered concrete. Outside the church, at piazza del Gesù 45, you can visit the rooms of St Ignatius, which contain a wonderful painted corridor featuring trompe l'oeil special effects by Pozzo, and mementoes of the saint, including his death mask.

Museo Barracco di Scultura Antica

Corso Vittorio Emanuele 166 (06 687 5657, www.museobarracco. it). Bus 40Exp, 46, 62, 64, 916. **Open** *Oct-May 10am-4pm Tue-Sun. June-Sept 1-7pm Tue-Sun.* **Admission** *free.* **Map** *p78 G9.*

This small collection of mostly pre-Roman art was amassed during the first half of the 20th century by Giovanni Barracco. The nobleman's artistic interests covered the whole gamut of ancient art, as seen in the collection of Assyrian reliefs, Attic vases, Egyptian sphinxes and Babylonian stone lions, as well as Roman and Etruscan exhibits and Greek sculptures. Don't miss the copy of the *Wounded Bitch* by the fourth-century BC sculptor Lysippus, on the second floor.

♥ Museo Ebraico

Lungotevere Cenci (06 6840 0661, www.museoebraico.roma.it). Bus 23, 63, 280, 780/ tram 8. **Open** *Apr-Sept 10am-6pm Mon-Thur, Sun; 9am-4pm Fri. Oct-Mar 10am-5pm Mon-Thur, Sun; 9am-2pm Fri. Closed Jewish hols.* **Admission** *€11; €5 reductions.* **Map** *p78 J11.*

Inscriptions and carvings line the entrance passage to this fascinating museum, which holds a collection that details the history of the city's Jewish community. The recently extended and refurbished display is housed beneath the magnificent neo-Assyrian, neo-Greek Great

Synagogue that was inaugurated in 1904. As well as luxurious crowns, Torah mantles and silverware, this museum presents vivid reminders of the persecution that was suffered by Rome's Jews at various times throughout the city's history. Copies of the 16th-century papal edicts that banned Jews from a progressively longer list of activities are a disturbing foretaste of the horrors forced on them by the Fascists and Nazis. The Nazi atrocities are in turn represented by stark photographs and heart-rending relics derived from the concentration camps, as well as film footage tracing developments in the post-war period. There are also a number of displays on the ancient Roman synagogue excavated at Ostia in 1964, as well as Jewish items from the city's catacombs. The entrance to the museum includes a guided tour of the two Synagogues housed in the building.

Portico d'Ottavia

Via Portico d'Ottavia. Bus 23, 30Exp, 44, 63, 81, 83, 160, 170, 280, 628, 715, 716, 780, 781, H. **Open** *9am-6pm daily.* **Admission** *free.* **Map** *p78 J10.*

Great ancient columns and a marble frontispiece, held together with rusting iron braces, now form part of the church of Sant'Angelo in Pescheria. They were originally the entrance of a massive colonnaded square (*portico*) containing temples and libraries, built in the first century AD by Emperor Augustus and dedicated to his sister Octavia (this, in turn, had been built over a first-century BC square). The mighty structure was decorated with 34 bronzes by Lysippus depicting bellicose events from the life of Alexander the Great; these are long lost. The isolated columns outside, and the inscription above, date from a later restoration, undertaken by Septimius Severus in AD 213. After lengthy digs and restoration work in the 1990s, a walkway was opened allowing you to stroll through the *forum piscarium* – the ancient fish market, hence the name of the church. The walkway continues through the excavation past a graveyard of broken columns and dumped Corinthian capitals to the **Teatro di Marcello**, one of the strangest sights in Rome: a Renaissance palace grafted on to an ancient Roman theatre and now housing luxury apartments.

San Giorgio in Velabro

Via del Velabro 19 (06 6979 7536, www.sangiorgioinvelabro.org). Bus 30Exp, 44, 63, 81, 83, 160, 170, 628, 715, 716, 780, 781, H. **Open** *10am-12.30pm, 4-6.30pm daily.* **Map** *p78 K11.*

In the know
Gesù's saintly spectacle

Flashing lights and piped heavenly choirs herald an eye-popping performance of religious theatricality at the Gesù. A bizarre daily *son et lumière* on the life, but mostly the death, of the Jesuits' founder Ignatius Loyola (*see above*) offers 15 minutes' respite from the dizzying frescoes and sheer opulence of the Gesù's fixtures and fittings. Be there at 5.30pm prompt: proceedings start with mechanical precision.

After the recent discovery of the original nine-metre (30-foot) altarpiece painted by Jesuit brother Andrea Pozzo, restoration began on the complex Baroque mechanics once used to raise and lower the giant altarpiece. These were designed as a show to inspire awe and reverence in amazed onlookers. Baroque art is all about trickery, magic, delight and astonishment. Pozzo here (and at nearby Sant'Ignazio) showed himself to be a master.

The soft light from the windows in the clerestory gives a peaceful aura to this austere little church of the fifth century. A swingeing restoration in 1925 did away with centuries of decoration and restored its original Romanesque simplicity. The 16 columns, pilfered from the Palatine and the Aventine hills, are all different. Pieces of an eighth- or ninth-century choir, including two slender columns, are incorporated into the walls. In the apse is a restored fresco by the school of Pietro Cavallini showing St George with a white horse and the Virgin on one side of the central Christ figure, and St Peter and St Sebastian opposite. The 12th-century altar is a rare example of the Byzantine-inspired 'caged and architraved' ciborium, a canopy on columns. A church was first built here by Greeks and was dedicated to St Sebastian, who was believed to have been martyred in the swampy area hereabouts. It was later re-dedicated to St George of Cappadocia (of dragon-slaying fame); a piece of the skull of the valorous third-century saint is kept under the altar.

Santa Maria in Cosmedin

Piazza della Bocca della Verità 18 (06 678 7759). Bus 30Exp, 44, 63, 81, 83, 160, 170, 628, 715, 716, 780, 781, H. **Open** *9.30am-5.50pm daily.* **Map** *p78 J12.*

Despite an over-enthusiastic restoration, this is a lovely jumble of early Christian, medieval and Romanesque church design – with a touch of kitsch. Santa Maria in Cosmedin was built in the sixth century and enlarged in the eighth. The beautiful bell tower was a 12th-century addition. Between the 11th and 13th centuries much of the decoration was replaced with cosmati-work, including the spiralling floor, throne, choir and 13th-century *baldacchino*.

In the sacristy/souvenir shop is a fragment of an eighth-century mosaic of the Holy Family, brought here from St Peter's. In the crypt are ruins of the Ara maximus, a monument to Hercules over which the church was built. The name Cosmedin comes from the Greek, meaning splendid decoration; this has always been the church of the Greek community, many of whom were expelled from Constantinople in the eighth century: Byzantine rite services are still held here at 10.30am on Sundays.

The church is better known as the *bocca della verità* (the mouth of truth) as, according to legend, anyone who lies while their hand is in the mouth of the mask of the horned man on the portico wall will have that hand bitten off. It was reportedly used by Roman husbands to determine the fidelity of their wives.

Restaurants

Open Baladin €€

Via degli Specchi 6 (06 683 8989, www.openbaladin.com). Bus 30, 40, 46, 62, 63, 64, 70, 81, 87, 271, 492, 628, 780, 916, H/tram 8. **Open** *noon-midnight daily. Closed 2wks Aug.* **Map** *p78 H10* ④
International

Dynamic northern Italian brewer Teo Musso is turning more and more of his fellow countryfolk into beer drinkers. Open Baladin, with its 'wall of beer' – about 100 labels served bottled, displayed up one wall of this buzzing venue – and a choice of 40 or more on tap, is his first Roman venture. Bar-snack food, from mounds of chicken wings to gourmet hamburgers, melt-in-the-mouth mozzarella and a signature scrambled egg with bacon helps the brews from many of Italy's smallest and most interesting producers slip down nicely. This is not a venue for a romantic tryst: most nights, downstairs is utter chaos, upstairs only slightly less so. But if you're seeking beer and bustle, this is your place.

❤ Il Pagliaccio €€€€
Via dei Banchi Vecchi 129 (06 6880 9595, www.ristoranteilpagliaccio. it). Bus 40, 46, 62, 64, 916. **Open** 7.30-10.30pm Tue; 12.30-2pm, 7.30-10.30pm Wed-Sat. Closed 1wk Feb, 3wks Aug. **Map** p78 F9 ⑤
International

Though prices have climbed – pushed up, perhaps, by a second Michelin star – chef Anthony Genovese still offers a true gourmet experience. The menu successfully incorporates both Mediterranean and oriental influences and his sure touch is evident in innovative combinations such as roasted squid with rhubarb or foie gras served with amberjack. There's also an interesting wine list. Leave plenty of space to try one of the excellent desserts, which are prepared by Alsatian pastry chef-genius Marion Lichtle. Ten-course (€170) and eight-course (€150) taster menus can be arranged.

Pianostrada Laboratorio di Cucina €€
Via delle Zoccolette 22 (06 8957 2296, www.facebook. com/pianostrada). Bus 23, 30, 40, 46, 62, 63, 64, 70, 81, 87, 492, 628, 916, H/tram 8. **Open** 1-4pm, 7pm-midnight Tue-Fri, 10am-midnight Sat, Sun. Closed 3wks Aug. **Map** p78 G10 ⑥
Mediterranean

The all-female squad of Pianostrada recently left their cramped premises in Trastevere to this new, larger location over the river, complete with a pretty interior garden and large open kitchen. Freshly baked bread and *foccacia* are used to make excellent *panini* (such as the signature burger of salt cod served in a squid-ink bun) and there are creative salads, pastas and *secondi* as well as home-made desserts and cakes.

❤ Il Sanlorenzo €€€€
Via dei Chiavari 5 (06 686 5097, www.ilsanlorenzo.it). Bus 30, 40, 46, 62, 63, 64, 70, 81, 87, 492, 628, 916, H/tram 8. **Open** 7.30-11.45pm Mon, Sat; 12.45-14.45pm, 7.30-11.45pm Tue-Fri. Closed 1wk Aug. **Map** p78 H10 ⑦ *Seafood*

You'll travel a long way to find fish to rival what is served in this classically elegant restaurant: for both freshness and preparation, Il Sanlorenzo certainly ranks among Rome's finest. From the exquisite raw seafood *antipasto* through the unbeatable spaghetti with sea urchins and the daily catch baked simply in a crust of salt, this is seafood at its very best, though straight from the island of Ponza, south of Rome. The price tag is high, but it's worth it; and wonderfully graceful service without a hint of smart-dining pomposity makes the whole experience a special one.

> **In the know**
> **A temple under a church**
>
> You don't need much imagination to picture the ancient temple to Aesculapius (the god of medicine) that lies beneath the church of **San Bartolomeo** (piazza di San Bartolomeo all'Isola, www. sanbartolomeo.org) on the Tiber Island. The precious marble columns in the nave of the original temple, which was inaugurated in 293 BC. If you need help to imagine how things were when Otto III built this church in 998, then check out the massive bronze vessel (protected by an iron grille on the right-hand wall of the nave, by the altar) in which the 18-year-old German-born Holy Roman Emperor brought relics of the apostle Bartholomew from Benevento.

❤ Sora Margherita €€

Piazza delle Cinque Scole 30 (06 687 4216). Bus 30, 40, 46, 62, 63, 64, 70, 81, 87, 492, 628, 916, H/tram 8. **Open** *12.45-2.45pm daily; 7.30-10.30pm Mon, Wed; 8-11.20pm Fri, Sat. Closed 1wk Aug.* **No cards. Map** *p78 H10* ❽ *Jewish-Roman*

This spit-and-sawdust, hole-in-the-wall trattoria offers a great local dining experience. Tables are crammed into a couple of narrow rooms, and the din generated by 20 simultaneous conversations, with orders shouted over the top, is quite bewildering. Sora Margherita is not for health freaks, and if you're on a diet, forget it; but no one argues with serious Roman Jewish cooking at these prices. The menu of classic pasta and meat dishes includes a great *pasta e fagioli* (pasta and bean stew) and *ossobuco* (veal shank) washed down with rough-and-ready house wine. Dessert consists of home-made *crostate* (jam or ricotta tarts).

Cafés, bars & pubs

Il Goccetto

Via dei Banchi Vecchi 14 (06 686 4268, www.facebook.com/Ilgoccetto). Bus 40, 46, 62, 64, 916. **Open** *6.30pm-midnight Mon; noon-3pm, 6pm-midnight Tue-Sat. Closed 3wks Aug.* **Map** *p78 F9* ❺ *Wine bar*

One of the more serious *centro storico* wine bars, occupying part of a medieval bishop's house, Il Goccetto has original painted ceilings, dark wood-clad walls and a cosy, private-club feel. Wine is the main point here, with a satisfying range by the glass from €4, but if you're peckish, there's a choice of cheeses, salamis and salads too.

Il Vinaietto – Antica Vineria

Via Monte della Farina 37 (06 6880 6989). Bus 30, 40, 46, 62, 63, 64, 70, 81, 87, 492, 571, 628, 780, 916, H/tram 8. **Open** *10.30am-3pm, 6.30-10.30pm Mon-Sat. Closed 1wk Aug.* **Map** *p78 H10* ❻ *Wine bar*

First and foremost a carry-out bottle shop, this long-running establishment near campo de' Fiori becomes a laid-back bohemian-chic stop of an evening, with standing-only customers spilling out into the picturesque street to sip wine by the glass at very reasonable prices.

Bakeries, pasticcerie & gelaterie

Alberto Pica

Via della Seggiola 12 (06 686 8405). Bus 30, 40, 46, 62, 63, 64, 70, 81, 87, 271, 492, 628, 780, 810, 916, H/tram 8. **Open** *Jan-Mar, Oct, Nov 8.30am-2am Mon-Sat. Apr-Sept, Dec 8.30am-2am Mon-Sat; 3pm-midnight Sun. Closed 1wk Aug.* **No cards. Map** *p78 H10* ❶ *Café*

Horrendous neon lighting, surly staff... and some seriously good ice-cream: these are the hallmarks of this long-running café close to the justice ministry. The rice specialities stand out: imagine eating frozen, partially cooked rice pudding and you'll get the picture. *Riso alla cannella* (cinnamon rice) is particularly wonderful.

❤ Il Forno Campo de' Fiori

Vicolo del Gallo 14 (06 6880 6662, www.fornocampodefiori.com). Bus 30, 40, 46, 62, 63, 64, 70, 81, 87, 116, 492, 628, 810, 916, H/tram 8. **Open** *7.30am-2.30pm, 5-8pm Mon-Sat. Closed Sat pm July & Aug.* **No cards. Map** *p78 G9* ❷ *Bakery*

This little bakery does the best takeaway sliced pizza in the campo de' Fiori area by far. The plain *pizza bianca* base, dressed with extra-

Il Pagliaccio p91

❤ Borini
*Via dei Pettinari 86 (06 687 5670).
Bus 23, 63, 271, 280, 780, H/tram
8.* **Open** *10.30am-7.30pm Mon-Sat.
Closed 2wks Aug.* **Map** *p78 G10* **7**
Shoes
Franco Borini's shop is busily
chaotic, packed with clued-in
shoe-lovers. In unusual hues and
effortlessly elegant, his durable shoes
vary from latest trends to timeless
classics. Prices are not low, but for
this kind of quality, they're fair.

Laboratorio Marco Aurelio
*Via dei Cappellari 21 (348 276 2842,
www.laboratoriomarcoaurelio.it).
Bus 30, 40, 46, 62, 63, 64, 70, 81,
87, 492, 628, 780, 810, 916, H/tram
8.* **Open** *by appt only 4-8pm Tue-
Sat. Closed mid Aug-mid Sept.* **No
cards**. **Map** *p78 G9* **8** *Jewellery*
Designer Marco Aurelio creates
stunning and often unconventional
pieces using hammered and wrought
silver, on site. Sizeable stones and
intricate patterns vaguely recall the
styles of ancient Roman.

Leone Limentani
*Via Portico d'Ottavia 47 (06 6880
6686). Bus 23, 63, 271, 280, 780,
H/tram 8.* **Open** *10am-7.30pm
Mon-Sat. Closed 2wks Aug.* **Map** *p78
J10* **9** *House & home*
A treasure-trove of high-piled
crockery and kitchenware is on
display here – at bargain-basement
prices. Many big-name brands are
reduced by up to 20%.

❤ Marta Ray
*Via della Reginella 4 (06 6873714,
www.martharay.it). Bus 23, 40Exp,
46, 62, 64, 916, H/tram 8.* **Open**
10am-8pm daily. **Map** *p78 H10* **10**
Accessories
Designer Marta Ratajczak's
gorgeous leather bags and
shoes combine contemporary
style with quality materials and
craftsmanship. From snazzy
ballerina flats to buttery soft

virgin olive oil, is delicious in itself,
but check out the one with *fiori
di zucca* (courgette flowers) too.
Close by, at campo de' Fiori 22, is
the main shop, which turns out a
variety of delicious breads, biscuits
and cakes.

Shops & services

Beppe e i suoi formaggi
*Via Santa Maria del Pianto
9/A (06 6819 2210, www.
beppeeisuoiformaggi.it). Bus 23,
40Exp, 46, 62, 64, 916, H/tram
8.* **Open** *9am-10.30pm Mon-Sat.
Closed 1wk Aug.* **Map** *p78 H10* **6**
Delicatessen
Walking into Beppe Giovale's
shop in the Jewish Ghetto is like
entering a cheese wonderland.
The vast counter displays an
overwhelming selection from the
familiar parmesan, pecorino and
mozzarella, to strong and stinky
varieties, many of which hail from
Beppe's home region of Piedmont.
There is also a small restaurant
area which serves cheese tastings
and a few seasonal dishes for lunch
and dinner.

93

satchels and wallets in a spectrum of colours, this stuff is made to last. The practical prices are an added bonus. **Other locations** via dei Coronari 121/122 (piazza Navona).

Momento

Piazza Benedetto Cairoli 9/via dei Giubbonari (06 6880 8157). Bus 30, 40, 46, 62, 63, 64, 70, 81, 87, 492, 628, 780, 810, 916, H/tram 8. Open 10am-7.30pm Mon-Fri; 10am-1.30pm, 3.30-7.30pm Sat. Map p78 H10 ⑪ *Fashion*

The poshest of princesses and her boho cousin will be equally awed over the collection of clothes and accessories at this treasure trove. Definitely for the fearless and colourful, all pieces from jumpers to evening gowns are flirty, feminine and fun. Also a fabulous spot for knock-'em-dead shoes and handbags in colour combos you've got to see to believe.

Entertainment

Oratorio del Gonfalone

Via del Gonfalone 32 (06 687 5952, www.oratoriogonfalone.eu). Bus 23, 40Exp, 46, 62, 64, 116, 190, 280, 870, 916. Box office 10am-4pm Mon-Fri. No cards. Map p78 F9 ② *Theatre*

This beautiful frescoed little auditorium is located in a 16th-century oratory adjacent to the Baroque church of the Gonfalone. It provides a suitable home for one of the city's most precious organs.

Teatro di Roma – Argentina

Largo Argentina 52 (06 684 0001, www.teatrodiroma.net). Bus 30Exp, 40Exp, 46, 62, 63, 64, 70, 81, 87, 492, 628, 780, 916, H/tram 8. Box office 10am-2pm, 3-7pm Tue-Sun. Map p78 H9 ③ *Theatre*

Rome's plush flagship theatre has a wide-ranging programme, including some dance and poetry.

Quirinale & Fontana di Trevi

Water is the dominant theme in the area nestling beneath the immense **Palazzo del Quirinale**, begun in 1574 for Pope Gregory XIII, once home to popes and kings and now the official residence of Italy's president. The water that cascades into the **Fontana di Trevi** is from the *acqua vergine* spring, said to be Rome's best, and used by Grand Tourists to make their tea. (Don't try drinking straight from the fountain: it's full of coins and chlorine.)

The surrounding medieval streets conceal many other testimonies to the importance of water, including the 'miraculous' well in the church of **Santa Maria in Via** (via Mortaro 24), from where cupfuls of healing liquid are still dispensed.

The Trevi district was a service area for the palace from the 16th century, home to the printing presses, bureaucratic departments and service industries that oiled the machinery of the Papal States. Aristocratic families, such as the Barberinis and Colonnas, built their palaces close by; their art collections are now on view at **Palazzo Barberini** and **Galleria Colonna**. Under the stern eye of the papal authorities, the **Galleria dell'Accademia di San Luca** (piazza dell'Accademia 7, www.accademiasanluca.eu) kept the flame of artistic orthodoxy burning.

Sharing the Quirinale hill with the president's palace are two of Rome's finest small Baroque churches, **San Carlo** and **Sant'Andrea**, and a crossroads with four fountains (1593) representing river gods.

Fontana di Trevi

acqua vergine spring – legend says the source was revealed to the troops of Agrippa by a virgin – the sparkling water of the fountain is full of chlorine (though there's a chlorine-free spout hidden in a bird-bath-shaped affair at the back of the fountain to the right).

It was an altogether different affair in 19 BC, when spring water – 100,000 cubic metres (3.5 cubic feet) of the stuff daily – was transported here by an aqueduct from the 12th kilometre of the via Collatina, to the east of Rome. The only aqueduct to pass underground along its whole route into the city, it was the sole survivor of barbarian destruction and other horrors of the early Middle Ages. In 1570 Pius V restored the conduit but it wasn't until 1732 that Pope Clement XII called for designs for a new *mostra* – a magnificent fountain to mark the end of the aqueduct. Completed decades later to a design by Nicolò Salvi, the *mostra* – the Trevi Fountain – immediately became a draw for tourists who drank the prized waters to ensure a return to Rome, as folklore has it.

Tucked away in a tiny piazza and almost always surrounded by jostling crowds, the fountain's stark travertine (cleaned in 2016 in a project sponsored by Fendi) gleams beneath powerful torrents of water and constant camera flashes. It's a magnificent rococo extravaganza of rearing sea horses, conch-blowing tritons, craggy rocks and flimsy trees, erupting in front of the wall of Palazzo Poli. Nobody can quite remember when the custom started of tossing coins in to the waters. The fountain is drained every Monday morning and the money goes to the Red Cross. Visit as early or as late as you can to have a chance of avoiding the crowds.

Sights & museums

❤ Fontana di Trevi

*Piazza di Trevi. Bus 52, 53, 62, 63, 71, 80Exp, 81, 83, 85, 116, 160, 492, 628. **Map** p78 K8.*
For recent generations, it was Anita Ekberg who made this fountain famous when she plunged in wearing a strapless black evening dress in Federico Fellini's classic film *La Dolce Vita*. Don't even think about trying it yourself – wading, washing and splashing in fountains are strictly against local by-laws. And unlike the Grand Tourists, you don't want to drink from it either: channelled from the ancient

Sala Grande, Galleria Colonna

Galleria Colonna

Via della Pilotta 17 (06 678 4350, www.galleriacolonna.it). Bus 40Exp, 60Exp, 64, 70, 117, 170, H. **Open** *9am-1.15pm Sat, or by appt. Closed Aug.* **Admission** *€12; €10 reductions. No cards.* **Map** *p78 K9.*

Saturday mornings are your only chance to see this splendid gallery, completed in 1703 by Prince Filippo II Colonna whose descendants still live in the palace. (Among others, the Colonnas produced a pope, a saint and an excommunicated cardinal.) The entrance leads to the Room of the Column, originally the throne room of Prince Filippo and his successors, who would have sat in state by the ancient column, back-lit by light shining through the window behind, and with a view across to a triumphal arch dedicated to Marcantonio Colonna, the family hero. (Audrey Hepburn behaved regally here, too, in *Roman Holiday*.) The cannonball embedded in the stairs down to the Great Hall lies where it landed during the French siege of Rome

on 24 June 1849. The mirrored hall may be the work of Gian Lorenzo Bernini, inspired by his visit to Versailles in 1665, while the immense frescoed ceiling pays tribute to Marcantonio, who led the papal fleet to victory against the Turks in the great naval battle of Lepanto in 1571. The gallery's most famous and much-reproduced picture is Annibale Caracci's earthy peasant *Bean Eater*. Private tours can be arranged of the gallery as well as the private apartments at other times during the week. When the weather permits the café on the pleasant terrace is worth a visit.

♥ Palazzo Barberini – Galleria Nazionale d'Arte Antica

Via delle Quattro Fontane 13 (06 481 4591, bookings 06 32 810, barberinicorsini.org). Metro Barberini/bus 52, 53, 61, 62, 63, 80Exp, 85, 492, 590. **Open** *8.30am-7pm (last entry 6pm) Tue-Sun.* **Admission** *€10 incl Palazzo Corsini (ticket valid 10 days, see p121); €5 reductions.* **Map** *p78 L7.*

Top architects like Maderno, Bernini and Borromini queued up to work on this vast pile, which, despite its size and attention to detail, was completed in just five years, shortly after Maffeo Barberini became Pope Urban VIII in 1623. Bernini did the main staircase, a grand rectangular affair now marred by an ill-placed lift. Borromini, whose uncle Carlo Maderno drew up the original palace plans, added the graceful oval staircase. After lengthy restoration and extension of the gallery into newly acquired parts of the palace, three floors of paintings are now visible. The main show is the splendid first floor *salone* with the extraordinary ceiling painting by Pietro da Cortona. The *Allegory of Divine Providence* (1629) is the most Baroque of all Baroque extravanganzas and worth the ticket price all by itself. Highlights of the main first-floor 16th- and 17th-century collection are Raphael's *Fornarina* (said, probably wrongly, to be a portrait of the baker's daughter he may have been engaged to at the time of his death in 1520), Holbein's pompous *Henry VIII*, Caravaggio's *Judith and Holofernes* and Titian's *Venus and Adonis*.

Palazzo del Quirinale
Piazza del Quirinale (06 3996 7557, www.quirinale.it). Bus 40Exp, 52, 53, 60, 61, 62, 63, 64, 70, 80Exp, 85, 170, 492, 590, C3, H. **Open** *8.30am-noon Sun. Closed July, Aug.* **Admission** *€10.* **Map** *p78 K8.*
The new St Peter's still wasn't finished when Pope Gregory XIII started building this pontifical summer palace on the highest of Rome's seven hills; begun in 1573, the Quirinale was not completed until over 200 years later. The risk that a pontiff (they were not, on the whole, renowned for their youthful vigour) might keel over during the holidays was such that it was

decided to build somewhere that was also suitable to hold a conclave to elect a successor. The Quirinale's Cappella Paolina (named after Paul V) was designed by Carlo Maderno and finished in 1617; it is a faithful replica of the Vatican's Sistine Chapel, minus the Michelangelos. Accommodation for the cardinals was provided in the *Manica lunga*, the immensely long wing that runs the length of via del Quirinale to the rear of the palace. Bernini added the main entrance door in 1638.

Concerts are held in the Pauline chapel of the Palace at noon on Sundays throughout much of the year. Concerts are free but advance booking is required (palazzo. quirinale.it).

The presidential guard changes with a flourish on the piazza del Quirinale at 4pm on Sundays from October to May, and at 6pm from June to September. The palazzo is closed during the summer months of July and August, and occasionally in April and December, so do check before visiting.

♥ San Carlo alle Quattro Fontane
Via del Quirinale 23 (06 488 3261, www.sancarlino.eu). Metro Barberini/bus 40Exp, 52, 53, 60, 61, 62, 63, 64, 70, 80Exp, 85, 170, 492, 590, C, H. **Open** *10am-1pm Mon-Sat; 11am-1pm Sun.* **Map** *p78 L7.*
Carlo Borromini's first solo composition (1631-41), and the one of which he was most proud, San Carlo (often called Carlino, due to its diminutive scale) is one of the star pieces of the Roman Baroque. The most remarkable feature is the dizzying oval dome: its geometrical coffers decrease in size towards the lantern to give the illusion of additional height – Borromini is all about illusion – and the subtle illumination, through hidden windows, makes the dome appear

to float in mid-air. There is also an austere adjoining courtyard and a sobering crypt.

Sant'Andrea al Quirinale

Via del Quirinale 29 (06 487 4565, santandrea.gesuiti.it). Bus 40Exp, 52, 53, 60, 61, 62, 63, 64, 70, 80Exp, 85, 170, 492, 590, H. **Open** *8.30am-noon, 2.30-6pm Tues-Sat; 9am-noon, 3-6pm Sun.* **Map** *p78 L8.*

With funding from Prince Camillo Pamphilj, the Jesuits commissioned Gian Lorenzo Bernini to build a church for novices living on the Quirinale. The site was small and awkward, but Bernini solved the problem by designing an oval church (1658) with the entrance and the high altar very unusually on the short axis. Above the door, a section of the wall seems to have swung down on to the columns, creating an entrance porch. Inside, the church is richly decorated with the figure of St Andrew (by Antonio Raggi, Bernini's star pupil) floating heavenwards through a broken pediment above the high altar.

Antica Birreria Peroni

Via di San Marcello 19 (06 679 5310, www.anticabirreriaperoni. net). Bus 53, 62, 63, 80, 81, 83, 85, 117, 492, 628, C3. **Open** *noon-midnight Mon-Sat. Closed 2wks Aug.* **Map** *p78 J8* ❼ *Birreria*

This long-standing *centro storico birreria* is the perfect place to grab a quick beer or an informal lunch or dinner. Service is rough-and-Roman but generally friendly, and the food – a few hot pasta dishes, fried snacks and some cold cuts – is good and relatively cheap. Sausage, though, is the main draw: three different types of German-style *wurstel* are on offer. The *birreria* still retains its original art nouveau

decor, with a chiaroscuro frieze featuring such slogans as 'drink beer and you'll live to be 100'.

Il Gelato di San Crispino

Via della Panetteria 42 (06 679 3924, www.ilgelatodisancrispino. it). Bus 52, 53, 62, 63, 71, 80, 83, 85, 117, 492, 590, C3. **Open** *noon-12.30am Mon-Thur, Sun; noon-1.30am Fri, Sat.* **No cards.** **Map** *p78 K7* ❸ *Gelateria*

A few years ago, when Rome's ice-cream sector languished in a mire of self-satisfaction, Il Gelato di San Crispino came along to shake things up. Obsessive control over the whole production process, from the choice of superlative raw materials to every stage of mixing and freezing, resulted in an ice-cream that reached new heights and prompted a wave of imitations. Although, in recent years, it has lost a little of its loyal following to some of the new kids on the block, for many punters San Crispino remains one of the best ice-creams anywhere. **Other locations** piazza della Maddalena 5, Pantheon (06 9760 1190); Fiumicino airport, Terminal A.

Sala Trevi

Vicolo del Puttarello 25 (06 678 1206, www.fondazionecsc.it). Bus 52, 53, 62, 63, 71, 80Exp, 81, 83, 85, 492, 628. **Map** *p78 K8* ❹ *Cinema*

This 100-seater cinema belongs to Italy's national film archive. It shares its basement location with a 400sq m (4,300sq ft) archaeological site based around two ancient Roman *insulae* (apartment blocks), which can be seen through the glass panels at the side of the main screening room.

Villa Borghese & Tridente

Until the 1870s, when Rome became the capital of newly united Italy and speculators set to work to house the soaring population, the city was dotted with splendid private estates. An act of unusual foresight by the state in 1901 saved Villa Borghese from the carve-up, and left us with this delightful green space.

Descending south from the park, via Vittorio Veneto (known simply as via Veneto) was the haunt of the famous and glamorous in the *dolce vita* years of the 1950s and '60s. These days, it's home to insurance companies, luxury hotels and visitors wondering where the stars and paparazzi went.

Best ancient history
Museo dell'Ara Pacis *p109*
Museo Nazionale Etrusco di Villa
Giulia *p101*

Best for a shopping splurge
Furla *p114*
L'Olfattorio – Bar à Parfums *p114*
Sermoneta *p114*

Best for coffee or cocktails
Caffè Canova-Tadolini *p113*
Hotel Locarno Bar *p113*

Best art through the ages
Galleria Borghese *p104*
La Galleria Nazionale *p101*
MAXXI *p112*
Museo Carlo Bilotti *p101*
Santa Maria del Popolo *p110*

Best for English tourists
Babington's Tea Room *p112*
Keats-Shelley Memorial
House *p108*
Spanish Steps *p110*

Also south of Villa Borghese is the wedge-shaped Tridente, with its English banks and English bookshops. It was a home-from-home for the Grand Tourists of the 18th and 19th centuries, when English 'milords' took lodgings in and around piazza di Spagna. Even today, there are visitors who never make it further than the Tridente's array of glorious fashion retailers.

Villa Borghese

In the first century BC, Rome's most extensive gardens, the Horti Sallustiani, spread over the valley between the Quirinale hill and the Pincio. During the Renaissance, the area was colonised by aristocratic families such as the Borghese and Boncompagni-Ludovisi, who attempted to outdo one another with the lavishness of their vast suburban estates. In fact, up until the building boom in Rome during the late 1800s, only the odd villa or decorative pavilion interrupted the tranquil and leafy parkland that stretched from the Pincio to Porta Pia.

When Rome was made capital of Italy in 1871, this green idyll was seen as prime building land, to be dug up and replaced by street after

street of grandiose *palazzi*; of the estates, only the Villa Borghese was saved from the property vultures; it is now the city's most central public park.

Villa Borghese is a great repository of art and culture, encompassing not only the superb Baroque-crammed **Galleria Borghese** (*see p104*), but also **La Galleria Nazionale** for post-19th century art, the **Museo Nazionale Etrusco di Villa Giulia** for Etruscan objects and the small **Museo Carlo Bilotti** for modern art. Plus you'll find one of Rome's greatest views from the **Pincio** hill, over piazza del Popolo to the dome of St Peter's. The park also houses the **Bioparco-Zoo** (www.bioparco.it) and the **Casa del Cinema**.

Sights & museums

❤ La Galleria Nazionale

Viale delle Belle Arti 131 (06 3229 8221, www.lagallerianazionale. com). Bus 61, 89, 160, 490, 495/ tram 3, 19. **Open** *8.30am-7.30pm Tue-Sun.* **Admission** *€10; €5 reductions. Exhibition price varies. No cards.* **Map** *p102 J2.*

Several of the villas dotted around the park are the remains of a world exposition held here in 1911, and this neo-classical palace dedicated to 19th- and 20th-century art is one of the most eye-pleasing. (For 21st century *see p112* MAXXI.) A rehang in 2017 broke with the traditional chronological layout.

Major Italian works include the bombast of Canova's *Hercules* (1795), the melancholy of Modigliani, Boldini's society portraits with a twist, the metaphysical masterpieces of De Chirico, not to mention Lucio Fontana and Burri.

International stars include *The Three Ages* by Klimt (1905) and *The Gardener* (1889) and *Madame Ginoux* (1890) by Van Gogh. Cézanne, Braque, Rodin and Henry Moore are also represented here.

❤ Museo Carlo Bilotti

Viale Fiorello La Guardia (06 0608, www.museocarlobilotti.it). Bus 61, 89, 160, 490, 491, 495. **Open** *Oct-May 10am-4pm Tue-Fri; 10am-7pm Sat, Sun. June-Sept 1-7pm Tue-Fri; 10am-7pm Sat, Sun.* **Admission** *free.* **Map** *p102 K4.*

This small museum of modern art is housed in a *palazzo* that was bought by Scipione Borghese in 1616 and used as a resting place during hunts. Damaged by French cannon fire in 1849, it was then variously used as a storehouse for oranges, a religious institute and city offices; it opened as a gallery in 2006 to house the superlative collection of billionaire tycoon Carlo Bilotti. The De Chirico paintings and sculptures that form the nucleus of the 22 works in the permanent collection (first floor) perhaps influenced Bilotti to choose Rome as the city in which to display them (De Chirico spent much of his life in Rome, and died here in 1978.) Also on the first floor, an entire room is devoted to the Bilotti family: the highlights are a Larry Rivers portrait of Signor Bilotti posing before a Dubuffet canvas, and a poignant 1981 Warhol portrait of Bilotti's wife and daughter. A wall of photographs capture the family schmoozing with various high-profile figures on the contemporary art scene. The ground floor hosts temporary art exhibitions.

❤ Museo Nazionale Etrusco di Villa Giulia

Piazzale di Villa Giulia 9 (06 322 6571). Bus 52, 926/tram 2, 19. **Open** *8.30am-7.30pm Tue-Sun.* **Admission** *€8; €4 reductions. No cards.* **Map** *p102 H2.*

Founded in 1889 at the splendid Villa Giulia, this collection charts the development of the sophisticated, mysterious

→ Getting around

Villa Borghese is best accessed from the Spagna metro stop on line A. Either take the unprepossessing underground walkway and escalator, climb the Spanish Steps, or use the lift just inside the metro station entrance. These lead you to the ridge of the Pincio. Alternatively, walk up via Veneto from Barberini metro stop (a gentle ten-minute uphill stroll). The Tridente area is very walkable, and easily navigated using the main road arteries as guides.

Via F. Jacovacci
Via Michele Mercati
Via B. Buozzi
Via Giuseppe Mangili
Viale delle Belle Arti
Via Antonio Gramsci
Via Ulisse Aldrovandi
Via F. Flaminia
British School at Rome
Via di Villa Giulia
Giardino Zen
Museo Nazionale Etrusco di Villa Giulia
La Galleria Nazionale
Via Giovanni Vincenzo Gravina
Lungotevere delle Navi
Viale delle Belle Arti
Via Omero
Piazzale Firdusi
Piazza della Marina
Museo Pietro Canonic
Viale Madama Letizia
Via di Valle
Museo Hendrik Christian Andersen
Via Pasquale Stanislao Mancini
Via degli Orti Giustiniani
VILLA BORGHESE
Giardino del Lago
Silvano Toti Globe Theatre
Lungotevere Arnaldo da Brescia
Via degli Scialoja
Via Giambattista Vico
Stazione di Piazzale Flaminio
Viale Fiorello
Museo Carlo Bilotti
Via David Lubin
Via Pietro Canonica
Piazza Victor Hugo
La Guardia
Piazza d. Canestre
Ponte Metropolitana Pietro Nenni
Via Luisa di Savoia
Via Domenico Romegnosi
Flaminio Ⓜ
Via Giorgio Washington
Viale del Muro Torto
Viale della Magnolie
Viale San Paolo del Brasile
Via Gian
Piazzale Flaminio
Via delle Magnolie
V.M. Cristina
Principessa Clotilde
Santa Maria del Popolo
Via Valadier
Viale dei Bambini
Viale dell'Ippocastano
Ponte Regina Margherita
Via Maria Adelaide
Piazza del Popolo
Piazzale Napoleone I
Pincio
Via delle Magnolie
Piazza della Libertà
❻
Galoppatoio
Via della Penna
Via del Borghetto
Piazza Bucarest
❺
Viale del Galoppatoio
Viale del Muro Torto
Via Ennio Quirino Visconti
Via Angelo Brunetti
❹
✚
Casina Valadier
Giardino di Villa Medici
Via Giuseppe Gioacchino Belli
Via del Vantaggio
Via di Fontanella
Viale della Trinità dei Monti
Villa Medici
Passeggiata di Ripetta
Via del Fiume
Via Laurina
Via del Corso
Via di Gesù e Maria
Via Margutta
❶
Via Pietro Cossa
Via del Babuino
Via di San Giacomo
Via dei Greci
❸
Lungotevere in Augusta
Via Antonio Canova
Via della Frezza
TRIDENTE
✚
Spagna Ⓜ
Via Marianna Dionigi
Museo dell'Ara Pacis
Via di Ponlelici
Via Vittoria
Via della Bocca di Leone
Via della Croce
❹❷
Piazza di Spagna
❸❷
Trinità dei Monti
Via Vittoria Colonna
Via Fontanella Borghese
Mausoleo d'Augusto
Via delle Carrozze
❶
Via del Corso
Spanish Steps
Keats-Shelley House
Via F. Crispi
Fiume Tevere
San Rocco
Via di Ripetta
Piazza Augusto Imperatore
Via di Leoncino
Via delle Convertite
❺
Piazza Mignanelli
Via Sistina
Museo delle Anime del Purgatorio
Ponte Cavour
Santi Ambrogio e Carlo al Corso
Largo Carlo Goldoni
Via di Condotti
Borgognona
Piazza dei due Macelli
Via Gregoriana
Lungotevere Marzio
San Girolamo degli Illirici
Via della Vite
Palazzo Borghese
Via di Campo Marzio
Via del Leone
Piazza di San Lorenzo in Lucina
Via Frattina
Posta Centrale
Via Mercede
Galleria d'Arte Moderna di Roma Capitale
Ponte Umberto I
Via Nicosia
San Lorenzo in Lucina
Via del Clementino
Via del Leone
Via della Scrofa
Via di Monte Brianzo
❷
Piazza del Parlamento
Via di Campo Marzio
Piazza San Silvestro
Via Bufalo
Largo d Tritone
Via Metastasio
Palazzo di Montecitorio
V. d. San Claudio
Galleria dell'Accademia
Piazza Poli
Palazzo Chigi
Piazza di Montecitorion
Piazza Colonna
Fontana di Trevi
Via In Arcione
Via delle Crociferi
Via del Lavatore
V.N. In Arcione

0 300 m
0 300 yds

© Copyright Time Out Group 2017

G   H   J   K

Bioparco Zoo

Via Ulisse Aldrovandi

Via Giacomo Carissimi

Piazza Giuseppe Verdi

Via Saverio Mercadante

Via Giovanni Battista Martini

Via Giovanni Paisiello

V. Claudio Monteverdi

Via Gaspare Spontini

Via Gaetano Donizetti

Viale del Giardino Zoologico

Via Ruggero Giovannelli

Via Metauro

Via Tagliamento

Via Arno

2

Viale Regina Margherita

Via Tirso

Via G. Po

Via Sele

Via Saverio Mercadante

Via Pietro Raimondi

Via Jacopo Peri

Via Sameto

Via Basento

Piazzale dei Daini

Viale dei Daini

Villa Giorgina

Via Adda

Giardini di Villa Albani

Viale dell'Uccelliera

Parco dei Daini

Via Gregorio Allegri

Via Salaria

3

Viale dei Cavalli Marini

Galleria Borghese

Piazzale Scipione Borghese

Via Pinciana

Via Po

Via Livenza

Via Tevere

Via di Villa Albani

Via Savoia

Via Nizza

V. Reggio Emilia

Piazza di Siena

Piazzale del Museo Borghese

Via Isonzo

Via Salaria

Via Rieti

Via Veletri

Via Brescia

Via Mantova

4

Viale del Pupazzi

Via di Santa Teresa

Via Aniene

Via Nizza

Via Bergamo

Via G. Paglia

Piazza Alessandria

Viale Alberto Sordi

Via Giacomo Puccini

Piazza Fiume

Via S. Massimo

Via G. A. Alessandria

ale Goethe Sordi

Via del Museo Borghese

Corso d'Italia

Piazza Salaria

Via Valenziani

Piazzale di Porta Pia

Sottovia Ignazio Guidi

1

Casa del Cinema

Via Pinciana

Via Campania

Via Sicilia

Via Lucania

Via Calabria

Via S. Massimo

Via Piave

Giardino di Villa Paolina

Porta Pia

5

Piazza Brasile

Corso d'Italia

Via Sardegna

Via Puglie

Piazza Sallustio

Via Flavia

Via Palestro

QUARTIERE LUDOVISI

Via Lazio

Via Toscana

Via Abruzzi

Via Romagna

PIAZZA SALLUSTIO & PORTA PIA

2

Via Cernaia

British Embassy

Via Lombardia

Via Sicilia

Via Piemonte

Via Quintino Sella

Via Castelfidardo

Via Goito

6

Via Marche

Via Boncompagni

Via Servio Tullio

Via Castelfidardo

v. Ludovisi

Via Aurora

Via Emilia

Via Lucullo

Via Sallustiana

Via Aureliana

Via XX Settembre

Via Montebello

Via Goito

VIA VENETO

Villa Margherita

Via Gaeta

Via Pastrengo

Via Pietro Barbieri

Terme di Diocleziano

Piazza dell' Indipendenza

Via Vittorio Veneto

Via Giosue Carducci

V. Mario Pagano

V. Antonio Salandra

Via XX Settembre

Santa Maria della Vittoria

Via Solferino

Museo e Cripta dei Frati Cappuccini

Via Leonida Bissolati

Via di San Basilio

Via di San Nicola da Tolentino

Via Parigi

Via Vittorio Emanuele Orlando

Santa Maria degli Angeli

Via Enrico de Nicola

v. di Purificazione

Via Vittorio Veneto

Salita di S. Nicola da Tolentino

Via Firenze

Via Torino

Termini Ⓜ

7

Via Sistina

Barberini Ⓜ

Piazza Barberini

Palazzo Barberini

Via XX Settembre

Repubblica Ⓜ

Piazza della Repubblica

Largo di Villa Peretti

Piazza del Cinquecento

Stazione Termini

v. di Avignonesi

Via Rasella

Giardini di Palazzo Barberini

San Paolo dentro le Mura

Teatro dell'Opera

Palazzo Massimo alle Terme

Via Giovanni Giolitti

Giardino del Quirinale

Palazzo delle Esposizioni

Via Nazionale

Via Napoli

Piazza Beniamino Gigli

L

M

N

Teatro Umberto I

Palazzo del Quirinale

Palazzo del

103

💜 Galleria Borghese

Piazzale del Museo Borghese 5 (06 32 810, www.galleriaborghese. it). Bus 52, 53, 160, 490, 495, 910. **Open** *9am-7pm Tue-Sun.* **Admission** *€15; €8.50 reductions. Exhibition price varies.* **Map** *p102 M3.*

Begun in 1608 by Flaminio Ponzio and continued by Jan van Santen (Italianised to Giovanni Vasanzio) upon his death, the *Casino nobile* was designed to house Cardinal Scipione Borghese's art collection. One of Bernini's greatest patrons, the cardinal had as good an eye for a bargain as for a masterpiece: he picked up many works – including the odd Caravaggio – at knock-down prices after they were rejected by the disappointed or shocked patrons who had commissioned them.

The building's imposing façade was originally adorned with sculptures and ancient reliefs, which, along with many of the gallery's priceless gems, were sold to Napoleon in 1807 and are now conserved in the Louvre.

Inside, a curved double staircase leads to the imposing entrance salon, with fourth-century AD floor mosaics showing gladiators fighting wild animals; the spectacular trompe l'oeil ceiling fresco (Mariano Rossi, 1775-78) shows Romulus received as a god on Olympus by Jupiter and other tales of Roman glory.

In Room 1 is one of the gallery's highlights: Canova's 1808 waxed marble figure of Pauline, sister of Napoleon and wife of Prince Camillo Borghese, as a topless Venus reclining languidly on a marble and wood sofa, which once contained a mechanism that slowly rotated it. Prince Camillo thought the work so provocative that he forbade even the artist from seeing it after completion.

Rooms 2 to 4 contain some spectacular sculptures by Gian Lorenzo Bernini, made early in his career and already showing flashes of his genius. His *David* (1624) merits observation from different points of view in Room 2; the tense, concentrated face on the biblical hero as he is about to launch his shot is a self-portrait of the artist. Room 3 houses perhaps Bernini's most famous piece: *Apollo and Daphne* (1625), a seminal work of Baroque sculpture. In Room 4, Pluto's hand presses fiercely into Proserpina's marble thigh in The *Rape of Proserpina* (1622), as she flexes her toes in tearful struggle.

Room 5 contains important pieces of classical sculpture, many of them Roman copies of Greek originals. Among the most renowned are a Roman copy of a

The Rape of Proserpina (Bernini, 1622)

Greek dancing faun and a copy of sleeping Hermaphroditus, who was the offspring of Hermes and Aphrodite, displayed with his/her back to the onlooker so that the breasts and genitals are invisible. Bernini's *Aeneas, Anchises and Ascanius* (1620) dominates Room 6, showing the family fleeing as Troy burns, a theme reflected in the ceiling with Pecheux's painting of the gods deciding the fate of the city. Room 7 is Egyptian-themed: the ceiling paintings by Tommaso Maria Conca (1780) include an allegory of the richness of Egypt. The six Caravaggios in Room 8 include the *Boy with a Basket of Fruit* (c1594) and the *Sick Bacchus* (c1593), which is believed to be a self-portrait.

Upstairs, the picture gallery is packed with one masterpiece after another. Look out in particular for: Raphael's *Deposition*, Pinturicchio's *Crucifixion with Saints Jerome and Christopher* and Perugino's Madonna and Child (Room 9); Correggio's *Danaë*,

commissioned as 16th-century soft porn for Charles V of Spain (Room 10); a dark, brooding *Pietà* by Raphael's follower Sodoma (Room 12); two self-portraits and two sculpted busts of Cardinal Scipione Borghese by Bernini (Room 14); Jacopo Bassano's *Last Supper* (Room 15); and Rubens' spectacular *Pietà* (Room 18). Titian's *Venus Blindfolding Cupid* and *Sacred and Profane Love*, the work that originally put the gallery on the map, are the centrepieces of Room 20. In 1899, the Rothschilds offered to buy the latter work at a price that exceeded the estimated value of the entire gallery and all its works put together; the offer was turned down.

Note: booking is obligatory, and if you haven't booked well in advance you may find the gallery fully booked from April to October. You should have no trouble getting in midweek in low season. Visitors are assigned a two-hour slot, entering every two hours from 9am until 5pm. You must leave at the end of your slot.

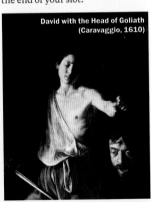

David with the Head of Goliath (Caravaggio, 1610)

Etruscans. The villa was originally constructed in the mid 16th century as a sumptuous summer residence for Pope Julius III; Michelangelo gave his friend Vignola a hand with the design. The rustic façade leads into an elegantly frescoed loggia. Across the courtyard, stairs go down to the nymphaeum.

In the main body of the museum, a number of rooms are dedicated to objects found at the Etruscan necropolis at Cerveteri; the centrepiece is the almost life-size terracotta sarcophagus. Dating from the sixth century BC, it shows a married couple as if they are reclining at a dinner party (or indeed their own funerary banquet). The Etruscan fondness for eating and drinking is apparent from the vast number of bronze cooking utensils, as well as ceramic cups and amphorae (often decorated with scenes from imported Greek myths). The Room of the Seven Hills (a frescoed frieze names them) contains the Castellani collection of extraordinarily delicate jewellery from the eighth century BC right up to the 19th century. Next door is the Room of Venus, with pieces unearthed at the fifth-century BC temples of Pyrgi. The Etruscans went well prepared to their graves, and the majority of the collection comes from excavations of tombs: hundreds of vases, pieces of furniture and models of buildings made to accompany the dead. Detailed notes in English explain the excavation sites and provide information on how gold, bronze and clay were worked in times gone by. The last room before one exits contains one of the museum's absolute masterpieces, the delicate terracotta sixth-century BC *Apollo of Veio*. In the gardens there is a reconstruction of an Etruscan temple, and a pleasant café which is sadly only open sporadically.

Entertainment

Casa del Cinema
Largo Marcello Mastroianni 1 (060608, www.casadelcinema.it). Bus 61, 89, 120, 150, 160, 490, 495. **Map** *p102 L4* ❶ *Cinema*
In the Villa Borghese park, the Casa is used for film-related presentations and screenings. Many of the films shown during the Casa's festivals and retrospectives are in *lingua originale*. Even if you're not there to see a film, the Cinecaffè inside the Casa del Cinema is a great place for a coffee or lunch.

Via Veneto & around

Leading south from Villa Borghese, via Veneto struggles to live up to its *dolce vita* glory days, when Fellini made it Rome's most glamorous hangout. Modern-day Taylors and Burtons, when they're in town, do their hell-raising elsewhere, but this elegant tree-lined slalom curve still manages to rake in the euros, mainly thanks to its vast luxury hotels groaning under the weight of their own chandeliers, and its cripplingly expensive, glass-enclosed pavement cafés, aimed entirely at expense-account travellers and unwitting tourists. The area either side of via Veneto is known as the **Quartiere Ludovisi**, after the 17th-century Villa Ludovisi which occupied this space until the 1870s.

At the southern end of via Veneto is **piazza Barberini**. In ancient times, erotic dances were performed here to mark the coming of spring. The square's magnificent centrepiece, Bernini's **Triton fountain**, was once in open countryside. Now he sits – his two fish-tail legs tucked beneath him on a shell supported by four dolphins – amid thundering traffic.

▶ *For Palazzo Barberini and its art collection, see p96.*

Sights & museums

Museo e Cripta dei Cappuccini

Via Veneto 27 (06 4201 4995, www. cappucciniviaveneto.it). Metro Barberini, bus 52, 53, 61, 63, 80, 83, 1 160. **Open** *Church 7am-noon, 3pm-7pm daily. Museum & crypt 9am-7pm daily.* **Admission** *Church free. Museum & crypt €8.50; €5 reductions.* **Map** *p102 L6.*

The spooky Capuchin crypt that unsuspecting tourists once happened across has become a well-packaged tourist attraction – sad, but inevitable. Fortunately, the monks have done the transformation with some taste. Visitors are channelled through a series of rooms full of artefacts (a knotted whip for self-flagellation, anyone?) and minor artworks celebrating the order, its saints and missions. Here, too, is the early 17th century painting of *St Francis in Meditation*, which the monks are still, bravely, defending as a work by Caravaggio, though this is almost certainly wishful thinking. The real draw comes at the end, in the crypt, which holds Rome's most macabre sight: the skeletons of thousands of monks, meticulously dismantled and arranged in swirls, sunbursts and curlicues through four subterranean chapels. Delicate ribs hang from the ceiling in the form of chandeliers, and inverted pelvic bones make the shape of hourglasses – a reminder (as a notice states) that 'you will be what we now are'.

The Baroque church upstairs – officially the church of Santa Maria dell'Immacolata Concezione, but known to all as *i Cappuccini* (the Capuchins) after the long-bearded, brown-clad Franciscan sub-order to which it belongs – has a *St Michael* (1635) by Guido Reni (first

chapel on the right), a major hit with English Grand Tourists, and a fine *St Paul's Sight Being Restored* (1631) by Pietro da Cortona (first chapel on the left).

Restaurants

Osteria dell'Arco €€

Via G Pagliari 11 (06 854 8438, www.osteriadellarco.net).Bus 38, 60, 62, 80, 90, 490, 495. **Open** *1-3pm, 8-11pm Mon-Fri; 8-11pm Sat. Closed lunchtime in Aug.* **Map** *p102 N4* **①** *Osteria*

The lively neighbourhood just outside Porta Pia is on the up and up, with a sprinkling of new places to eat. One of the best is this wine-oriented *osteria*, all brick vaulted ceiling and bottle-lined walls, which offers creative *trattoria* cooking at competitive prices. A frequently changing menu might have ravioli with broccoli and anchovies, while desserts are mostly play-safe standards such as *crema catalana*. Vegetarians will find a better-than-average selection here, and the worthwhile wine list includes several by-the-glass options.

Pinsere €

Via Flavia 98 (06 4202 0924, www. pinsaromana.info/pinsere-roma). Bus 38, 60, 62, 90, 492, 910. **Open** *9am-8pm Mon-Fri. Closed 2wks Aug.* **Map** *p102 N5* **②** *Pizzeria*

Named after *la pinsa*, an ancient Roman forerunner of pizza, Pinsere sells its oval flatbreads individually with generous, great-quality toppings which range from the classic margherita to more unique seasonal creations such as prosciutto with fresh figs. It's a tiny place with a handful of seats but with prices hovering around the €4-€5 mark for a whole *pinsa* it's a great value and satisfying lunch spot.

Tridente

The Tridente was built as a showpiece. At its northern tip is **piazza del Popolo**, used for executions for centuries and given its oval form by architect Giuseppe Valadier during the early 19th century. The obelisk in the centre was brought from Egypt by Augustus and stood in the Circo Massimo until 1589, when it was moved to its present site by Pope Sixtus V. The porta del Popolo, built by Pope Sixtus IV in 1475 and remodelled by Bernini in 1655, replaced the Roman porta Flaminia, which was the northern entrance into the ancient city. Next to it is the church of **Santa Maria dei Popolo**. On the south side, the churches of Santa Maria dei Miracoli and Santa Maria di Monte Santo demarcate the 'trident' of streets that emanate from the piazza into the city.

Leading out centrally from the square is the Tridente's principal thoroughfare, **via del Corso**, which passes high-street clothing retailers en route to piazza Colonna (named after its second-century **colonna di Marco Aurelio**), and piazza Venezia. Just off piazza Colonna is the prime minister's office in **Palazzo Chigi** and the Lower House of Parliament in **Palazzo di Montecitorio**.

Via Ripetta heads south from piazza del Popolo towards Augustus's mausoleum and the **Ara Pacis**, while the third street, chic **via del Babuino**, runs past a series of tempting antique and designer stores to the **Spanish Steps** and the **Keats-Shelley Memorial House**. The super-smart grid of streets at the foot of the steps has been attracting the rich and famous since the 18th century, when Grand Tourists (*see p111*) met for coffee at the (long gone) Caffè degli Inglesi on the corner of via delle Carrozze. To the south-east, the **Galleria d'Arte Moderna** (via F Crispi 24, galleriaartemodernaroma. it) has an intriguing collection of 20th-century Roman art. Parallel to via del Babuino, tucked right below the Pincio hill, is via Margutta, fondly remembered as the focus of the 1960s art scene and 'home' to Gregory Peck in the 1953 classic *Roman Holiday*. Fellini also lived on this artsy alley. Criss-crossing the three arteries are the boutique-lined streets, such as via Condotti, that have given Rome its reputation as a major fashion centre.

Sights & museums

Colonna di Marco Aurelio

Piazza Colonna. Bus 52, 53, 62, 63, 71, 80Exp, 81, 83, 85, 117, 492, 590, 628, C3. **Map** *p102 J8.*
The 30-metre (100-foot) column of Marcus Aurelius was built between AD 180 and 196 to commemorate the victories on the battlefield of that most intellectual of Roman emperors. Author of the *Meditations*, he died while campaigning in 180. The reliefs on the column, modelled on the earlier ones on Trajan's Column (*see p69*) in the Imperial Fora, are vivid illustrations of Roman army life. In 1589 a statue of St Paul replaced that of Marcus Aurelius on top of the column.

❤ Keats-Shelley Memorial House

Piazza di Spagna 26 (06 678 4235, www.keats-shelley-house.org). Metro Spagna/bus 52, 53, 62, 63, 71, 80Exp, 83, 85, 117, 160, 492, 590, C3. **Open** *10am-1pm, 2-6pm Mon-Sat.* **Admission** *€5; €4 reductions.* **Map** *p102 K6.*
The house at the bottom of the Spanish Steps where 25-year-old John Keats died in 1821 is

Colonna di Marco Aurelio

♥ Museo dell'Ara Pacis

Via Ripetta/lungotevere in Augusta (06 0608, www.arapacis.it). Bus 30Exp, 70, 81, 87, 117, 280, 492, 628, 913. **Open** *9.30am-7.30pm daily.* **Admission** *€10.50, €8.50 reductions. Exhibition price varies.* **Map** *p102 H6.*

Now in a striking and luminous container – designed by Richard Meier and opened amid great controversy – Augustus' great monument, the Ara Pacis Augustae, was inaugurated in 9 BC; this altar of Augustan peace celebrated the end of the civil war and strife that had characterised the last years of the Republic, and the wealth and security brought by Augustus' victories. Originally located a few hundred metres away (off via in Lucina, behind the church of **San Lorenzo in Lucina**; *see below*), the *ara* was designed to overlook the urban stretch of via Flaminia (now via del Corso) by which Augustus had re-entered the city after three years' absence in Spain and Gaul. The altar as we see it now was reconstructed in the 1930s (by Mussolini who called himself 'the New Augustus') – after major excavations under the *palazzo* that had been built over the altar – its position known from fragments discovered during building work in the 16th century, and an equally major trawl through the world's museums looking for missing bits.

San Lorenzo in Lucina

Piazza San Lorenzo in Lucina 16A (06 687 1494). Bus 52, 53, 62, 63, 71, 80Exp, 81, 83, 85, 117, 160, 492, 590, 628, C3. **Church** *8am-8pm daily.* **Roman remains** *guided tour 5.15pm 1st Sat of mth.* **Admission** *Church free. Roman remains €2. No cards.* **Map** *p102 J7.*

This 12th-century church was built on the site of a *titulus*, which in turn is believed to stand on the site of an ancient well sacred to Juno. The church's exterior

crammed with mementos. A lock of Keats' hair and his death mask, a minuscule urn holding tiny pieces of Percy Bysshe Shelley's charred skeleton, along with copies of documents and letters, and a massive library make this a Romantics enthusiast's paradise. Bring a box of tissues: even the hardest-hearted can be moved to tears by the sight of manuscripts written by consumptive poets with shaky hands.

On the floor directly above the museum, an apartment, replete with period decor and now managed by the Landmark Trust (www.landmarktrust.org.uk), can be rented for holiday stays.

▶ *Devotees should also make the pilgrimage to the Cimitero Acattolico (Protestant Cemetery; see p139) where both Keats and Shelley are buried.*

incorporates Roman columns, while the 17th-century interior contains a Bernini portrait bust of a papal physician in the Fonseca Chapel, a kitsch 17th-century *Crucifixion* by Guido Reni and a monument to French artist Nicolas Poussin, who died in Rome in 1665. In the first chapel on the right is a grill, reputed to be the one on which the martyr St Lawrence was roasted to death.

❤ Santa Maria del Popolo
Piazza del Popolo 12 (06 361 0836, www.santamariadelpopolo.it). Metro Flaminio/bus 61, 89, 117, 160, 490, 495, 628, 926/tram 2. **Open** *7am-noon, 4-7pm Mon-Thur; 7am-7pm Fri, Sat; 7.30am-1.30pm, 4.30-7.30pm Sun.* **Map** *p102 H4.*
According to legend, Santa Maria del Popolo occupies the site of a garden where the ashes of the hated Emperor Nero were scattered. The site was still believed to be haunted by demons 1,000 years later; in 1099 Pope Paschal II built a chapel there to dispel them. Nearly four centuries later, beginning in 1472, Pope Sixtus IV rebuilt the chapel as a church.

In the choir (behind the high altar, ask the custodian for permission to pass beyond the curtain) are, unusually for Rome, stained-glass windows, a northern touch created by French artist Guillaume de Marcillat in 1509. The apse itself was designed by Bramante, while the choir ceiling and first and third chapels in the right aisle were frescoed by Pinturicchio, the favourite artist of the Borgias. In Pinturicchio's exquisite works (1508-10), the Virgin and a host of saints keep company with some very pre-Christian sibyls. Most intriguing is the Chigi Chapel, designed by Raphael for wealthy banker Agostino Chigi. The mosaics in the dome depict God creating the sun and the seven planets, and Agostino's personal horoscope:

with binoculars you can just about make out a crab, a bull, a lion and a pair of scales. The chapel was finished by Bernini, who, on the orders of Agostino's descendant Pope Alexander VII, added the statues of Daniel and Habakkuk. The church's most-gawped-at possessions, however, are the two masterpieces by Caravaggio to the left of the main altar, in the Cerasi Chapel. On a vast scale, and suffused with lashings of the maestro's particular light, they show the martyrdom of St Peter and the conversion of St Paul. To the left of the main door is a memorial to 17th-century notable GB Gisleni: grisly skeletons, chrysalids and butterflies remind us of our brief passage through this life before we exit the other end.

❤ Spanish Steps
Metro Spagna/bus 52, 53, 62, 63, 71, 80Exp, 83, 85, 117, 160, 492, 590. **Map** *p102 K6.*
Piazza di Spagna takes its name from the Spanish Embassy to the Vatican, but is chiefly celebrated for the elegant cascade of stairs down from the church of **Trinità dei Monti**. Known in Italian as the Scalinata di Trinità dei Monti, the English Grand Tourists referred to them as the Spanish Steps. Completed in 1725, they might more accurately be called French: they were funded by French diplomat Etienne Gueffier, who felt the muddy slope leading up to the church – itself built with money from a French king – needed a revamp. At the foot of the stairs is a delightful boat-shaped fountain, the *barcaccia*, designed in 1627 by Gian Lorenzo Bernini and/or his less famous father Pietro; it's ingeniously sunk below ground level to compensate for the low pressure of the delicious *acqua vergine* that feeds it. The steps are best seen first thing in the morning before the crowds arrive.

Grand Tourists

Well-to-do gentlemen flock to Rome

A burgeoning fascination with the classical world brought a procession of international travellers to Rome. The 17th century saw the arrival of artists such as Nicholas Poussin and Claude Lorrain who parlayed Roman decay into dreamy landscapes punctuated by the ruins of vanished greatness.

But it was in the 18th and early 19th centuries that the trickle turned into a flood.

A stopover in Rome was an essential part of any young gentleman's education, with English *milords* leading the pack. They put up in the smartest part of the city, between via del Corso and piazza di Spagna, where they could find hotels, cafés, carriage repair workshops (in via delle Carrozze) and an ever-growing band of *ciceroni* (tour guides) who would accompany them around the city.

Inspired by the great art around them, many would take up a brush themselves. To cater to them, a whole art industry sprung up, with artists' models hanging out on the Spanish Steps or in vicolo dei Modelli waiting to pose in return for payment, and impoverished artists both Italian and northern European keen to show them the rudiments.

Writers – particularly of the Romantic variety – flocked too. Byron claimed that Rome was the city of his soul, but he spent less than a month here. Keats came in the hope that the climate would cure his consumption. It didn't. He coughed his last at the bottom of the Spanish Steps, in what is now the **Keats-Shelley Memorial House** (*see p108*); he is buried in the wonderfully romantic **Cimitero Acattolico** (*see p139*). Shelley's ashes are interred there too, though he drowned in a sailing mishap off the Tuscan coast.

Goethe, whose Roman abode on via del Corso is one of the city's most charming house-museums, was less than impressed by the city which he described as intolerably noisy and prone to messy murders.

Restaurants

Matricianella €€
Via del Leone 3-4 (06 683 2100, www.matricianella.it). Bus 52, 53, 62, 63, 71, 80, 81, 83, 85, 116, 116T, 117, 119, 160, 175, 492, 590, 628, C3. **Open** *12.30-3pm, 7.30-11pm Mon-Sat. Closed 3wks Aug.* **Map** *p102 H7* ❸ *Trattoria*
This is a friendly, bustling upscale *trattoria* with fair prices – for the *centro storico*. The menu is cover-to-cover Roman with pasta classics such as *bucatini all'amatriciana* (thick spaghetti with bacon, tomatoes and pecorino) and *rigatoni con coda alla vaccinara* (rigatoni with braised oxtail), while,

for the more adventurous, there are also the local *quinto quarto* (offal) dishes featuring tripe, intestine and sweetbreads. The well-chosen wine list is a model of honest pricing; service is friendly but no-nonsense. It's almost always packed so be sure to book ahead. There are a few, highly sought-after tables outside.

Pastificio Guerra €
Via della Croce 8 (06 679 3102). Metro Spagna/bus 52, 53, 62, 63, 71, 80, 81, 83, 85, 117, 160, 492, 590, 628. **Open** *1-9pm daily.* **No cards.** **Map** *p102 J6* ❹ *Streetfood*
This tiny purveyor of fresh pasta has gained fame as a cheap and cheerful lunch destination in one of

North of the Centre

Travel a little further afield for culture and cuisine

For centuries, the dead-straight via Flaminia was the route along which most travellers entered the Eternal City. Nowadays it passes through affluent residential Roma nord, or Flaminio, as it shoots north from piazza del Popolo to a hopping new hub of art and culture around the hyperactive **Auditorium-Parco della Musica** (see p43) and the Zaha Hadid-designed **MAXXI** art gallery. The MAXXI (www.maxxi.art) displays a permanent collection of works by mainly Italian contemporary artists; it's the dramatic building itself, however, that holds centre stage. Across the river is the wonderfully camp fascist-era Foro Italico sports complex, which includes the **Stadio Olimpico** (see p46).

To the north-east, Nomentano offers some charming art nouveau buildings. Its green lung is the **Villa Torlonia** (www. museivillatorlonia.it): home of the aristocratic Torlonia family from 1797; glorified as Mussolini's suburban HQ in the 1930s and trashed by Anglo-American forces when they made it their high command base (1944-47). Beneath the main house (the pretty *Casino nobile*), Mussolini's bunker can be visited by appointment. Contemporary art enthusiasts flock to the **MACRO** gallery (www. museomacro.org), housed in a stunningly converted brewery.

North of the city you'll also find the city's only three-star Michelin restaurant atop the Monte Mario. **La Pergola** (www.romecavalieri.com), on the top floor of the Cavalieri hotel, has a panoramic view over the city, and Chef Heinz Beck's technical dexterity and unerring taste and texture combinations never fail to impress.

the priciest parts of the city. There are no frills here, just a choice of two pasta dishes (which change daily) served on plastic plates to eat at the counter or take away. But at €4 a portion, which includes water and a cup of house wine, you would be hard pushed to find a better deal round here.

Cafés, bars & pubs

Antico Caffè Greco

Via Condotti 86 (06 679 1700, www.anticocaffegreco.eu). Metro Spagna/bus 52, 53, 62, 63, 71, 80, 81, 83, 85, 117, 492, 590, 628. **Open** *9am-9pm daily.* **Map** *p102 J6* ❶ *Café*

Founded in 1760, this venerable café – the oldest in Rome – was once the hangout of Casanova, Goethe, Wagner, Stendhal,

Baudelaire, Shelley and Byron. Opposition to the French Occupation of 1849-70 was planned here. Today its elegant interior is the very expensive hangout of bus-loads of tourists; locals, when they come, cram the foyer and down coffee on the hoof.

♥ Babington's Tea Room

Piazza di Spagna 23 (06 678 6027, www.babingtons.com). Metro Spagna/bus 52, 53, 62, 85, 117, 160, 301, 492, 628. **Open** *10am-9.15pm daily.* **Map** *p102 J6* ❷ *Tea room*

Homesick British expats have been heading to this quaint establishment at the foot of the Spanish Steps for a little taste of home ever since it opened its doors in 1893. The first place to serve tea in the Eternal City, it became a favourite meeting spot of visiting film stars and celebrities: Elizabeth Taylor and Richard Burton came here for romantic trysts during the filming of *Cleopatra* and even famed film director Federico Fellini was partial to the English muffins. Everything from breakfast, lunch and dinner is served here but it is the classic afternoon tea that draws the crowds with cucumber sandwiches and proper scones served on delicate patterned china.

♥ Caffè Canova-Tadolini
Via del Babuino 150A (06 3211 0702, www.canovatadolini.com). Metro Spagna/bus 117. **Open** *8pm-midnight daily.* **Map** *p102 J5* ❸ *Café/Bar*
Sculptor Antonio Canova signed a contract in 1818 to ensure that this property, in the heart of the old artists' quarter, would remain an atelier for sculpture. The master's wishes were respected until 1967: the workshop passed through many generations of the Tadolini family, descendants of Canova's favourite pupil and heir, Adamo Tadolini. Now refurbished as a museum-atelier, Canova's workshop has café tables among its stunning marble sculptures and a refined old-world feel: dark hardwood floors, wood-beamed ceilings, chandeliers and mustard-yellow leather banquettes and chairs. The small bar offers cocktails and assorted drinks, as well as tasty titbits, from canapés to cookies and pastries. The restaurant serves from noon to 11pm daily, but we recommend sticking to the café.

♥ Hotel Locarno Bar
Via della Penna 22 (06 361 0841, www.hotellocarno.com). Metro Flaminio/bus 81, 117, 590, 628, 926. **Open** *7am-1am daily.* **Map** *p102 H5* ❹ *Bar*
The glorious art nouveau bar of the Hotel Locarno is a treat at any time of day for coffee or tea in surroundings of slightly faded elegance, much favoured by visiting actors and film directors, and local intellectuals. But around 7pm the panorama changes as the bar itself and the delightful leafy terrace outside (patio heaters keep it open through the year) become the venue for one of the city's hottest *aperitivo* scenes. Trendy young Romans rub shoulders with in-the-know out-of-towners, vying for a terrace perch.

Rosati
Piazza del Popolo 5 (06 322 5859, www.barrosati.com). Metro Flaminio/bus 81, 117, 590, 628, 926. **Open** *7am-11.30pm daily.* **Map** *p102 H5* ❺ *Café/Bar*
Rosati is the traditional haunt of Rome's intellectual left: Calvino, Moravia and Pasolini were regulars. The art nouveau interior has remained unchanged since its opening in 1922. The coffee and *pasticceria* are excellent as are the cocktails; splash out on a pavement table with ringside view of stately piazza del Popolo to enjoy some serious people-watching.

Stravinskij Bar
Via del Babuino 9 (06 328 881, www.hotelderussie.it). Metro Spagna or Flaminio/bus 81, 117, 590, 628, 926. **Open** *9am-1am daily.* **Map** *p102 H5* ❻ *Bar*
Inside the swanky Hotel De Russie, this bar is divided into three sections: the small bar, a larger lounge area with sofas, and the outdoor patio. The first two are filled in cooler months with international business people, the hotel's celebrity guests and a gaggle of deep-pocketed regulars. But the real draw here is the fabulous patio, a sunken oasis of shady tables surrounded by orange trees and a gorgeous terraced garden. The drinks menu is pricey but interesting and the cocktails are well executed by some of Rome's top mixologists; try the signature

Stravinskij Spritz: prosecco mixed with a secret recipe of berries, citrus and spices.

Shops & services

Bottega del Marmoraro
Via Margutta 53B (06 320 7660). Metro Spagna/bus 117. **Open** *8am-1pm, 3.30-7.30pm Mon-Sat.* **No cards.** **Map** *p102 J5* ❶
Gifts & souvenirs
Stepping into this hole-in-the-wall shop, you'd be forgiven for thinking you'd been teleported back to the workroom of an ancient Roman craftsman: the tiny space is crammed with pseudo-classical inscriptions, headless statues and busts. The jolly *marmoraro* Enrico Fiorentini can make to order.

C.U.C.I.N.A
Via Mario de' Fiori 65 (06 679 1275, www.cucinastore.com). Metro Spagna/Bus 52, 53, 61, 62, 63, 80, 83, 85, 116, 116T, 150, 160, 175, 492, 590, C3. **Open** *11.30am-7.30pm Mon, Sun; 10.30am-7.30pm Tue-Sat.* **Map** *p102 J6* ❷ *House & home*
Even the most adventurous cooks will find a utensil their kitchen lacks at this culinary gadgetry shop. It sells a vast range of kitchenware, from bamboo rice steamers to a fine selection of jelly moulds.

❤ Furla
Piazza di Spagna 22 (06 6920 0363, www.furla.com). Metro Spagna/bus 52, 53, 62, 63, 80, 81, 83, 85, 116, 116T, 117, 119, 160, 175, 492, 590, 628, C3. **Open** *10am-8pm Mon-Sat; 10.30am-8pm Sun.* **Map** *p102 J6* ❸
Accessories
In eye-popping colours or as elegantly subdued classics, Furla's bags have spread like wildfire all over the city, not to mention the world. Prices won't reduce you to tears, and the line extends to shoes, sunglasses and wallets as well as watches.

❤ L'Olfattorio – Bar à Parfums
Via Ripetta 34 (bookings 06 361 2325, information 800 631 123, www.olfattorio.it). Metro Flaminio/bus 81, 117, 119, 224, 590, 628, 926. **Open** *10.30am-7.30pm daily. Closed Sun July, Aug & 2wks Aug.* **Map** *p102 H5* ❹ *Health & beauty*
It's strictly personal shopping at this innovative perfumery. A 'bartender' will awaken your olfactory organs and guide you expertly towards your perfect scent. Once determined, exclusive lines of hand-made English and French fragrances are available on site. Paradise for perfume-lovers.

❤ Sermoneta
Piazza di Spagna 61 (06 6791 960, www.sermonetagloves.com). Metro Spagna/ bus 117, 301, 492, 590, 913. **Open** *9.30am-8pm Mon-Sat, 10.30am-7pm Sun. Closed Sun in July & Aug.* **Map** *p102 J6* ❺
Accessories
Sermoneta's exquisite gloves are still made in the traditional method involving 10 skilled artisans and no fewer than 28 steps to produce each pair. The service is frosty but the choice is dizzying, with a selection of leathers from classic kidskin to more unique styles in suede, ostrich and boar, which come in every colour of the rainbow.

Entertainment

Nuovo Olimpia
Via in Lucina 16G (06 686 1068, www.circuitocinema.com). Bus 62, 63, 80, 83, 85, 117, 160, 492, 628. Closed Jul-Aug. **Map** *p102 J7* ❷
Cinema
Hidden away just off via del Corso, this two-screener belongs to the arthouse-oriented Circuito Cinema group; both screens usually show films in *lingua originale*.

San Giovanni in Laterano

East of the Centre

The Esquilino hill, around Termini railway station (if you've come to Rome on a budget deal there's a good chance you'll find yourself staying in a hotel around here), was once where the rich and powerful had their gardens and villas. Today – despite municipal attempts to bring about a 'renaissance' – there's no escaping the fact that Esquilino's *palazzi* are pretty grimy. There are, however, gems here, if you know where to look. The spur of the Esquiline closest to the Colosseum is the Colle Oppio park, with ruins of Trajan's baths. More picturesque and a whole lot buzzier, Monti has chaotic streets full of ethnic shops, eateries and lively bars.

Best sights
Palazzo Massimo alle Terme *p117*
San Clemente *p128*
Santa Maria Maggiore *p117*

Best for post-ruins recovery
Fatamorgana *p125*
Li Rioni *p129*
Taverna dei Fori Imperiali *p125*

Best night out
Black Market Art Gallery *p126*
Coming Out *p130*

Best for foodies
L'Asino d'Oro *p124*
Nuovo Mercato Esquilino *p120*
Trattoria Monti *p121*

Best for wine lovers
Ai Tre Scalini *p125*
Al Vino Al Vino *p125*
Trimani *p122*

EAST OF THE CENTRE

South of the Colle Oppio and nestling against the Colosseum is the Caelian hill (Celio), which still retains the bucolic character that made it the residential area of choice for Roman senators and nobility. To the east sits Rome's cathedral, San Giovanni in Laterano, which continues to attract religious visitors. Meanwhile, students and artists keep neighbouring San Lorenzo lively.

Esquilino

Despite assurances from local authorities that the area is on the up, the Esquilino can still feel rundown, and its after-dark characters may not be what you expected of the Eternal City. Don't despair, though, if you find you've booked yourself a hotel here: the area has its own charms and attractions.

After Italian Unification in the 1870s, the ancient ruins and Renaissance villas that dotted the area were swept away, and a whole new grid-like city-within-a-city was built. Piazza Vittorio Emanuele II – the city's biggest square, known simply as **piazza Vittorio** – was the new capital's showcase residential area, but its grand *palazzi* gradually fell into

decline. The area was given a new lease of life (if not prosperity) in the 1980s by a revamp of the piazza's central gardens and the emergence of a multi-ethnic community in the surrounding streets; **Nuovo Mercato Esquilino** food market in an ex-barracks on via Lamarmora bursts with exotic produce and smells (*see p120*).

Elsewhere, you'll find ancient artefacts in the **Palazzo Massimo alle Terme** and **Terme di Diocleziano**; one of Bernini's most extraordinary sculptures, *The Ecstasy of St Teresa*, in the Cornaro chapel of **Santa Maria della Vittoria** (via XX Settembre 17), and splendid mosaics in the basilica of **Santa Maria Maggiore**. You can also admire the extraordinary mid 20th-century design of Termini railway station.

Sights & museums

💜 Palazzo Massimo alle Terme

Largo di Villa Peretti 1 (06 480 201, www.archeoroma.beniculturali. it). See p180 Transport to Termini. **Open** *9am-7.30pm Tue-Sun.* **Admission** *€7; €3.50 reductions. Free 1st Sun of mth.* **Map** *p118 N7.*

Part of the Museo Nazionale Romano collection (*see p121* In the know), Palazzo Massimo has a basement display of coins from Roman times to the euro. On the ground and first floors are busts of emperors, their families and lesser mortals, in chronological order (allowing you to track changing fashions in Roman hairstyles). The ground floor covers the period up to the end of the Julio-Claudian line. In Room 5 is a magnificent statue of Augustus as *pontifex maximus*. Room 7 houses the undoubted stars of the ground floor, two bronzes found on the Quirinale showing a Hellenistic hero in the triumphant pose of Hercules and an exhausted boxer.

The first floor begins with the age of Emperor Vespasian (AD 69-79); portrait busts in Room 1 show the gritty no-nonsense soldier. Room 5 has decorations from Imperial villas – statues of Apollo and of a young girl holding a tray of religious objects are both from Nero's coastal villa at Anzio, and a gracefully crouching Aphrodite taking her bath is from Hadrian's Villa at Tivoli. Room 6 has two discus throwers, second-century marble copies of a Greek bronze original from the fifth century

Santa Maria Maggiore

BC. In Room 7 is a peacefully sleeping hermaphrodite, another second-century AD copy of a Greek original.

The real highlight of the Palazzo Massimo, though, lies on the second floor, where rare wall paintings from assorted villas have been reassembled.

💜 Santa Maria Maggiore

Piazza Santa Maria Maggiore (06 6988 6800, www.vatican. va). Bus 16, 70, 71, 75, 105, 360, 590, 649, 714, 717/tram 5, 14. **Church** *7am-7pm daily. Museum 8.30am-6.30pm daily.* **Loggia** *(booking essential, groups only) 8.30am-6.30pm daily.* **Admission** *Church free. Museum €3. Loggia €5. No cards.* **Map** *p118 N9.*

Behind this blowsy Baroque façade is one of the most striking basilica-form churches in Rome. Local tradition says a church was built on this spot in c366; documents place it almost 100 years later. The fifth-century church was first extended in the 13th century, then

➜ Getting around

The areas of Monti, Celio and Colle Oppio are a short walk from the Forum/Colosseum area. For Esquilino, *see p180* Transport to Termini, which lists all transport options going to or passing by the station. A little further afield, the area of San Lorenzo is served by tram 3. To reach San Giovanni take metro line A to the stop of the same name.

EAST OF THE CENTRE

Highlight

❤ Nuovo Mercato Esquilino

*Via Lamarmora. Metro Vittorio/
bus 70, 71, 105, 150, 360, 590, 649/
tram 5, 14.* **Open** *5am-3pm Mon-
Sat.* **Map** *p118 P9* ❶ *Market*

Tucked between the jumble
of ancient and industrial
archaeology (railway lines,
tram lines, aqueduct, part of a
grand Roman dining pavilion)
by Termini and the faded *fin de
siècle* grandeur of piazza Vittorio
Emanuele is the lively and chaotic
Esquiline market. The area has
long been a multicultural hub, and
that is reflected in the market's
rich arrays of produce both wildly
exotic and as Roman as they come.
African and Asian stalls stock
fruits, vegetables and spices that
are hard to come by in other parts
of the city, while alongside them
more traditional greengrocers,
fishmongers and butchers noisily

vie to attract customers. It all
starts winding up by lunchtime
so get there early, and then pop
over to nearby Mercato Centrale
in Termini station for a snack.
In a separate building there are
exotic fabrics, and rather less
interesting selections of clothes
and household goods.

again prior to the 1750 Holy Year,
when Ferdinando Fuga redid the
interior and attached the façade
that we see today. Inside, a flat-
roofed nave shoots between two
aisles to a triumphal arch and apse.
Above the columns of the nave,
heavily restored fifth-century
mosaics show scenes from the
Old Testament. There are also
13th-century mosaics in the apse by
Jacopo Torriti, which show Mary,
dressed as a Byzantine empress,
being crowned Queen of Heaven
by Christ.

The Virgin theme continues
in fifth-century mosaics on the
triumphal arch. The ceiling in the
main nave is said to have been
made from the first shipment of
gold extracted from the Americas

by Ferdinand and Isabella of
Spain, and was presented to
the church by the Borgia Pope
Alexander VI. The Borgias'
heraldic device of a bull is very
much in evidence. In the 16th
and 17th centuries two incredibly
flamboyant chapels were added.
The first was the Cappella Sistina
(last chapel on the right of the
nave), designed by Domenico
Fontana for Sixtus V (1585-90),
and decorated with multicoloured
marble, gilt and precious stones.
Directly opposite is the Cappella
Paolina, an even gaudier Greek-
cross chapel, designed in 1611
by Flaminio Ponzio for Paul V to
house an icon of the Madonna
(dating from the ninth, or possibly
the 12th, century) on its altar.

To the right of the main altar a plaque marks the burial place of Rome's great Baroque genius, Gian Lorenzo Bernini. In the loggia, high up on the front of the church (book tours in advance; notes are provided in English), are glorious 13th-century mosaics that decorated the façade of the old basilica, showing the legend of the foundation of the church. The lower row shows Mary appearing to Giovanni the Patrician, who, with Pope Liberius, then sketches the plan for the basilica. The legend goes that the Virgin told Giovanni to build a church on the spot where snow would fall the next morning. The snow fell on 5 August 352, a miracle that is commemorated on that day every year, when thousands of flower petals are released from the roof of the church in the Festa della Madonna delle Neve (*see p58*). The Cappella Paolina also contains a relief (1612) by Stefano Maderno showing Liberius tracing the plan of the basilica in the snow.

Terme di Diocleziano

Via Enrico de Nicola 79 (06 3996 7700, archeoroma.beniculturali. it). See p180 Transport to Termini. **Open** *9am-7.45pm Tue-Sun.* **Admission** *€7; €3.50 reductions. Free 1st Sun of mth.* **Map** *p118 N6.* Part of the Museo Nazionale Romano (*see below*), Diocletian's baths were built in AD 298-306, and

were the largest bath complex ever built in the Roman Empire, able to accommodate an estimated 3,000 people at a time. For an idea of the immense size of the structure, tour the remaining fragments: the tepidarium and part of the central hall are in Santa Maria degli Angeli; a circular hall can be seen in San Bernardo alle Terme (piazza San Bernardo); and the Aula Ottagona (octagonal hall) – which used to house Rome's planetarium and now is occasionally used for exhibitions – is in via Romita.

A convent complex was built around the largest surviving chunk of the baths by Michelangelo in the 1560s: it now contains inscriptions and other items from the Museo Nazionale Romano ancient artefacts collection, including some of the hut-shaped funerary urns found in Lazio, which give an idea of what eighth-century BC houses looked like.

Restaurants

❤ Trattoria Monti €€

Via di San Vito 13A (06 446 6573). Metro Vittorio/bus 16, 70, 71, 75, 105, 360, 590, 649, 714, 717/tram 5, 14. **Open** *12.45-2.45pm, 7.45-11pm Tue-Sat; 12.45-2.45pm Sun. Closed 1wk Aug, Dec.* **Map** *p118 O9* ❶
Trattoria

This upmarket trattoria is more difficult to get into than many top restaurants – so book well in advance. The reasons for its popularity are simple: friendly service and ambience, excellent food and a huge wine list with reasonable markups. The cuisine, like the family that runs the place, is from the region of Le Marche – so meat, fish and game all feature on the menu. Vegetarians are well served by a range of *tortini* (pastry-less pies); pasta-hounds can enjoy such treats as *tagliolini* with anchovies, pine nuts and pecorino cheese.

Cafés, bars & pubs

Fiddler's Elbow

*Via dell'Olmata 43 (06 487 2110,
www.thefiddlerselbow.com). Metro
Cavour/bus 16, 70, 71, 75, 360, 590,
649, 714, 717.* **Open** *4pm-1.30am
daily.* **Map** *p118 N9* ❶ *Pub*

One of the oldest, best-known pubs
in Rome, the Fiddler's Elbow has a
basic wooden-benched interior that
hasn't changed for years. Though
Italy's smoking ban means it's no
longer a fume-filled dive, it still
succeeds in giving the impression
of being one. Check the website for
live music dates.

Shops & services

❤ Trimani

*Via Goito 20 (06 446 9661). Metro
Termini/bus 38, 85, 92, 140, 217,
360.* **Open** *9am-8.30pm Mon-Sat.
Closed 1wk Aug.* **Map** *p118 O6* ❷
Food & drink

In the family since 1821, Trimani
is Rome's oldest and best wine
shop with a spectacular choice of
labels from all over Italy which
can be shipped anywhere in the
world. Around the corner at Via
Cernaia 37/b the same family
recently opened a wine bar to serve
wines by the glass as well as lunch
and dinner.

Entertainment

Teatro dell'Opera di Roma – Teatro Costanzi

*Piazza B Gigli 1 (06 4816 0255,
www.operaroma.it). Metro
Repubblica/bus 40Exp, 60Exp, 64,
70, 71, 170, H.* **Box office** *9am-5pm
Tue-Sat; 9am-1.30pm Sun; until
15mins after performances begin.*
Map *p118 M7* ❶ *Theatre*

The lavish late 19th-century *teatro
all'italiana* interior comes as quite
a surprise after the grey, angular,
Mussolini-era façade. There are
towering rows of boxes, and loads

Domus Aurea

of stucco, frescoes and gilding.
The acoustics vary: the higher
(cheaper) seats are unsatisfactory,
so splash out on a box, if you can.

Monti & Colle Oppio

The **Monti** quarter is altogether
more picturesque than the
Esquilino hill above. In ancient
times, this was the giant,
thunderous Suburra slum,
where life expectancy was short.
Nowadays, the alleyways of Monti
are still noisy and bustling, the
difference being that this area is
now seriously hip.

Flanking Monti to the north-
west, via Nazionale is a traffic
artery that runs south-west from
piazza della Republica; halfway
down is the huge **Palazzo delle
Esposizioni** gallery, and, at
the southern end, the **Villa
Aldobrandini** park, which has
superb views over the city. To the
east, two stunning early churches
dedicated to sister saints, **Santa
Prassede** and **Santa Pudenziana**
(via Urbana 160), glow with
extraordinary mosaics.

To the south, on Colle Oppio,
Nero fiddled in his **Domus Aurea**,
entertaining his guests with his
imperial twanging. These days,
this stretch of green is peopled by
Roman mums and their offspring
during the day, and some very

dubious characters after dark. On the western slope of the park, **San Pietro in Vincoli** contains important relics and a mighty Michelangelo, while, to the east, the **Museo Nazionale d'Arte Orientale** provides an exotic break from ancient Rome.

Sights & museums

Domus Aurea

Via della Domus Aurea (06 3996 7700, www.coopculture. it). Metro Colosseo/bus 53, 75, 80, 85, 87, 117, 810/tram 3. **Open** *Sat, Sun 8.45am-6pm by appt only.* **Map** *p118 M11.*

▶ *At present, access is only possible by following guided tours pre-booked online. Visits may be suspended or cancelled in the winter months or in case of bad weather.*

In the summer of AD 64 fire devastated a large part of central Rome. (Some blame Nero for setting the blaze intentionally but fire was a real risk and a common occurrence.) The ashes of patrician palaces mingled with those of slums. Afterwards, anything in the area east of the Forum left unsinged was knocked down to make way for a home fit for the sun-god that Nero liked to imagine he was.

Work began on the emperor's Domus Aurea (Golden House) immediately after the fire had died down. A three-storey structure, its main façade faced south and was entirely clad in gold; inside, every inch not faced with mother-of-pearl or inlaid with gems was frescoed by Nero's pet aesthete Fabullus. Fountains squirted perfumes, and baths could be filled with sea or mineral water. In one room, Suetonius claimed, an immense ceiling painted with the sun, stars and signs of the zodiac revolved constantly, keeping time with the heavens. Lakes were dug,

forests planted and a 35-metre-high (116-foot) gilded bronze statue of Nero erected.

After Nero's death in AD 68, a *damnatio memoriae* was issued and work was begun to eradicate every vestige of the hated tyrant. Vespasian drained the lake to build his amphitheatre (the tight-fisted emperor kept Nero's colossus, simply putting a new head on it, and so the stadium became known as the Colosseum), and Trajan used the brickwork as a foundation for his baths. So thorough was the cover-up job that for decades after the house's frescoes were rediscovered in 1480, no one realised it was the Domus Aurea that they had stumbled across. The frescoed 'grottoes' became an obligatory stopover for Renaissance artists, inspiring – among other things – Raphael's weird and wonderful frescoes in the Vatican (and also giving us the word 'grotesque'). The artists' signatures can still be seen scratched into the ancient stucco.

Museo Nazionale d'Arte Orientale

Via Merulana 248 (06 4697 4832 www.museorientale.beniculturali. it). Bus 16, 714, 717, C3/tram 3. **Open** *8am-7pm Tues-Sun.* **Admission** *€6; €3 reductions. No cards.* **Map** *p118 O10.*

If you've had enough of ancient and papal Rome, try this impressive collection of Oriental art, in a dusty *palazzo* near Santa Maria Maggiore. It's arranged geographically and roughly chronologically. First are ancient artefacts from the Near East – pottery, gold, votive offerings – some from the third millennium BC. Then come 11th- to 18th-century painted fans from Tibet, sacred sculptures, and some Chinese pottery from the 15th century. Perhaps most unusual are artefacts from the Swat culture, from Italian-funded excavations in Pakistan.

Palazzo delle Esposizioni

Via Nazionale 194 (06 3996 7500, www.palazzoesposizioni.it). Bus 40Exp, 60, 64, 70, 71, 170, H. **Open** *10am-8pm Tue-Thur, Sun; 10am-10.30pm Fri, Sat.* **Admission** *€8-€12.* **Map** *p118 L8.*

This imposing 19th-century purpose-built exhibition space continues to produce excellent shows on a host of historical, artistic and contemporary-icon themes. Often more than one exhibit is running simultaneously around the 10,000sq m (108,000sq ft) space. If you're under 30, it's free from 2pm to 7pm on the first Wednesday of the month. You don't need a ticket to access the basement bookshop and café – this latter a great place to grab a light lunch.

Santa Prassede

Via Santa Prassede 9A (06 488 2456). Bus 16, 70, 71, 75, 84, 360, 590, 649, 714. **Open** *7.30am-noon, 4-6.30pm Mon-Sat; 8am-noon, 4-7pm Sun.* **Map** *p118 N9.*

This church was built in the ninth century on the spot where St Praxedes is said to have harboured Christians. The saint, the story says, sponged up the blood of 23 martyrs who were discovered and killed before her, throwing the sponge into a well; its location is now marked by a porphyry disc on the floor of the nave. This tale is depicted in the 1735 altarpiece by Domenico Muratori. The church is a scale copy of the old St Peter's, a ninth-century attempt to recreate an early Christian basilica, although uneven brickwork shows that the Romans had lost the knack.

Pope Paschal I was looking for artists to decorate the chapel of San Zeno as a mausoleum dedicated to his mother, St Theodora. With the Roman Empire long dead, the pick of mosaic artists was thriving across in Byzantium, where the traditionally Roman art of mosaic took on a flashier and more colourful style, with coloured glass tesserae often backed with gold or silver. Undoubtedly the finest expression of Byzantine art in Rome, the chapel is topped with a vault showing a fearsome Christ supported by four angels, while around the walls are various saints, including St Theodora herself with the blue square halo that tells us she was still alive when she posed for her mausoleum mosaic.

Restaurants

❤ L'Asino d'Oro €€

Via del Boschetto 73 (06 4891 3832, www.facebook.com/asinodoro). Bus 40, 60, 64, 70, 71, 117, 170, H. **Open** *12.30-3pm, 7.30-11pm Tue-Sat. Closed 2wks Aug.* **Map** *p118 L9* ❷ *Trattoria*

Chef Luca Sforza moved his restaurant 'The Golden Donkey' from the Umbrian town of Orvieto to Rome back in 2011 and continues to pull in the crowds, making it difficult to get a table. The short, Tusco-Umbrian-inspired menu changes regularly, based on what is freshest and best at any given time. There is often a touch of sweet and sour in his creations: wild boar in chocolate sauce, cod with raisins and chestnuts, or goose

Fatamorgana

with stewed apple are frequently featured. The €16 fixed lunch menu is arguably one of Rome's best gourmet offers, but even during the evening the price/quality ratio of both the food and wine is exceptional.

❤ Taverna dei Fori Imperiali €€€
*Via della Madonna dei Monti 9 (06 679 8643, www. latavernadeiforiimperiali.com). Metro Cavour/bus 75, 117. **Open** 12.30-3pm, 7.30-10.30pm Wed-Mon. Closed 2wks Aug, 1wk Sept. **Map** p118 L10* ❸ *Trattoria*

This cosy, family-run restaurant hidden behind the Imperial Forum has gained a legion of loyal fans thanks to the warm, friendly atmosphere and focus on quality cuisine. The family's menu always features several seasonal specials and a few creative combinations alongside more standard Roman fare. The attention to detail and popularity have pushed the prices a little above the average trattoria but the ambience, location and food make it worth the extra splurge.

Cafés, bars & pubs

❤ Ai Tre Scalini
*Via Panisperna 251 (06 4890 7495, www.facebook.com/aitrescalini). Bus 40, 60, 64, 70, 117, 170, H. **Open** 12.30pm-1am daily. Closed 1wk Aug. **Map** p118 L9* ❷ *Wine bar*

This atmospheric, rustic wine bar is the *aperitivo* destination of choice for Monti arty, creative types. It is always packed on summer evenings when crowds spill out onto pretty, vine-covered Via Panisperna and it is a struggle to get through the door, let alone the bar. Earlier in the day it is an altogether calmer affair with friendly staff, excellent wines (many also served by the glass) and an all-day menu of food chalked up on the blackboard.

❤ Al Vino Al Vino
*Via dei Serpenti 19 (06 485 803). Bus 40, 60, 64, 70, 117, 170, H. **Open** 10.30am-2.30pm, 6pm-1am daily. Closed 2wks Aug. **Map** p118 L9* ❸ *Bar*

This hostelry on lively via dei Serpenti has a range of over 500 wines, with more than 25 available by the glass. But its speciality is *distillati*: dozens of fine grappas, whiskies and other strong spirits. The food is so-so but light snacks are fine for soaking up the alcohol. Shame the staff can be less than charming.

La Bottega del Caffè
*Piazza Madonna dei Monti 5 (06 474 1578). Metro Cavour/bus 53, 75, 80, 85, 87, 117. **Open** 8am-2am daily. **Map** p118 L9* ❹ *Café*

With tables outside on the pretty square (patio heaters keep them warm through winter) this café draws locals – and weary sightseers from the nearby Roman and Imperial Fora – for breakfast, lunch and *aperitivi*. Friendly staff serve morning coffee or afternoon tea with tiny *cornetti* or biscuits. There's generally a cooked option alongside the usual range of sandwiches and filled rolls at lunch.

Bakeries, pasticcerie & gelaterie

❤ Fatamorgana
*Piazza degli Zingari 5 (06 4890 6955, www.gelateriafatamorgana. it). Metro Cavour/bus 40, 60, 64, 70, 75, 117, 170, H. **Open** 1pm-midnight daily. **Map** p118 M9* ❶ *Gelateria*

Organic, no additives, gluten-free and superb: the wonderful product whipped up by Maria Agnese Spagnuolo for her Fatamorgana mini-chain (and previously only available in the 'burbs) can now be found in several new easily accessible *centro storico* locations, including this one in the hip Monti district's pretty piazza degli Zingari. There are all the classic flavours (with twists), plus specialities such as black cherries and beer, pears and gorgonzola, and baklava. **Other locations** via Roma Libera 11, Trastevere; via Laurina 10, Tridente ; piazza degli Zingari 5, Monti; via Aosta 3, San Giovanni; via Leone IV 50, Prati; via dei Chiavari 37, Campo de' Fiori.

Shops & services

Abito – Le Gallinelle
Via Panisperna 61 (06 488 1017, www.facebook.com/ABITO61). Metro Cavour/bus 40, 60, 64, 70, 71, 117, 170. **Open** *11am-8pm Mon-Sat. Oct-Jan also open noon-8pm Sun. Closed 2wks Aug.* **Map** *p118 M9* **❸** *Fashion*
Wilma Silvestri founded Le Gallinelle in 1989 and sells gorgeous, reworked vintage and ethnic garments along with new contemporary designs which she creates in her workroom at the back of the shop. Items can be tailored or made-to-measure on demand. For those who shun the outlandish, there are classic linen suits for men and women.

Mercato Monti
Via Leonina 46 (www. mercatomonti.com). Metro Cavour/ bus 40, 64, 70, 75, 117. **Open** *Sept-June 10am-8pm Sat, Sun.* **Map** *p118 M10* **❹** *Market*
Mercato Monti perfectly reflects the arty, hipster vibe of the Monti district. Almost every weekend young creatives set up shop at the back of the Hotel Palatino to sell their wares which include innovative jewellery and accessories, vintage-inspired clothing and unique crafts and homewares. Check the website for dates.

Entertainment

❤ Black Market Art Gallery
Via Panisperna 101 (339 822 7541, www.blackmarketartgallery.it). Metro Cavour/bus 40, 64, 70, 75, 117, 170, H, 8N, 9N, 15N. **Open** *6pm-2am daily.* **Admission** *free; extra for big acts.* **Map** *p118 M9* **❷**
Live music
If you're looking for a very intimate concert, this is the place to be. The unplugged live sessions bring to Rome indie-rock and jazz musicians, who play in a tiny space in the back (with roughly 50 seats) fitted with vintage furniture and sofas, for a retro-cool feel. Their website is unreliable, so check their Facebook page for an updated list of events. If you show up impromptu, you might have to stand, but can always grab a cocktail and a bite at the bar. Admission is free, as are most of the concerts. There may be a charge when more popular bands play.

San Lorenzo

San Lorenzo was planned in the 1880s as a working-class ghetto, with few public services or amenities. Unsurprisingly, it soon developed into Rome's most politically radical district. These days it retains some of its threadbare, jerry-built, working-class character. But it's more radical-chic than just plain radical: a constant influx of artists and students mingles with the few surviving salt-of-the-earth locals. And, besides the many emporia selling tombstones, coffins and memorial lanterns, there's a happy mix of artisans, second-hand clothing shops, clubs and restaurants.

Along the north-east side is the vast Verano cemetery, with the basilica of **San Lorenzo fuori le Mura** by its entrance.

To the north-west, the **Città universitaria** (the main campus of Europe's biggest university, La Sapienza), has buildings designed in the 1930s by Marcello Piacentini and Arnaldo Foschini.

Sights & museums

San Lorenzo fuori le Mura

Piazzale del Verano 3 (06 491 511). Bus 71, 88, 163, 492/tram 3, 19. **Open** *Apr-Sept 7.30am-noon, 4-8pm daily. Oct-Mar 7.30am-12.30pm, 3.30-7pm daily.* **Map** *p118 S7.*

This spacious church, with its unusual chancel and ethereal light, gives an atmosphere of calm, a feature of the Romanesque tradition to which it belongs. Like most Roman places of worship, the building has been formed from a patchwork of 'improvements' over the centuries. St Laurence, whose remains lie in a crypt beneath the church, was martyred in the mid third century; convert-Emperor Constantine had a basilica built over his tomb during the fourth century. Several popes were subsequently laid to rest in the same underground catacombs.

In the late sixth century, Pope Pelagius II rebuilt the basilica; from this incarnation comes the broad chancel with its Corinthian columns, marble ciborium and stylised Byzantine mosaic of Pelagius and St Laurence, with Christ seated on an orb. The nave is a 13th-century addition by Pope Honorius, even though much is a faithful restoration undertaken after it was demolished by American bombs in 1943. In the portico are 13th-century frescoes depicting the life of the saint. A lovely courtyard encloses gardens and a piece of the errant bomb that wreaked havoc on the church. A ramp on the right leads behind the chancel to the crypt of Blessed Pope Pius IX, the last pope to rule over the Vatican States; his reportedly uncorrupted body lies with a creepy silver mask over his face.

Entertainment

Le Mura Live Music Club

Via di Porta Labicana 24 (www. lemuramusicbar.com). Bus 71, 492, 10N, 11N/tram 3. **Open** *8.30pm-2am daily.* **Admission** *free with annual membership card (€7). No cards.* **Map** *p118 Q9* ❸
Live music

Friendly and lively, Le Mura has a policy of encouraging upcoming Italian bands: the quality varies greatly. But this live-music club also fields better-known Italian and international names, as well as offering live-mic nights, jazz, good DJ sets and the occasional '60s event by retro one-night crew Twiggy.

Muccassassina

Qube, via di Portonaccio 212 (06 541 3985, www.muccassassina. com). Metro Tiburtina/bus 409, 440, 545. **Open** *11pm-4am Fri.* **Admission** *€15 (incl 1 drink). No cards.* **Map** *p118* ❹ *Gay club night*

The Mario Mieli crew (*see p189*) were trailblazers of the gay one-nighter a few years ago – and their Friday-night fest at the Qube still packs them in. Three floors of pop and house create a great atmosphere throughout, which tends to get hot (literally). There are also some one-off events on other evenings: check the website for details.

Celio

Celio was (like the rest of Rome) overrun in AD 410 by Alaric the Goth. Its patrician villas and shops remained largely deserted for centuries afterwards, crumbling back to nature. Today, the hill itself retains a bucolic character, giving a glimpse of what ancient, early Christian and medieval Rome might have been like; much of it is occupied by monasteries and convents, churches and nursery schools.

In the tight grid of streets south-east of the Colosseum, around the verdant and lovely **Villa Celimontana** park, is a whole slew of ancient churches. These include impressive Baroque **San Gregorio al Celio** (piazza di San Gregorio Magno 1) and **Santa Maria in Domnica** (via della Navicella 10) with its pretty mosaics. There's also multi-layered **San Clemente** and **Santi Quattro Coronati**, which is blessed with several extraordinary frescoes.

Sights & museums

♥ San Clemente

Via San Giovanni in Laterano (06 774 0021, www.basilicasan clemente.com). Metro Colosseo/bus 53, 75, 80, 85, 87, 117, 810/tram 3. **Open** *9am-12.30pm, 3-6pm Mon-Sat; noon-6pm Sun.* **Admission** *Church free. Excavations €10; €5 reductions.* **Map** *p118 N11.*

A favourite with kids for its dungeon-like underground level, this 12th-century basilica is a three-dimensional Roman timeline, a church above a church above an even older Imperial building – a full 18 metres (60 feet) of Roman life separate the earliest structure from the one we see today.

In 1857 the Irish Dominicans – who have run the church since the 17th century – began digs that unearthed the church's fourth-century predecessor, and, beneath, an early Christian *titulus* (meeting place). The fourth-century structure was razed in the Norman sack of 1084, but the *schola cantorum* (choir), with its exquisite carving and mosaic decorations,

survived and was moved upstairs to the new church, where it still stands.

Also in the upper church is the 12th-century mosaic in the apse, still in Byzantine style but with a theological complexity unusual for its period. Against a gold backdrop, cobalt blues, deep reds and multi-hued greens make up the crucified Christ. From the drops of Christ's blood springs the vine representing the Church, which swirls around peasants at their daily tasks, Doctors of the Church spreading the divine word and a host of animals. Above the cross, the hand of God links heaven and earth, while below, sheep represent Christ and the 12 apostles. The Latin inscription above the sheep says 'I am the vine, you are the branches'. Towards the back of the church, in the chapel of St Catherine of Alexandria, a series of frescoes by Masolino (c1430), possibly with help from Masaccio, depict the life of the saint – she is shown calmly praying as her torturers prepare the wheel to which she was strapped and stretched to death (and for which the firework was later named) – as well as Christ on the cross in between the two thieves.

Santi Quattro Coronati

Via dei Querceti (06 7047 5427, www.monacheagostinianes antiquattrocoronati.it). Bus 53, 85, 117/tram 3. **Church** *6.30am-12.45pm, 3-7.45pm daily.* **Cloister** *10-11.45am, 4-5.45pm Mon-Sat.* **Oratory** *8.30-11.45am, 4-5.45pm daily.* **Map** *p118 N12.*

The secret places in the basilica of the Four Crowned Saints make it another good candidate for dragging listless kids to. The church dates from the fourth century and was probably named after four Roman soldiers who refused to pray before the statue of Esculapius, the

Roman god of healing. Another version has it dedicated to early stonemasons who refused to sculpt the aforementioned deity, making the church especially dear to present-day masons. Like San Clemente and Santi Giovanni e Paolo, it was burned down by rampaging Normans in 1084. It was rebuilt as a fortified monastery, with the church itself reduced to half its original dimensions; the outsize apse, visible as you look uphill along via dei Santi Quattro, remains from the original church. The early basilica form is still discernible, and the columns that once ran along the aisles are embedded in the walls of the innermost courtyard. The church has a fine cosmatesque floor and an upper-level *matronium*, to which women were relegated during religious functions. There is also one of Rome's most beautiful cloisters, dating from about 1220, with lovely, slender columns supporting delicate arches and a double-cupped fountain amid its flowerbeds. The musty chapel of Santa Barbara conceals a pair of frescoes: a 12th-century *Madonna and Child* and a ninth-century unidentified saint. Just ring the bell at the door on the left side of the nave and a kind-hearted nun will probably let you have a peek.

Villa Celimontana

Via della Navicella/via San Paolo della Croce. Bus 75, 80, 81, 117, 673/ tram 3. Open dawn-dusk daily. Map p118 N13.
This is a pretty, leafy walled garden, with a rather pokey playground; which does not stop swarms of local kids from climbing, running and holding birthday picnics here. The pleasant lawns are dotted with pieces of marble from the collection of the Mattei family, which owned the property from 1553 until 1928, when it became a public park. The graceful family villa, now housing

the Italian Geographic Society, was built in the 16th century. Forlorn and forgotten at the southern end is one of Rome's Egyptian obelisks. During the summer, the villa becomes the gorgeous venue for evening jazz concerts.

Restaurants

♥ Li Rioni €€
Via dei Santi Quattro 24 (06 7045 0605, lirioni.it) Metro Colosseo/bus 53, 75, 80, 81, 85, 87, 117, 673/tram 3. Open 7pm-midnight Wed-Mon. Closed 2wks Aug. Map p118 N11 ❹
Pizzeria
A hit with locals and tourists alike, Li Rioni churns out wafer-thin *pizza romana* from its wood-fired oven at an impressive rate, and at more than reasonable prices given its location just a short stroll from the Colosseum. The (slightly kitsch) interior is decked out like a Roman street with shuttered windows and terracotta hues and in summer extra tables are set up outside on the pavement. Expect it to be packed, and very noisy; exactly as a Roman pizzeria should be.

Luzzi €€
Via Celimontana 1 (06 709 6332, www.trattorialuzzi.it). Metro Colosseo/bus 53, 75, 80, 81, 85, 87, 117, 673/tram 3. Open noon-midnight Mon, Tue, Thur-Sun. Closed 2wks Aug. Map p118 N11 ❺
Trattoria
When it's busy (and it almost always is), this heaving neighbourhood trattoria is the loudest and most crowded 40sq m in the whole of Rome. It isn't the place for a romantic tête-à-tête, nor for gourmet dining, but it is cheap, lively and handy for the Colosseum. And the menu's range of Roman staples and pizzas is competently done, though expect the service to be a little erratic. The outdoor tables operate all year round.

Cafés, bars & pubs

Café Café
Via dei Santi Quattro 44 (06 700 8743, www.cafecafebistrot.it). Metro Colosseo/bus 53, 75, 80, 81, 85, 87, 117, 673/tram 3. **Open** *9.30am-4.30pm daily. Closed 1wk Aug.* **Map** *p118 M11* ⑤ *Café*
This attractive place offers smoothies, teas, wines, salads and sandwiches for travellers weary after a romp around the Colosseum. There's a brunch buffet from 11.30am to 4pm on Sundays.

Caffè Propaganda
Via Claudia 15 (06 9453 4255, www.caffe propaganda.it). Metro Colosseo/bus 53, 75, 80, 81, 85, 87, 117, 186, 271, 571, 673, 810/tram 3. **Open** *noon-2am daily.* **Map** *p118 M12* ⑥ *Café*
With its leather banquettes, monochrome décor and French artwork, Caffè Propaganda looks more Paris bistro than Roman drinking hole. Its diverse clientele consists of well-heeled Romans mixed with tourists who stumble in after a trek around the Colosseum down the road. Lunch and dinner are served but prices are high and the service can be patchy making it best to drop by for afternoon tea or coffee (accompanied by one of the exquisite pastries).

❤ Coming Out
Via San Giovanni in Laterano 8 (06 700 9871, www.comingout.it). Metro Colosseo/bus 53, 85, 87, 117, 571, 673, 10N, 11N. **Open** *7am-2am daily.* **Map** *p118 M11* ⑦ *Gay bar*
The epicentre of the 'Gay Street' in Rome, this very popular LGBT pub offers breakfasts, quick lunches, evening snacks, beers and cocktails to a predominantly youthful crowd of men and women. It's a useful address if you need somewhere to meet before heading off in search of something a bit more adventurous. There's a

San Giovanni in Laterano

6.30-8.30pm happy hour; plus a DJ set from 11pm on Wednesday (and Thursday – but not during the summer, as the place is already quite packed).

San Giovanni

East of the Celio, amid traffic, smog and drab post-unification apartment buildings, are some of Christianity's most important churches – including Vatican-owned **San Giovanni in Laterano** itself, Rome's cathedral. After Emperor Constantine legalised Christianity in the fourth century, he donated land on which the basilica (originally dedicated to the Saviour) was built. This was ground-breaking in that it brought the new religion out into the open, but was fence-sitting in the sense that, at the time, this neighbourhood was as far as you could get from the city's centre of power.

To the south of the basilica are the sunken brick remains of the **Porta Asinaria**, an ancient gate in the third-century AD Aurelian wall. A park follows the ancient wall north to **Santa Croce in Gerusalemme**, which is surrounded by a panoply of easily visible Roman ruins.

Sights & museums

San Giovanni in Laterano
*Piazza San Giovanni in Laterano 4 (06 6988 6409, www.vatican.va). Metro San Giovanni/bus 16, 81, 85, 87, 117, 218, 650, 714/tram 3. **Church** 7am-6.30pm daily. **Baptistry** 7.30am-12.30 pm, 4-6.30pm daily. **Cloister** 9am-6pm daily. Museum 10am-5.30pm daily. **Admission** Church free. Cloister €3. Museum €4. No cards. Map p118 P12.*

The Catholic faithful earn indulgences for visits to this major basilica. Along with the Lateran palace, it was the site of the original papal headquarters until the move across the river to St Peter's and the Vatican during the 14th century. Constantine's second wife, Fausta, gave the plot of land to Pope Melchiades to build the papal residence and church in 313. There are few traces of the original basilica, which was destroyed by fire, earthquake and barbarians. It has been heavily restored and reconstructed: the end result is a vast, impersonal, over-decorated hangar.

The façade, with its 15 huge statues of Christ, the two Johns (Baptist and Evangelist) and 12 Doctors of the Church, is part of the 1735 rebuilding by Alessandro Galilei. The interior bears the stamp of Borromini, who transformed it in 1646. A few treasures from earlier times survive: a much restored 13th-century mosaic in the apse, a fragment of a fresco attributed to Giotto (hidden behind the first column on the right) showing Pope Boniface VIII announcing the first Holy Year in 1300, and the Gothic *baldacchino* over the main altar.

From the left aisle, you can access the 13th-century cloister, with delicate twisted columns and fine cosmatesque work by the Vassalletto family. A small museum off the cloister contains papal vestments and some original manuscripts of music by Palestrina.

The north façade was designed in 1586 by Domenico Fontana, who also placed Rome's tallest Egyptian obelisk outside. This was part of Pope Sixtus V's 16th-century urban renewal scheme. Also on this side is the octagonal baptistry that Constantine had built. The four chapels surrounding the font have mosaics from the fifth and seventh centuries, and bronze doors said to come from the Baths of Caracalla.

Santa Croce in Gerusalemme
*Piazza Santa Croce in Gerusalemme 12 (06 7061 3053, www.santacroceroma.it). Bus 81, 649/tram 3. **Open** 7am-12.45pm, 3.30-7.30pm daily. **Map** p118 R11.*

Founded in 320 by St Helena, mother of Emperor Constantine (who legalised Christianity in 313), this church began as a hall in her home, the Palatium Sessorium, a palace that originally belonged to the Emperor Septimius Severus (193-211). The church was rebuilt and extended in the 12th century, and again in 1743-44. Helena had her church constructed to house relics brought back from the Holy Land by the redoubtable lady herself. The emperor's *mamma* came back with an enviable shopping-bagful: three chunks of Christ's cross, a nail, two thorns from his crown and the finger of St Thomas – allegedly the very one that the doubting saint stuck into Christ's wound. All these are displayed in a chapel at the end of a Fascist-era hall at the left side of the nave. Apart from the wood, those venerable objects are rather hard to identify, inside their gold reliquaries. In the mosaic-ceilinged lower chapel (under the altar) is Helena's stash of soil from Jerusalem. Helena's Holy Land souvenir collecting sparked a relic-craze exploited to the full for centuries by the wily merchants of the Holy Land; when Jesus-related bits were in short supply, scraps of saints and martyrs were fair game too.

The basilica's gorgeous vegetable garden, restored and lovingly tended by monks of the adjoining monastery, is unfortunately closed to the public.

▶ *The grave of St Helena can be seen in the Aracoeli (see p74)... though the pretty little church of Sant'Elena in Venice also claims to have the great lady's body.*

Scala Santa & Sancta Sanctorum

Piazza di San Giovanni in Laterano 14 (06 772 6641, www. scala-santa.com). Metro San Giovanni/bus 16, 85, 87, 218, 650, 665, 714/tram 3. **Scala Santa** *Apr-Sept 6.15am-1pm, 3-6.30pm Mon-Sat; 7am-12.30pm Sun. Oct-Mar 6.15am-1pm, 3-6pm Mon-Sat; 7am-12.30pm Sun.* **Sancta Sanctorum** *(booking obligatory) 9.30am-12.30pm, 3-5.10 pm Mon-Sat.* **Admission** *Scala Santa free. Sancta Sanctorum €3.50. No cards.* **Map** *p118 P12.*

According to tradition, these steps (now covered with wooden planks) are the very ones Jesus climbed in the house of Pontius Pilate only to see the Roman governor wash his hands of the self-styled messiah. Emperor Constantine's mother St Helena brought these back in the fourth century. A crawl up the Scala Santa (on your knees) has been a

fixture on every serious pilgrim's list ever since. In 1510 Martin Luther gave it a go, but halfway up he decided that relics were a theological irrelevance and walked back down again. Don't climb them unless you know 28 different prayers (one for each step); walking up is not allowed. Prepare for a queue on Good Friday.

At the top of the Holy Stairs (but also accessible by non-holy stairs to the left) is the Sancta Sanctorum ('Holy of Holies'), the *privatissima* chapel of the popes and one of the only monuments around here that escaped Sixtus V's revamping. Some of the best early Christian relics were kept in the crypt under the altar at one time – including the heads of saints Peter, Paul and young Agnes. Most of them have been distributed to other churches around the city, but displayed in a glass case on the left wall is a fragment of the table on which the Last Supper was supposedly served. The real treasures here, however, are the 13th-century frescoes in the lunettes and on the ceiling, attributed to Cimabue. Once, no one but the *pontifex maximus* himself was allowed to set foot in the Sancta Sanctorum.

Entertainment

Bunker

Via Placido Zurla 68, Suburbs: east (06299929/34 85793760, www. bunkerclubroma.com). Bus 81, 105, N16. **Open** *10pm-3am Thur, Sun; 10pm-4am Fri-Sat.* **Admission** *free with Acil card.* **Map** *p118* ⑤
Gay club

The biggest gay men's disco cruising club in Rome, with glory holes, underground red zone, maze, video screens, dance floor and cocktail bar. On Thursday/Saturday/Sunday underwear/naked night, on Friday free entry and free dress code.

South of the Centre

The leafy, upmarket Aventine hill just steps from the Colosseum couldn't be more different from the busy, workaday districts of Testaccio and Ostiense that lie at its southern feet, yet there's a grudging respect between them that runs both ways. Without the proximity of Testaccio's bars and markets, and Ostiense's burgeoning cultural and nightlife scene, the Aventine would be nothing but a lifeless enclave of privilege; whereas inhabitants of the hectic lower areas are grateful for a respite from the bustle and din by wandering up to the peaceful hill that overlooks them. Quiet attractions abound south of the centre, from the Terme di Caracalla (Baths of Caracalla) to the Cimitero Acattolico and via Appia Antica.

Best sights
Centrale Montemartini *p141*
Cimitero Acattolico *p139*
Museo delle Mura *p145*
Terme di Caracalla *p136*

Best for re-charging your batteries
Barberini *p140*
Tram Depot *p140*
Trapizzino *p138*

Best for rubbing shoulders with the locals
Da Remo *p138*
Flavio al Velavevodetto *p138*
Masto *p138*
Mercato Testaccio *p142*

Best night out
Akab *p142*
Goa Club *p144*
Casa del Jazz *p137*
Teatro Palladium *p144*

Aventine & San Saba

The Aventine hill is a lovely place for a stroll. Dozens of orange trees and a spectacular view over the city, especially at sunset, make **Parco Savello** – surrounded by the crenellated walls of a 12th-century fortress – worth a visit. In nearby piazza Cavalieri di Malta, peek through the keyhole of the priory of the Knights of Malta to enjoy the surprise designed by Gian Battista Piranesi: a telescopic view of the dome of St Peter's.

Across busy viale Aventino is the similarly well-heeled **San Saba** district and, beyond the white cuboids of the UN's Food and Agricultural Organisation, the giant **Terme di Caracalla**, where opera is performed in summer (*see p59* Opera at Terme di Caracalla).

Sights & museums

Santa Sabina
Piazza Pietro d'Illiria 1 (06 5794 0600). Bus 81, 160, 175, 628, 715. Open 7am-6.30pm daily. Map p135 J13.
Try to visit Santa Sabina on a sunny day, when the light shines softly into this magnificent, solemn basilica. It was built in the fifth century over an early Christian titulus believed to have belonged to a martyred Roman matron named Sabina; the only trace of this ancient place of worship is a bit of mosaic floor visible through a grate at the entrance. The church was subjected to a merciless restoration in the 1930s: nevertheless, what you see today is arguably the closest thing – give or take a 16th-century fresco or two – in Rome to an unadulterated ancient basilica.

➔ Getting around
Just south of the centre of town, the Aventine is eminently walkable from the Colosseum area. Further afield, take metro line B for stops in Testaccio, Ostiense and EUR. For via Appia Antica take bus 660 from Colli Albani metro station (line A) to the junction of via Appia Antica and via Cecilia Metella and either walk or hire bikes from Parco Appia Antica Punto Informativo Other buses that service the area include no.118 (from Piramide metro) and no.218 (from piazza San Giovanni).

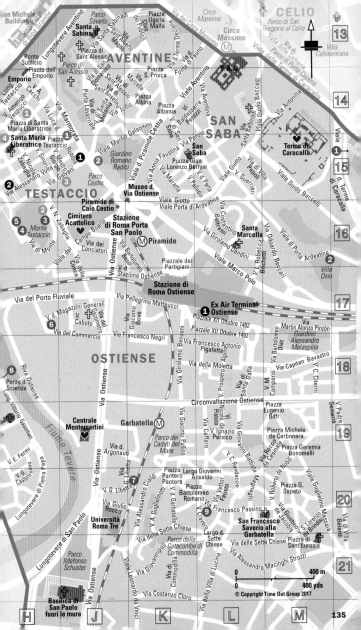

Terme di Caracalla

❤ Terme di Caracalla

*Viale delle Terme di Caracalla 52
(06 3996 7700, www.coopculture.
it). Bus 118, 160, 628.* **Open**
*9am-2pm Mon; 9am-sunset Tue-
Sun.* **Admission** *€6; €3 reductions.
No cards.* **Map** *p135 M15.*

The high-vaulted ruins of the Baths
of Caracalla, surrounded by trees
and grass, are pleasantly peaceful
today, but were anything but
tranquil in their heyday, when up
to 1,600 Romans could sweat it out
in the baths and gyms. You can get
some idea of the original splendour
of the baths – built between AD
213 and 216 – from the fragments
of mosaic and statuary littering
the grounds, although the more
impressive finds are in the Vatican
Museums (*see p164*) and the Museo
Archeologico in Naples.

The two cavernous rooms down
the sides were the *gymnasia*, where
Romans engaged in strenuous
sports like toss-the-beanbag.
There was also a large open-air
natatio (pool) for lap-swimming.
After exercising, they cleansed
themselves in saunas and a series
of baths of varying temperatures.
The baths were usually open
from noon until sunset and were
social centres where people came
to relax after work. The complex
also contained a library, a garden,
shops and stalls. Underneath it all
were 9.5km (six miles) of tunnels,
where slaves scurried about,
treading the giant wheels that
pumped clean water up to bathers
and tending to huge braziers that
heated the chambers from below
the tiles and through pipes in the
walls. Caracalla's baths were in use
for more than 300 years: the fun
dried up in 537 when the Visigoths
sacked Rome and severed the
city's aqueducts.

Discovered in 1912 but never
opened to the public, Rome's
largest mithraeum is situated in
the tunnels beneath the baths; it is
currently open for evening guided
tours. See www.coopculture.it or
www.060608.it for information.

▶ *If visiting in summer, try to
catch an opera at the Caracalla –
even if you're not an opera lover, the
setting will convince you (see p59).*

Entertainment

Angelo Mai Altrove

Via delle Terme di Caracalla 55A, Aventine (329 448 1358, www. angelomai.org). Bus 118, 160, 628. **Open** *varies.* **Admission** *varies. No cards.* **Map** *p135 N15* ❶
Nightclub

This highly active *centro sociale* is one of the few remaining alternative semi-legal arts social, arts and entertainment hubs operating in central Rome nowadays. Check out the website for the programme of live music and dance events, all of which are guaranteed to be very far off the beaten musical track.

❤ Casa del Jazz

Viale di Porta Ardeatina 55, San Saba (06 704 731, www.casajazz.it). Bus 160, 715. **Open** *10am-midnight on concert eves.* **Admission** *€5-€15. No cards.* **Map** *p135 M16* ❷
Live music

This city council-owned jazz venue in a plush villa confiscated from a local organised-crime boss and situated behind the Terme di Caracalla (*see p136*) offers a packed programme of high-class Italian and international jazz performers. There's a café and restaurant, too, set in the villa's beautiful grounds.

Testaccio & Ostiense

Home to Rome's most vibrant nightlife scene, Testaccio is bustling, noisy and workaday, despite an influx of young(ish) professionals into an area traditionally populated by brusquely salt-of-the-earth long-term residents. Locals of all stripes mix contentedly in the gardens of **piazza Santa Maria Liberatrice** on warm evenings, linked by an almost universal devotion to the AS Roma football team and an indulgent fondness for the few remaining elderly ladies who still traipse to **Mercato Testaccio** in their slippers of a morning.

There are no major monuments here, just traces of Testaccio's hard-working past, such as the ancient port, **Emporio**, whose remains can be seen near ponte Sublicio, and the rubbish tip of carefully stacked pieces of around 50 million amphorae that forms **Monte Testaccio**; you can see the broken clay pieces piled up in some spots along via Galvani. Other noteworthy stops include the charming **Museo della via Ostiense**; the **Cimitero Acattolico** (non-Catholic cemetery; *see p139*), with its illustrious company of defunct foreign artists and writers; and the totally out-of-place **Piramide di Caio Cestio**, the mausoleum of a Roman with an inflated ego.

Due south from Testaccio, via Ostiense slices through the once-run-down area of the same name, now destined for greater things. To the east of this ancient road is a concentration of nightspots, especially around via Libetta and the shiny, bustling new campus of the Università Roma Tre. The signs of change and renewal have been visible for a while – ever since the **Centrale Montemartini** power station was converted into one of the capital's most striking museums (*see p141*), the revamped **Teatro Palladium** reopened with a fascinating programme, and Testaccio's vibrant after-hours activity began seeping south.

Follow via Ostiense southwards and you reach one of Rome's major basilicas, **San Paolo fuori le Mura** (piazzale San Paolo 1, www.basilicasanpaolo.org).

Sights & museums

Museo della via Ostiense

Via Raffaele Persichetti 3, Testaccio (06 574 3193, archeoroma. beniculturali.it). Metro Piramide/ bus 23, 30Exp, 75, 83, 118, 271, 280, 716, 769/tram 3. **Open** *Sept-July 9am-1.30pm Tue-Sun; Aug 9am-1.30pm Tue-Sat.* **Admission** *free.* **Map** *p135 K15.*

This humble but oddly charming museum contains artefacts and prints pertaining to via Ostiense and Ostia Antica, the ancient port to which this consular road led.

Restaurants

❤ Da Remo €€

Piazza Santa Maria Liberatrice 44, Testaccio (06 574 6270). Bus 23, 75, 95, 170, 280, 716, 781/tram 3. **Open** *7pm-1am Mon-Sat. Closed 3wks Aug.* **Map** *p135 H14* ❶ *Pizzeria*

The best place in town for authentic *pizza romana*, Remo is a Testaccio institution, with a prime location on the district's main piazza. You can sit at wonky tables balanced on the pavement, or in the cavernous interior, overseen by Lazio players in various team photos. The *bruschette al pomodoro* are the finest in Rome. A park with swings right across the road makes this a great place to eat with kids. You can try booking but they probably won't accept: get here early if you don't want to queue.

❤ Flavio al Velavevodetto €€

Via Monte Testaccio 97, Testaccio (06 574 4194, www. flavioalvelavevodetto.it). Bus 23, 30Exp, 75, 95, 170, 280, 716, 781/ tram 3. **Open** *12.30-3pm, 7.45-10.45pm daily.* **Map** *p135 H16* ❷ *Trattoria*

With its rear walls made of the piled-up amphora shards that constitute the strange urban feature called Monte Testaccio, Flavio al Velavevodetto (the name means 'I told you so') has all the hallmarks of a genuine Testaccio osteria. The traditional fare is hearty and *onesto* – not hugely refined but filling and generally good – the service is friendly in a hurried Roman way, and the atmosphere is buzzy, noisy and young (with a strong contingent from the nearby music school as well as clubbers starting their night out). There are some outside tables for warm-weather dining.

❤ Masto €€

Via Galvani 39/41, Testaccio (06 9521 5816, www.facebook.com/ MASTO-1734866006762281). Bus 23, 30, 75, 83, 170, 280, 673, 716, 719, 781/tram 3. **Open** *9am-midnight Mon-Sat, noon-11pm Sun. Closed 1wk Aug.* **Map** *p135 J15* ❸ *Delicatessen/Wine bar*

During the morning Masto operates as a delicatessen with the locals wandering in to stock up on the excellent prosciutto, salami and cheese. At mealtimes it transforms into an informal dining spot serving light meals, salads and their signature *taglieri*: huge wooden chopping boards loaded with cured meats and cheeses. Towering shelves display a decent selection of wines and the exuberant owners Rita and Emiliano keep clients entertained with their lively antics.

❤ Trapizzino €

Via G Branca 88, Testaccio (06 4341 9624, www.trapizzino.it). Bus 23, 30, 75, 83, 170, 280, 673, 716, 719, 781/tram 3. **Open** *Sept-July noon-1am Tue-Sun; Aug 6pm-1am Tue-Sun. Closed 1wk Aug.* **Map** *p135 H15* ❹ *Streetfood*

Pizza maker Stefano Callegari took Rome by storm in 2009 when he invented the *trapizzino* from his tiny pizza joint in Testaccio. Almost a decade and a major refit later, the expanded shop now focuses almost

💜 Cimitero Acattolico

*Via Caio Cestio 6, Testaccio (06 574 1900, www.cemeteryrome.it). Metro Piramide/bus 23, 30Exp, 75, 83, 118, 280, 716, 769/tram 3. **Open** 9am-5pm Mon-Sat; 9am-1pm Sun. Closed 10 days Aug. **Admission** €3 donation requested. **Map** p135 J16.*

This heavenly oasis of calm in the midst of a ruckus of traffic has been Rome's final resting place for non-Catholic foreigners since 1784. Verdant and atmospheric, it's popular with modern-day travellers keen to recapture the atmosphere of the Grand Tour. Unofficially known as the Protestant Cemetery, this charmingly old-world corner of the city also hosts Buddhists, Russian Orthodox Christians and atheists: a sign points to the grave of Antonio Gramsci, founder of the Italian Communist Party. In the older sector, close to the first-century Pyramid of Caius Cestius, is the grave of John Keats, who coughed his last at the age of 25, after only four months in Rome; in fine Romantic fashion his anonymous epitaph concludes: 'Here lies one whose name was writ on water.' This was all the poet wanted; his executors added the rest. Next to him lies the friend who ministered to him on his death bed, Joseph Severn (who died six decades later). The larger, newer section is much more crowded, and slopes up to the crenellations of the Aurelian Wall. At the top, slightly to the left of the tower, is the tomb of Shelley, who died a year after Keats in a stormy shipwreck in the Bay of la Spezia, having unfortunately ignored a shipbuilder's advice in favour of his personal modifications to his boat. Just in front of his tombstone is the small monument to Belinda Lee, a Devon-born film star who lived in Rome but was killed in a car accident in California in 1961, aged 25.

solely on these triangular pockets of pizza dough stuffed with classic recipes ranging from oxtail stew to cuttlefish and peas; several more offshoots of the Trapizzino brand have popped up throughout the city. Also on offer are a range of *supplì* (deep-fried rice balls) and a selection of Italian craft beers.

Cafés, bars & pubs

L'Oasi della Birra

Piazza Testaccio 41, Testaccio (06 574 6122). Bus 23, 30, 75, 83, 170, 280, 716, 781/tram 3. **Open** *4.30pm-12.30am Mon-Sat, 6pm-12.30am Sun. Closed 1wk Aug.* **Map** *p135 J15* ❶ *Bar*

In the basement of an *enoteca* on Testaccio's market square, this 'Oasis of Beer' has more than 500 brews on offer – or so it claims – though in fact when you put your order in, you may find that the one(s) you want are temporarily unavailable... In fact, the wine collection upstairs (where an off-licence is open all day) is more impressive and can be enjoyed by the glass. From 7pm to 9pm every night, customers can pile up a plate from the very generous *aperitivo* buffet to accompany their glass of wine. An à la carte menu includes snacks, cheese and cured meat platters, as well as dishes with a Teutonic slant. The outdoor tables operate year-round, weather permitting.

♥ Tram Depot

Via Marmorata 13, Testaccio (06 575 4406, www.facebook.com/tramdepotroma). Bus 23, 30, 75, 83, 170, 280, 716, 781/tram 3. **Open** *mid Mar-Oct 8am-2am daily.* **Map** *p135 J15* ❷ *Café/Bar*

With drinks and *panini* served from a disused tram carriage on the corner of via Marmorata to be consumed at the outside tables (accompanied by a frantic soundtrack of traffic and sirens), Tram Depot is certainly a quaint place to take a break. The most evocative time to visit is after sunset when young folk stop by for pre-dinner cocktails, the trees are bedecked with fairy lights and the atmosphere is one of friendly conviviality.

Bakeries, pasticcerie & gelaterie

♥ Barberini

Via Marmorata 41 (06 5725 0431, www.pasticceriabarberini.it). Bus 23, 30Exp, 75, 95, 170, 280, 716, 781/tram 3. **Open** *6am-9pm daily. Closed pm in Aug.* **Map** *p135 J15* ❶ *Café/Pasticceria*

The *testaccini* have been flocking to Barberini for their morning coffee and pastries for almost a century, and continue to do so despite a recent refit which saw the rather charming old bar replaced with a sparkling modern counter and the previous dusty decor transformed into a slick, pastel interior. The mouth-watering array of cakes are all made onsite and include fresh fruit tarts, decadent cream-filled creations and a feather-light mini tiramisù served in a tiny chocolate cup.

Shops & services

Eataly

Air Terminal Ostiense, piazzale XII Ottobre 1492, Ostiense (06 9027 9201, www.roma.eataly.it). Metro Piramide (follow signs to Ostiense, then air terminal) or Garbatella/bus 670, 673, 715, 716. **Open** *10am-midnight daily.* **Map** *p135 L17* ❶ *Food & drink/House & home*

The three sprawling floors of this temple to Italian cuisine is a food lover's paradise. On offer are kitchenware and cookbooks to dedicated sections of produce, meat, fish, cheese, wine and much

♥ Centrale Montemartini

*Via Ostiense 106 (06 574 8030, 06 0608, www.centralemontemartini. org). Metro Garbatella/bus 23, 769. **Open** 9am-7pm Tue-Sun. **Admission** €7.50, €5.50 reductions. **Map** p135 J19.*

Once a state of the art power station, the early 20th-century Centrale Montemartini was chosen in the late 1990s to house part of the collection of the Capitoline Museums during work on the atrium (which was being built to house Marcus Aurelius). The temporary exhibition 'Machines and Gods' was such a success that it became permanent. Ancient statuary is set off beautifully by the industrial setting; fauns and Minervas, bacchic revellers and Apollos

are all oddly at home against the imposing machinery of the decommissioned generating station. Highlights include incredibly detailed mosaics depicting marine themes, a spectacular early fourth-century mosaic depicting a hunting scene, pediment decorations which once adorned the Temple of Apollo Sosianus next to the Theatre of Marcellus, and the giant head and foot of a goddess found at Largo Argentina. Occasional musical events, including jazz concerts among the statues, are not to be missed.

You can buy a combined ticket for €12.50, which also gives you entry to the Capitoline Museums (€16 when a temporary exhibition is on).

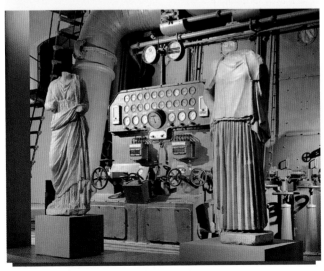

Mercato Testaccio

more. Dotted throughout are a myriad of specialist eateries serving food throughout the day as well as a wine bar and craft beer pub. Food festivals, cooking classes and tastings are held frequently so check the website for the programme of events.

♥ Mercato Testaccio
Between via Galvani & via A Volta, Testaccio (www.mercatoditestaccio. it). Bus 23, 30, 75, 83, 170, 280, 716, 781/tram 3. **Open** *7am-3.30pm Mon-Sat.* **Map** *p135 H15* ❷ *Market*
In 2012 Testaccio's slightly dilapidated market moved into squeaky-clean new premises. Almost all the old vendors made the move and the eccentric selection of stalls selling shoes, clothes, household goods and fresh produce are all still in business. However an influx of new gastronomic stalls have created a delightful juxtaposition of old and new as well as breathing a new lease of life into the market.

Michelin-starred chef Cristina Bowerman's modern delicatessen Romeo (box 30/44), delicious Roman sandwiches at Mordi e Vai (box 15) and gourmet snacks and streetfood at FoodBox (box 66), along with many more, have all contributed to raising the modern profile of both the market and the Testaccio neighbourhood.

Entertainment

♥ Akab
Via di Monte Testaccio 68/69, Testaccio (06 5725 0585, www. facebook.com/akabclubufficiale). Metro Piramide/bus 23, 30Exp, 75, 83, 130, 673, 719, 3N, 9N, 10N, 11N/ tram 3. **Open** *11pm-3am Tue-Sat.* **Admission** *€10-€25 (incl 1 drink).* **Map** *p135 H16* ❸ *Nightclub*
Formerly a carpenter's workshop, this place is now a busy, long-term fixture of the Testaccio nightlife scene, hosting various well-known international DJs. Depending

Goa Club p144

on the night you choose, music may be retro, R&B or house. Akab has two levels: an underground cellar and a street-level room, as well as a garden.

L'Alibi

Via di Monte Testaccio 40-44, Testaccio (06 574 3448, www. lalibi.it). Metro Piramide/bus 23, 30, 75, 83, 170, 280, 673, 716, 719, 3N, 9N, 10N, 11N/tram 3. **Open** *11.30pm-5am Thur-Sun.* **Admission** *€10-€20 (incl 1 drink).* **Map** *p135 H16* **4** *Gay club*

The gay club Alibi paved the way for Testaccio's boom as a nightlife quarter with an alternative feel. An increasingly straight-friendly approach, and the fact that it's showing its age rather, has diluted its success with punters. It's still a good place to bop the night away, however, with a well-oiled sound system covering two floors in winter and three in summer, when the roof garden comes into its own. If you can

get yourself on to the guest list, admission is cheaper.

Caruso Café de Oriente

Via di Monte Testaccio 36, Testaccio (06 574 5019, www. carusocafe.com). Metro Piramide/ bus 23, 30Exp, 75, 83, 130, 673, 719, 3N, 9N, 10N, 11N/tram 3. **Open** *Sept-May 11pm-4am Tue-Sun.* **Admission** *€8-€15, free Sun. No cards.* **Map** *p135 H16* **5** *Live music*

A must for lovers of salsa and the like, this club offers Latin American tunes every night and live acts almost daily. Shimmy your way in between scores of dancing couples to enjoy the warm atmosphere in these three, ethnic-themed, orange-hued rooms – or head up to the roof terrace. It's usually packed (some would say to an annoying degree) and service can be rude. In the summer months from June to August, Caruso moves venue to **Fiesta** (via delle Tre Fontane 24, Suburbs: EUR, www.fiesta.it).

Teatro Palladium

In trendy Ostiense, this is one of the best of Rome's fashionable clubs. The quality of the Italian and international DJs that it books is generally above the competition. Note that the doormen can be picky.

Teatro di Roma – India
Lungotevere Vittorio Gassman 1 (06 6840 00311, www.teatrodiroma. net). Bus 170, 766, 775, 780, 781, C6. **Box office** *from 5pm before shows (3pm Sun), or at Teatro di Roma – Argentina (see above).* **No cards.** **Map** *p135 H18* ❽ *Theatre*
This converted industrial space, with three stages, is used for more experimental offerings.

🖤 Teatro Palladium
Piazza Bartolomeo Romano 8 (06 5733 2768, www.teatro-palladium. it). Metro Garbatella/bus 670, 673, 715, 716. **Box office** *4-8pm Tue-Sun.* **No cards.** **Map** *p135 L20* ❾ *Theatre*
This beautiful theatre dates from the 1920s. Now furnished with brightly coloured chairs, it provides a fascinating mix of electronic music, cutting-edge theatre and art performances. It is one of the venues of choice for the exciting and eclectic annual RomaEuropa Festival (*see p57*).

Via Appia Antica

To the east of Ostiense lies the beginning of the Appian Way. Appius Claudius Caecus, censor of 312 BC, had the inspired idea of building a road (taking advantage of a lava stream from a volcanic eruption 270,000 years earlier) to move troops and goods easily between towns. In ancient times, the Appian Way was a prime spot for the real estate of the afterlife; the remains of the dead had to be kept outside the *pomerium* (a sacred city boundary), and well-to-do Roman families set

G I Am
Planet Roma, via del Commercio 36, Ostiense (340 753 8396, www. facebook.com/GIAMRoma). Metro Piramide/bus 23, 271, 769, 2N, 3N. **Open** *11pm-4am Sat.* **Admission** *€10. No cards.* **Map** *p135 H17* ❻ *Gay club night*
This gay one-nighter, held at the cavernous Planet Roma (formerly the Alpheus) club is a rather glamorous affair, featuring drag shows and programming a host of good-quality guest and resident DJs. This isn't just one for the boys: there's often a women-only room (La Coco' Room) at the event too, hosted by the Venus Rising crew. During the summer weekends, G I Am is hosted at the Gay Village (*see p57*).

🖤 Goa Club
Via Libetta 13, Ostiense (06 9555 8820, www.goaclub.it). Metro Garbatella/bus 23, 271, 769, 770, 2N, 3N, 9N. **Open** *Sept-May 11pm-4am Thur-Sat; 5pm-1am Sun.* **Admission** *€10-€25.* **Map** *p135 K20* ❼ *Nightclub*

💜 Museo delle Mura

*Via di Porta San Sebastiano 18 (06
0608, www.museodellemuraroma.
it). Bus 118, 218.* **Open** *9am-2pm
Tue-Sun.* **Admission** *free.*
Map *p8.*

Rome's ancient walls run an 18-
km (12-mile) circuit around the
city. Built by Aurelian in the third
century, a desperate sign of the
city's imminent decline, they
were subsequently reinforced
and modified. They remained the
fortifications defending the papal
city until they were breached at
porta Pia in 1870, 16 centuries after

their construction. This small
and free museum is housed in
the ancient porta San Sebastiano.
There is a small collection of
artefacts associated with Roman
walls and roads, including a
couple of nice models. But the
main attraction is undoubtedly
the fine view from the ramparts
of the gate, looking out across the
verdant Parco dell'Appia Antica
towards the Alban Hills in the
distance. There is also a walkway
that leads along a section of the
wall, complete with arrow slits to
peer out at advancing invaders.

SOUTH OF THE CENTRE

up family mausoleums alongside this major road into the city. It was once lined with tombs, vaults, sarcophagi and every kind of magnificent decoration imaginable.

Christians, too, began burying their dead here, initially in common necropoli. Later, as land became too expensive, they laid them to rest underground, creating the estimated 300-kilometre (200-mile) network of underground cemeteries known as the **catacombs**.

The beginning of the Appia Antica is now considered to be at the **porta San Sebastiano**, the best-preserved of the gates that were built by Aurelian when he walled the city in AD 270. Inside the gate is the little **Museo delle Mura** (see p145), which allows access to a section of the wall. On the right, ten minutes' walk beyond the gate, is the **Parco Appia Antica Punto Informativo** (via Appia Antica 58/60, 06 513 5316, www.parcoappiaantica. it). The further south you go, the more the Appian Way returns to its ancient roots: the original volcanic paving stones that lie exposed beneath a canopy of pines and cypresses are those trod by the Roman infantry.

Sights & museums

Catacombe di San Callisto

Via Appia Antica 110 & 126 (06 513 0151, www.catacombe.roma.it). **Open** *9am-noon, 2-5pm Mon, Tue, Thur-Sun. Closed late Jan-late Feb.* **Admission** *€8; €5 reductions.* Buried in the 29km (18 miles) of tunnels were nine popes (venerated in a chapel known as *il piccolo Vaticano*), dozens of martyrs and thousands of Christians. Named after third-century Pope Callixtus, the area became the first official cemetery of the Church of Rome.

San Sebastiano & Catacombe di San Sebastiano

Via Appia Antica 136 (06 788 7035/06 785 0350, www.catacombe. org). **Church** *8am-1pm, 2-5.30pm daily.* **Catacombs** *10am-5pm Mon-Sat. Closed mid Nov-mid Dec.* **Admission** *Church free, Catacombs €8; €5 reductions.* The name 'catacomb' originated in this spot, where a complex of underground burial sites situated near a tufa quarry was described as being *kata kymbas* – 'near the quarry'. The guided tour will take you into the crypt of St Sebastian, the martyr always depicted nastily pierced by a hail of arrows, who was buried here. Visitors usually ignore the fourth-century basilica built over the catacombs; pilgrims taking a tour of Rome's great basilicas understand its importance: the remains of apostles Peter and Paul were hidden in the underlying catacombs in the third century, during the persecutions by Emperor Valerian.

Catacombe di San Callisto

Trastevere & Gianicolo

Trastevere is quaint but buzzing, historical but without the imposing ruins and galleries you feel you have to 'do' on the other side of the river. Here your main tasks will include rambling through narrow cobbled streets, soaking up the rustic charm, basking in the laid-back feel of the place and selecting the likeliest-looking of the over-abundant bars for *aperitivi*.

Through the Imperial period, much of the area was agricultural, with farms, vineyards, villas and gardens laid out for the pleasure of the Caesars. Trastevere was a working-class district in papal Rome, and remained so until well after Italian unification; nowadays, those peeling walls conceal top property prices and residents who can afford them.

Best for greenery
Orto Botanico *p155*

Best rustic eating experience
Da Enzo al 29 *p153*
I Supplì *p154*

Best blow-out dinner
Antico Arco *p153*
Glass Hostaria *p154*

Best bookshop browsing
Almost Corner Bookshop *p157*
Open Door Bookshop *p158*

Best for tasteful gifts
Elvis Lives *p157*
Romastore Profumi *p158*
Les Vignerons *p158*

Best for a holy moment
Santa Cecilia in Trastevere *p152*
Santa Maria in Trastevere *p151*

Best street party
Festa de' Noantri *p58*

Best gelato fix
Fior di Luna *p157*

Viale Trastevere slices the district in two. At the hub of the much-visited western part is **piazza Santa Maria in Trastevere**, with its eponymous church. Smoggy via della Lungara leads to the lovely **Orto Botanico** (botanical gardens; *see p155*), the **Villa Farnesina**, with its frescoes by Raphael, and **Palazzo Corsini**, which houses part of the national art collection.

Fewer tourists make it to the warren of cobbled alleys in the eastern half, where craftsmen still ply their trades around the lovely church of **Santa Cecilia in Trastevere** (*see p152*). In this achingly charming part of Trastevere look out for unexpected treats, such as the church of **San Francesco a Ripa**.

The Gianicolo is the highest of central Rome's hills, though not one of the official seven. A couple of winding roads lead up from Trastevere, past decidedly patrician villas, many of which are now embassies and cultural institutions. It's leafy up here and a calm place for a stroll. Up via Garibaldi is Bramante's lovely **Tempietto**, in the courtyard of the church of **San Pietro in Montorio**. It contrasts oddly with the squat Fascist-era monument across the road: the **Ossario Garibaldino**. The view from the grand belvedere at the **Fontana Paola** over the red roofs of the *centro storico* is quite, quite lovely.

West of here stretches the leafy, well-heeled suburb of Monteverde, home to the vast, green expanses of **Villa Pamphili**, a wonderful place for a stroll.

Sights & museums

Palazzo Corsini – Galleria Nazionale d'Arte Antica

Via della Lungara 10 (06 6880 2323, www.barberinicorsini.org). Bus 23, 280. **Open** *8.30am-7pm Wed-Mon.* **Admission** *€10 (incl Palazzo Barberini, valid 10 days); €5 reductions. No cards.* **Map** *p150 F10.*

In the 1933 film *Queen Christina*, Greta Garbo played the former owner of this palace as a graceful tussler with existential angst; in real life, the stout 17th-century Swedish monarch smoked a pipe, wore trousers and entertained female – and a fair number of (ordained) male – lovers. 'Queen without a realm, Christian without a faith, and woman without shame' ran one of the contemporary epithets on Christina. But, in addition to being brilliantly scandalous, Christina was also one of the most cultured and influential women of her age. The century's highest-profile convert to Catholicism, she abdicated her throne and established her glittering court here in 1662, filling what was then Palazzo Riario with her fabled library and an ever-expanding collection of fabulous old masters. She threw the best parties in Rome and commissioned many of Scarlatti and Corelli's hit tunes before dying here in 1689.

Today the palace – later redesigned by Ferdinand Fuga for the Corsini family – houses part of the national art collection. The galleries have beautiful frescoes and trompe l'oeil effects, and contain paintings of the Madonna by Van Dyck, Filippo Lippi and Orazio Gentileschi, two *St Sebastians* (one by Rubens and one by Annibale Carracci) and a pair of *Annunciations* by Guercino. Among the works by Caravaggio is an unadorned *Narcissus*. There's also a triptych by Fra Angelico and a melancholy *Salome* by Guido Reni.

San Francesco a Ripa

Piazza San Francesco d'Assisi 88 (06 581 9020). Bus 23, 44, 75, 115, 280, 780, H/tram 3, 8. **Open** *7am-1pm, 3-7pm daily.* **Map** *p150 H13.*

Rebuilt in the 1680s, this church took the place of a 13th-century one that held now-lost frescoes by Pietro Cavallini chronicling the life of St Francis of Assisi. The saint stayed in the adjoining convent when he visited Rome in 1229: if you ask the sacristan, he may show you the cell where St Francis lived and the rock on which he placed his head to sleep. An orange tree in the garden was supposedly planted by the saint. The metaphysical artist Giorgio de Chirico is buried here behind a gate off the first chapel on the left; ask the sacristan if you can have a look. *See p156 Bernini's Babes.*

➜ Getting around

Trastevere is on the west side of the River Tiber (a short stroll across the pedestrian Ponte Sisto from the campo de' Fiori area), and south of the Vatican. Either work up an appetite climbing the Gianicolo, or take a bus (no.44, 75) up the hill and walk down.

❤ Santa Maria in Trastevere

Piazza Santa Maria in Trastevere (06 581 4802, www.santamariaintrastevere.org). Bus 23, 44, 75, 280, 780/tram 3, 8. **Open** *Sept-July 7.30am-9pm daily. Aug 8am-1pm, 3-9pm daily.* **Map** *p150 G11.*

This stunning church, with its welcoming portico and façade with shimmering 13th-century mosaics, overlooks the traffic-free piazza of the same name. Santa Maria is the heart and soul of Trastevere. According to legend, a well of oil sprang miraculously from the ground where the church now stands the moment Christ was born, and flowed to the Tiber all day. A small street leading out of the piazza, via della Fonte dell'Olio, commemorates this.

The façade we see today was designed by Carlo Fontana in 1692, but the mosaics pre-date it by four centuries: they show Mary breastfeeding Christ on a solid gold background.

The present 12th-century Romanesque church, built for Pope Innocent II, replaced a basilica from the late third or early fourth century (though legend has it that it was founded by Pope Callistus I, who died in 222) – one of the city's oldest and the first dedicated to the Virgin. That in turn probably topped the site of a *titulus* – a place of worship in the house of an early Christian. The apse is made magnificent by a 12th-century mosaic of Jesus and the Virgin Mary; the figure on the far left is Pope Innocent. Further down, between the windows, are mosaics of the Virgin from the 13th century, attributed to Pietro Cavallini, whose relaxed, realistic figures represent the re-emergence of a Roman style after long years of the hegemony of stiff Byzantine models. The *Madonna and Child* with rainbow overhead is also by Cavallini.

Tempietto di Bramante & San Pietro in Montorio

Piazza San Pietro in Montorio 2 (06 581 3940, Tempietto 06 581 2806). Bus 44, 75, 115. **Tempietto** *10am-6pm Tue-Sun.* **Church** *8am-noon, 3-4pm daily.* **Map** *p150 F12.*

Located on one of the various spots where St Peter is believed to have been crucified (St Peter's is another), San Pietro in Montorio conceals one of Rome's greatest architectural jewels in its courtyard: the Tempietto, designed by Donato Bramante in 1508 for Cardinal Giuliano della Rovere, who was to become Pope Julius II (and who also got him working on St Peter's basilica). The small circular structure, with its Doric columns, has classical symmetry that was subsequently imitated by many architects. Bernini got his hands on it in 1628, adding the staircase that leads down to the crypt. The church next door, founded in the late ninth century and rebuilt in the late 15th century, contains a chapel by Bernini (second on the left) and one by Vasari (fifth on the right). Paintings include Sebastiano del Piombo's *Flagellation* (c1516). The name Montorio, or golden hill, refers to the way the sun hit sand on the Gianicolo, turning it gold.

Villa Farnesina

Via della Lungara 230 (06 6802 7268, www.villafarnesina.it). Bus 23, 280. **Open** *9am-2pm Mon-Sat; 9am-5pm 2nd Sun of mth.* **Admission** *€6; €3 reductions.* **Map** *p150 F10.*

Villa Farnesina was built between 1508 and 1511 to a design by Baldassare Peruzzi as a pleasure palace and holiday home for the fabulously rich papal banker Agostino Chigi. Treasurer to Pope Julius II, Chigi was one of Raphael's principal patrons. In its day the villa was stuffed to the rafters

💙 Santa Cecilia in Trastevere

Piazza Santa Cecilia 22 (06 589 9289). Bus 23, 44, 75, 115, 280, 780, H/tram 3, 8. Church 9.30am-12.30pm, 4-6pm Mon-Sat; 11.30am-12.30pm, 4-6pm Sun. Cavallini frescoes 10am-12.30pm Mon-Sat; 11.30am-12.30pm Sun. Archaeological site 9.30am-12.30pm, 4-6pm daily. Admission Frescoes €2.50. Archaeological site €2.50. No cards. Map p150 H12.

The current 16th-century church of this magnificent religious complex was built above a fifth-century basilica, which in turn incorporated a *titulus*, or house where early Christians met. In this case, gruesome legend relates, that house belonged to Roman patrician Valerio, who lived at the time of Emperor Marcus Aurelius. So impressed was Valerio by his wife Cecilia's vow of chastity that he too converted to Christianity. Valerio was murdered for his pains, and Cecilia was arrested while she tried to bury him. Doing away with the saintly Cecilia proved a difficult job for the Romans. After a failed attempt to suffocate her in the house's hot baths they tried to behead her. But only three strokes of the axe were permitted by law, and after the third failed to do the job, as she was slowly dying she sang, securing her place as the patron saint of music. When her tomb was reopened in 1599, her body was uncorrupted. Sculptor Stefano Maderno portrays her with her head turned away in an exquisite marble rendering beneath the altar. Her sarcophagus is in the crypt.

The excavations below the church provide extensive evidence of early Roman and palaeo-Christian buildings; here, too, is the pretty decorated crypt where Cecilia's body lies.

On the first floor, on the other hand, is a choir from where nuns from the adjoining convent could look down over the interior of the basilica from behind a grill. On one wall is what remains of what was possibly Rome's greatest 13th-century fresco – a *Last Judgement* by little-known genius Pietro Cavallini. With its rainbow-winged angels of all ranks and desperate sinners writhing hellwards, the once-monumental fresco shows Cavallini breaking away from the Byzantine style and giving new light and humanity to the figures.

with great works of art, although many were later sold to pay off debts. Chigi was known for his extravagant parties, where guests had the run of the palace and the magnificent gardens. Just to make sure his guests knew that money was no object, he would have his servants toss the silver and gold plates on which they dined into the Tiber – into underwater nets, to be fished out later and used again. The powerful Farnese family bought the villa and renamed it in 1577 after the Chigis went bankrupt.

The stunning frescoes are homages to the pagan and classical world; the works on the ground-floor Loggia of Psyche were designed by Raphael but executed by his friends and followers, including Giulio Romano; according to local lore, the master himself was too busy dallying with his mistress, *la fornarina* (baker's girl), to apply any more paint than was strictly necessary. The *Grace* with her back turned, to the right of the door, is attributed to him, though. Around the corner in the Loggia of Galatea, Raphael took brush in hand to create the victorious goddess in her seashell chariot. Upstairs, the Salone delle Prospettive was decorated by Peruzzi with views of 16th-century Rome. Next to it is Agostino Chigi's bedroom, with a fresco of the *Marriage of Alexander the Great and Roxanne* (1517) by a contemporary of Raphael, known by the nickname Il Sodoma. Like most of his paintings, this is a rather sordid number showing the couple being undressed by vicious cherubs.

Restaurants

❤ Antico Arco €€€€
Piazzale Aurelio 7 (06 581 5274, www.anticoarco.it). Bus 44, 75, 115, 710, 870, 871. **Open** *noon-midnight daily.* **Map** *p150 E12* ① *Italian*

The minimalist yet warm interior of Patrizia Mattei's Gianicolo restaurant provides the perfect backdrop for sampling the carefully creative menu which changes according to the season. Although prices have risen somewhat in recent years, Antico Arco remains steadfast in its popularity and reputation. The seven-course *degustazione* menu (€78) is good value and the wine list offers up some sensibly priced gems. Until 6pm there is also a fixed finger food menu of miniature versions of the main dishes. Book well in advance.

Casa Mia €€
Via della Renella 88-90 (06 8697 4870, www.casamiaintrastevere. com). Bus 23, 280, 780, H/tram 8. **Open** *noon-11pm daily.* **Map** *p150 G11* ② *Trattoria*

A friendly, relaxed trattoria off the main drag, Casa Mia offers solid Roman cuisine and seasonal blackboard specials. On Thursdays there are usually home-made gnocchi while on Fridays the focus is on fish. There is a decently priced wine list to match. Unlike most places the restaurant stays open between lunch and dinner for a quick afternoon drink or snack. Snag a table in the delightful courtyard to dine *al fresco* or sit at the front to peer through the large window to see the chefs at work.

❤ Da Enzo al 29 €€
Via dei Vascellari 29 (06 581 2260, www.daenzoal29.com). Bus 23, 280, 780, H/tram 8. **Open** *12.30-2.30pm, 7.30-11pm Mon-Sat. Closed 3wks Aug.* **Map** *p150 J12* ③ *Trattoria*

Don't expect a long, leisurely experience at this diminutive family-run trattoria. Space is limited, the noise level is high and the service is fast and furious but for typical *cucina romana* it is a reliable and atmospheric option. Prices are a little above the average

Glass Hostaria

of years. The menu changes frequently: expect novelties along the lines of chestnut tagliatelle with pumpkin, sausage and sage, or sumac-scented lamb with quinoa, beluga lentils and nuts. There are three tasting menus including one for vegetarians.

❤ I Supplì €

Via di San Francesco a Ripa 137 (06 589 7110, www.lacasadelsuppli.it). Bus 23, 280, 780, H/tram 8. **Open** *10am-9.30pm Mon-Sat. Closed 3wks Aug.* **No cards.** **Map** *p150 G12* ⑤ *Streetfood*
A hole-in-the-wall institution, you can spot the entrance to I Supplì from the crowd of people hovering outside devouring the famed *supplì* (a deep-fried ball of rice and ragù stuffed with mozzarella). Aside from the excellent *fritti* (fried snacks) there is also some very good pizza-by-the-slice and a daily-rotating selection of pasta and rice dishes which are scooped into aluminium containers and sold by portion.

but the quality of ingredients is assured and there is a nice selection of lesser-known Lazio wines. Bookings are taken, but only for the early evening seating so to catch one of the outside tables get there for an early lunch or be prepared to join a very long queue.

❤ Glass Hostaria €€€€

Vicolo del Cinque 58 (06 5833 5903, www.glass-hostaria.it). Bus 23, 280, 780, H/tram 8. **Open** *8pm-midnight Tue-Sun. Closed 1wk Jan/Feb & 2wks July/Aug.* **Map** *p150 G11* ④ *Italian/Fusion*
Despite the place being ultra-modern and vigorously kicking against the traditional Trastevere dining scene, Glass offers surprisingly warm service, an interesting wine list and a menu that is, yes, experimental and fusion-tinged but rather less pretentious than you might expect. Chef Cristina Bowerman's Michelin star has pushed prices up somewhat in the past couple

Cafés, bars & pubs

Bar San Calisto

Piazza San Calisto (06 583 5869). Bus 23, 280, 780, H/tram 8. **Open** *7.30am-2am Mon-Sat.* **No cards.** **Map** *p150 G12* ① *Coffee shop/Bar*
Green tourists get their coffee or beer on Piazza Santa Maria in Trastevere; locals who know better go to this bar. The place's harsh lighting would make Sophia Loren look wan, and the dingy space – inside and out – is no picture postcard. But it's cheap and as such it has always been the haunt of arty and fringe types (plus many questionable characters after sundown). The bohemian crowd will be here downing beers or an *affogato* (ice-cream swamped with liqueur), or savouring some of the best hot chocolate in Rome: deliciously thick with fresh whipped cream.

💜 Orto Botanico

Largo Cristina di Svezia 24 (06 4991 7107, www.ortobotanicoitalia. it). Bus 23, 280. **Open** *Apr-Oct 9am-6.30pm Mon-Sat. Nov-Mar 9am-5.30pm Mon-Sat. Closed public hols.* **Admission** *€8; €4 reductions. No cards.* **Map** *p150 E11.*

Providing nearly 30 acres (121,000sq m) of greenery hiding in central Rome (plus 21,500sq ft – 2,000sq m – of greenhouses), the city's Botanical Gardens were established in 1833 when the Italian state acquired the gardens of the Villa Corsini. However, this verdant area at the foot of the Gianicolo has had a much longer botanical past. It was first planted in the 13th century, by order of Pope Nicholas III, when it was devoted to simples (medicinal plants)

and citrus groves. Its fortunes rose and fell under successive popes, but thanks to the aqueduct of Trajan, restored in the early 17th century, it would become one of the leading botanical gardens in Europe under Pope Alexander VII. Today the Orto Botanico is run by the University of Rome's Environmental Biology department as a living museum, and offers a delicious haven from the rigours of a hot, dusty day, with its Baroque stairs flanked by cascading waterfalls, formal tableaux around fountains and statues, its bamboo grove, and varieties of exotic plants and flowers. Check out the cactus garden, the orchids and the touching and smelling collection for the vision-impaired. You may find it to be one of Rome's most under-appreciated gems.

TRASTEVERE & GIANICOLO

Bernini's Babes

All hail the master of racy religious art

One hand clutches her breast, her body writhes and her face looks heavenwards in rapturous agony. Is she in the throes of death or in the midst of an erotic encounter with the Holy Spirit?

Beata Ludovica Albertoni (1671), who graces the church of **San Francesco a Ripa** (see p149), is just one of many sexually and spiritually charged marble women scattered around Rome by Baroque genius Gian Lorenzo Bernini.

Lusty Bernini – father of 11 – was a highly religious individual for whom the distinction between the sensual and the sublime was blurred. Sculptor, architect and darling of a string of popes, Bernini (1598-1680) attended Mass every morning, took communion twice a week, and on the way home from work stopped by regularly at the church of the **Gesù** (see p88) where he reportedly underwent the rigorous Spiritual Exercises of the Jesuits.

Evidently, though, that didn't preclude a first-hand understanding of female joys and fears. Just look at the terror on the face of Proserpina as Pluto grabs her fleshy thigh in *The Rape of Proserpina* (1622); the woeful desperation of Daphne as she turns into a laurel tree to escape Apollo's embrace in *Apollo and Daphne* (1622-25); or the come-hither look of the laid-back *Truth Unveiled by Time* (1646-52), all of which can be admired in the **Galleria Borghese** (see p104).

Bernini designed – though his workshop may have carved – the *Four Virtues* group in **Sant'Isidoro** (via degli Artisti 41, 06 488 5359, by appt only), in which *Charity* offers her ample naked bosom with an encouraging smile – an outright solicitation that Bernini's patrons in 1662 didn't seem to find out of place in a church. (It was too much for 19th-century sensibilities, though: the bronze tunics that were added to cover her and one of her buxom sisters were not removed until 2002).

Energetic and disciplined, an indefatigable worker who was at home with popes and princes, Bernini lost his head just once, for Costanza Bonarelli, the wife of a fellow artist. So steamy was the affair that Urban VIII had to step in to put out the fire. Bernini subsequently married, had his numerous brood and lived happily until the age of 82. But not before completing, for himself, an exquisite bust of his beloved Costanza (1635, in the Bargello museum in Florence), with an intelligent face and loose blouse.

Beata Ludovica Albertoni (Bernini, 1671)

Open Door Bookshop *p158*

Cioccolata e Vino
*Vicolo del Cinque 11 (06 5830 1868).
Bus 23, 280, 780, H/tram 8.* **Open**
*6.30pm-2am Mon-Fri; 2pm-2am
Sat, Sun.* **No cards.** **Map** *p150
G11* ❷ *Café/Shop/Bar*
Half-shop, half-bar, this tiny
emporium is a joy to visit at almost
any hour: for hot chocolate, a
delicious espresso with chocolate
in the bottom of your cup, a
chocolate tasting or a glass of
wine from a small but interesting
selection. Late at night the pub-
crawlers stop here to grab one of
the renowned chocolate shots:
liqueurs and cocktails served in a
tiny chocolate cup.

Bakeries, pasticcerie & gelaterie

♥ Fior di Luna
*Via della Lungaretta 96 (06 6456
1314, www.fiordiluna.com). Bus
23, 280, 630, 780, H/tram 8.* **Open**
11.30am-12.30am daily. **Map** *p150
G11* ❶ *Gelateria*
Gelato connoisseurs will find little
to criticise at this popular location
in the heart of Trastevere. Small-
batch production and attention
to quality are the bywords here
and the choices rotate according
to season and availability of fresh
produce. The fresh fruit sorbets
are heavenly (look out for the fig in
July). For something unique try the
flavours made with donkey milk.

Sora Mirella
*Lungotevere degli Anguillara,
corner of Ponte Cestio. Bus 23, 280,
780, H/tram 8.* **Open** *10am-3am
daily.* **No cards.**
Map *p150 H11* ❷ *Gelateria*
Mirella styles herself as *la regina
della grattachecca* (the Queen of
Water Ices), and there appears
to be no reason to disagree. The
place gives you an opportunity
to sit on the Tiber embankment
wall as you tuck into the *speciale
superfrutta* – fresh melon, kiwi
fruit and strawberry (or whatever
fruit happens to be in season)
with syrups served in a specially
designed glass.

Shops & services

♥ Almost Corner Bookshop
*Via del Moro 45 (06 583 6942). Bus
23, 30, 44, 83, 170, 716, 280, 781, H/
tram 3, 8.* **Open** *10am-8pm Mon-
Sat; 11am-1.30pm, 3.30-8pm Sun.*
Map *p150 G11* ❶ *Books*
Not an inch of space is wasted in
this English-language bookshop: a
good selection of fiction, as well as
history, art, archaeology and more
is displayed on every surface. Check
the noticeboard if you're seeking
work, lodgings or Italian lessons.

♥ Elvis Lives
*Via di San Francesco a Ripa 27 (06
4550 9542, www.elvislives.it). Bus
23, 280, 630, 780, H/tram 8.* **Open**
*10am-2pm, 3.30-8pm Mon-Sat.
Closed 3wks Aug.* **Map** *p150 G12* ❷
Accessories/Tech
Run by two graphic designers
this small shop sells all your
hipster needs from slogan t-shirts,
watches and sunglasses to cutting-
edge Polaroid cameras and retro
record players.

View from the Gianicolo

Mercato San Cosimato

Piazza San Cosimato. Bus 23, 75, 83, 280, 716, 781/tram 3, 8. **Open** *6.30am-2.30pm Mon-Sat.* **No cards.** *Map p150 G12* ❸ *Market*
Trastevere's lively morning market offers a glimpse into the daily life of the local *Trasteverini* as they peruse the mountains of fresh produce while catching up on the neighbourhood gossip. There are also a few fixed stalls at the back selling meat, fish and cheeses.

❤ Open Door Bookshop

Via della Lungaretta 23 (06 589 6478, www.books-in-italy. com). Bus 23, 44, 83, 115, 170, 716, 280, 781, H/tram 3, 8. **Open** *Sept-June 10.30am-8pm Mon-Sat; July 4-8.30pm Mon, Sat; 11.30am-8.30pm Tue-Fri. Closed Aug. Map p150 H11* ❹ *Books*
Second-hand and antiquarian English books have been sold from this cramped, welcoming little space on the 'other', quieter side of Trastevere since 1976.

Porta Portese

Via Portuense, southwards from Porta Portese. Bus 23, 44, 83, 115, 170, 716, 280, 781, H/tram 3, 8/train to Trastevere. **Open** *5am-2pm Sun. Map p150 H13* ❺ *Market*
Rome's biggest and most famous flea market grew out of the city's thriving black market after the end of World War II. A lingering air of illegality still persists here, so watch out for pickpockets. Dealers peddle all manner of items: bootleg CDs, furniture, clothes, fake designer gear and car stereos of dubious origin.

❤ Romastore Profumi

Via della Lungaretta 63 (06 581 8789, www.romastoreprofumi. com). Bus 23, 115, 280, 780, H/tram 8. **Open** *10am-8pm daily. Map p150 G11* ❻ *Health & beauty*
Passers-by are always drawn in by the artistic window displays of this elegant perfume shop. A blissful sanctuary of lotions and potions, they stock an array of gorgeous scents: old-school Floris, Creed and Penhaligon's rub shoulders with modern classics such as home-grown Acqua di Parma and Lorenzo Villoresi. Staff can be very abrupt.

❤ Les Vignerons

Via Mameli 61/62 (06 6477 1439, www.lesvignerons.it). Bus 23, 280, 630, 780, H/tram 8. **Open** *4-9pm Mon; 11am-9pm Tue-Thur; 11am-9.30pm Fri, Sat. Closed 2wks Aug. Map p150 G12* ❼ *Wine shop*
Friendly wine shop with a focus on natural and biodynamic wines from small producers in Italy and beyond. The staff here are more than happy to discuss and recommend bottles from the extensive selection. There is also a good choice of craft beers.

Entertainment

Nuovo Sacher

Largo Ascianghi 1 (06 581 8116, www.sacherfilm.eu). Bus 44, 75, 125, H/tram 3, 8. Map p150 H13 ❶ *Cinema*
The Nuovo Sacher is owned and run by veteran director Nanni Moretti, and is a meeting place for local cinematic talent. VO films are usually shown on Mondays or Tuesdays.

Dome of San Pietro

Vatican & Prati

It goes without saying that no visit to Rome is complete without a trip to the Vatican City. The world's smallest state at half a square kilometre (one fifth of a square mile) is home to St Peter's Basilica and the Vatican Museums.

The area where the Vatican now stands was once a marsh, stretching from the Gianicolo to modern-day Monte Mario. Today huge crowds of worshippers pack St Peter's square when the pope is in Rome. Visitors also flock to view one of the world's finest collections of art and antiquities, including the largest array of pagan and non-Christian works.

The bourgeois district of Prati (meaning meadows, which these were until the 19th century) offers a pleasing antidote to all that history and culture with its excellent shopping and bustling streets.

Best Michelangelos
Cappella Sistina (Musei
Vaticani) *p164*
Pietà (St Peter's) *p163*

Best Raphaels
Stanze di Raffaello (Musei
Vaticani) *p166*

Best jazz joint
Alexanderplatz *p170*

Best holy experience
A glimpse of the pope *p167*
St Peter's *p163*

Best for a post-Vatican bite
200 Gradi *p169*
Pizzarium *p169*

Best retail therapy
Coin Excelsior *p170*

Vatican

The St Peter's that we see today
was consecrated in 1626; the
previous basilica on this spot was
consecrated in the early years
of the fourth century. The link
between this area and Christianity,
however, predates even that
earlier church.

In AD 54, Emperor Nero built
a circus in the *campus vaticanus*,
a marshy area across the river
from the city centre. Ten years
later, when fire destroyed two-
thirds of Rome, Nero blamed the
Christians, and the persecution
of this new cult began in earnest,
with much of the Christian-
bashing taking place in Nero's
circus: legend says they were
covered in tar and burned alive.
Top apostle Peter is traditionally
believed to have been crucified
here and buried close by on the
spot where, in 326, Emperor
Constantine built the first church
of St Peter.

Not all of the subsequent
popes resided in the Vatican
but, throughout the Christian
era, pilgrims have flocked to the
tomb of the founder of the Roman
Church. After the Sack of Rome
in 1527, the popes moved first to
the Lateran palace, next to San
Giovanni (*see p131*), and then to
the Quirinale palace (*see p97*).
Only in 1870, with the unification
of Italy, were they forced back
across the Tiber once more. Until
1929, the pope pronounced the
Italian state to be sacrilegious.
But on 11 February 1929, Pius XII
and Mussolini signed the Lateran
Pacts, awarding the Catholic
church a huge cash payment, tax-
free status and a constitutional
role that led to an important
and continuing influence over
legislation on social issues.

As well as St Peter's and the
Vatican Museums, the Vatican
walls surround splendid formal
gardens, which can visited on
guided tours. These must be
booked at least one week in
advance either at the Vatican
tourist office (*see p162*) or through
www.biglietteriamusei.vatican.va.

➔ **Getting around**
The closest metro station to the Vatican is Ottaviano (line A); useful buses
include 64, 40 and 23.

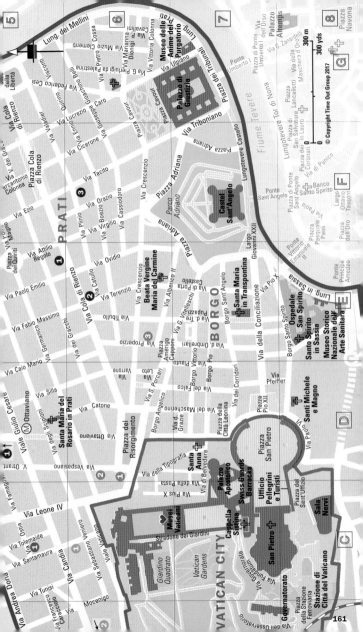

Vatican Essentials

It pays to be prepared

Dress code

The Vatican enforces its dress code strictly, both in St Peter's and in the Vatican Museums. Anyone wearing shorts or a short skirt, or with bare shoulders or midriff, will be turned away.

Must-haves

• **Sensible shoes**: these are absolutely essential if you are to attempt the ascent of the dome, as the 320 marble stairs after you emerge from the lift are worn and slippery.

• **Water**: in the Vatican Museums, only the Galleria degli Arazzi and the Sistine Chapel are air-conditioned and people have been known to keel over in the summer months. There are vending machines selling water at the museum entrance (by the lavatories and by the lifts), and there is a drinking fountain to fill up a bottle for free on the large terrace at the top of the entrance escalator.

• **Binoculars**: a good idea for looking at the details of frescoes in the Sistine Chapel, as well as for appreciating the view if you're planning an ascent of the dome.

Remember

• Entrances to St Peter's basilica and to the Vatican Museums are in separate places and involve two lengthy queues, as well as a ten-minute hike around the outside of the Vatican walls to get from one to the other.

You can significantly cut your waiting time at the museums by pre-booking a date and time for your visit online (mv.vatican.va; there's a €4-per-ticket surcharge) up to 60 days in advance.

• To minimise the often long security queue to enter St Peter's, arrive before 8.30am or after 5.30pm. Before you join the queue, make sure you're not going to be turned away once you get there because you're unsuitably dressed (no shorts above the knee, very short skirts, or bare midriffs or shoulders) and bear in mind that the doors close at the advertised times, no matter how many people are waiting outside.

Tourist information

The Vatican's tourist information office (06 6988 1662, open 8.30am-6.30pm Mon-Sat), situated on the left of St Peter's square as you face the basilica, dispenses information, organises guided tours, has a bureau de change, offers postal and philatelic services, and sells souvenirs and publications. The number of the Vatican switchboard is 06 6982; the general Vatican website, with information on papal activities, church business and museums and so on is vatican.va; www.vaticanstate.va has information about the Holy See in general.

Vatican gardens

Sights & museums

❤ San Pietro

Piazza San Pietro (06 6988 1662). Metro Ottaviano/bus 23, 34, 40Exp, 62, 64, 280. **No cards**. **Map** *p161 C7.*
Basilica *Open Apr-Sept 7am-7pm daily. Oct-Mar 7am-6.30pm daily.* **Admission** *free.*
Dome *Open Apr-Sept 8am-6pm daily. Oct-Mar 8am-5pm daily.* **Admission** *€6 (€8 with lift). Note: there are 320 steps to climb after the lift has taken you to the first level.*
Grottoes *Open Apr-Sept 8am-6pm daily. Oct-Mar 8am-5pm daily.* **Admission** *free.*
Necropolis *Apply at the Ufficio degli Scavi (06 6988 5318, scavi@fsp.va).* **Open** *Guided tours 9am-5pm Mon-Sat.* **Admission** *€13. Note: English-language tours must be booked at least 25 days in advance. Under-12s are not admitted; 12- to 15-year-olds must be accompanied by an adult.*
Treasury museum *Open Apr-Sept 9am-6.15pm daily. Oct-Mar 9am-5.15pm daily.* **Admission** *€7.*
The current St Peter's was consecrated on 18 November 1626 by Urban VIII, exactly 1,300 years after the consecration of the first basilica on the site. By the mid 15th century, the south wall of the original basilica was collapsing. Pope Nicholas V had 2,500 wagonloads of masonry from the Colosseum carted here, just for running repairs. It took the arrogance of Pope Julius II and his pet architect Donato Bramante to knock the millennia-old basilica down, in 1506.

Following Bramante's death in 1514, Raphael took over the work. In 1547, he too was replaced by Michelangelo, who died in 1564, aged 87, after coming up with a plan for a massive dome. Completed in 1590, this was the largest brick dome ever

constructed, and is still the tallest building in Rome. In 1607, Carlo Maderno designed a new façade, crowned by enormous statues of Christ and the apostles.

After Maderno's death, Bernini took over and became the hero of the hour with his sumptuous baldachin and elliptical piazza, built between 1656 and 1667. The oval measures 340m by 240m (1,115ft by 787ft) and is punctuated by the central Egyptian obelisk and two symmetrical fountains, by Maderno and Bernini. The 284-column, 88-pillar colonnade is topped by 140 statues of saints.

In the portico (1612), opposite the main portal, is a mosaic by Giotto (c1298), from the original basilica. Five doors lead into the basilica: the central ones come from the earlier church, while the others are both 20th century. The last door on the right is opened only in Holy Years by the pope himself.

Inside, a series of brass lines in the floor shows the lengths of other churches around the world that are not as big. Bernini's vast baldachin (1633), cast from bronze purloined from the Pantheon and hovering over the high altar, is the real focal point. Below the altar, two flights of stairs lead to the *confessio*, where a niche contains a ninth-century mosaic of Christ, the only thing from the old St Peter's that stayed in its original

---

In the know
Vatican facts

Vatican City is the world's smallest state. Despite having fewer than 800 residents, it has its own diplomatic service, postal service, army (the Swiss Guard), heliport, station, supermarket, and radio and TV stations. It has observer status at the UN, and issues its own stamps and currency.

♥ Musei Vaticani

*Viale del Vaticano (06 6988 3860,
mv.vatican.va). Metro Ottaviano
or Cipro-Musei Vaticani/bus 23,
32, 34, 49, 81, 492, 913, 990/tram
19. Open 9am-6pm Mon-Sat;
9am-2pm last Sun of mth. Also
open May-Sept 7pm-11pm Fri,
pre-booking essential. Closed
Catholic hols. Admission €16; €8
reductions. Free last Sun of mth.
Map p161 C7.*

One of the world's largest
museums is a sometimes
overwhelming maze,
incorporating areas, such as the
incomparable Sistine Chapel,
which were here long before
you could buy a ticket. The
museum began in 1503 as a
collection of ancient sculptures,
assembled by Pope Julius II in
his private summer palace, and
it's been added to ever since,
representing the accumulated
fancies and obsessions of a long
line of strong, often contradictory
personalities. The following are
selected highlights.

Apartamento Borgia

This six-room suite was
adapted for the Borgia Pope
Alexander VI (1492-1503) and
decorated by Pinturicchio with
a series of frescoes on biblical
and classical themes.

Cappella Sistina
(Sistine Chapel)

The world's most famous frescoes
cover the ceiling and one immense
wall of the Sistine Chapel, built
by Sixtus IV in 1473-84. For
centuries, it has been used for
popes' private prayers and papal
elections. In the 1980s and '90s,
the 930sq m (10,000sq ft) *Creation*
(on the ceiling) and *The Last
Judgement* (on the wall behind
the altar) were subjected to a
controversial restoration.

In 1508, Michelangelo was
commissioned to paint some
undemanding decoration on
the ceiling of the chapel. He
offered to do far more than that
and embarked upon his massive
venture alone, spending the next

Ceiling of the Cappella Sistina
(Michelangelo, 1508-1512)

four-and-a-half years standing on 18m-high (60ft) scaffolding. The ceiling work was completed in 1512, just seven months before the death of Julius, and shows a sequence of biblical scenes, from the Creation to the Flood, framed by monumental figures of Old Testament prophets and classical sibyls.

In 1535, aged 60, Michelangelo returned, inspired by the 1517 Protestant Reformation and by the sack of the city in 1527 by Imperial troops, which he saw as the wrath of God. *The Last Judgement* dramatically reflects this gloomy atmosphere. In among the larger-than-life figures, Michelangelo painted his own miserable face on the human skin held by St Bartholomew.

Before Michelangelo ever set foot in the chapel, the stars of the 1480s – Perugino, Cosimo Roselli, Botticelli, Ghirlandaio – had created the paintings on the walls. On the left-hand wall (as you look at the *Last Judgement*)

are depictions of Moses; on the right-hand wall are scenes from the life of Christ.

Galleria Chiaramonte
Founded by Pius VII in the early 19th century, this is an eclectic collection of Roman statues, reliefs and busts.

Gallerie dei Candelabri & degli Arazzi
The long gallery, studded with candelabra, contains Roman statues, while the next gallery has ten huge tapestries (*arazzi*), woven by Flemish master Pieter van Aelst from cartoons by Raphael.

Galleria delle Carte Geografiche
Pope Gregory XIII (who was responsible for the introduction of the Gregorian calendar) had a craze for astronomy; he built this 120m-long (394ft) gallery, with the Tower of the Winds observation point at the north end. Ignazio Danti drew the

Stanze di Raffaello

💙 Musei Vaticani *continued*

extraordinarily precise maps of Italian regions and cities, which were then frescoed (1580-83).

Museo Egiziano
Founded in 1839, this selection of ancient Egyptian art from 3,000 BC to 600 BC includes statues of a baboon god, painted mummy cases, real mummies and a marble statue of Antinous, Emperor Hadrian's lover.

Museo Etrusco
This collection contains Greek and Roman art as well as Etruscan masterpieces, including the contents of the Regolini-Galassi Tomb (c650 BC). This section is usually only open in the mornings.

Museo Pio-Clementino
The world's largest collection of classical statues fills 16 rooms. Don't miss the first-century BC Belvedere Torso by Apollonius of Athens, the Roman copy of the bronze *Lizard Killer* by Praxiteles and, in the octagonal Belvedere Courtyard, the exquisite *Apollo Belvedere* and dynamic *Laocoön*.

Pinacoteca
Founded by Pius VI, the Pinacoteca (picture gallery) holds many of the pictures that the Vatican managed to recover from France after Napoleon took them in the early 19th century. The collection includes several delicate Madonnas by Fra Filippo Lippi, Fra Angelico, Raphael and Titian; Raphael's last work, *The Transfiguration*; and Caravaggio's *Entombment*. The Pinacoteca usually closes at 3.30pm.

Stanze di Raffaello
Pope Julius II gave the 26-year-old Raphael carte blanche to redesign four rooms of the Papal Suite. The Study (Stanza della Segnatura, 1508-11) covers philosophical and spiritual themes. Raphael next turned to the Stanza di Eliodoro (1512-14), where the portrayal of God saving the temple in Jerusalem from the thieving Heliodorus was intended to highlight the divine protection enjoyed by Pope Julius. The Dining Room (Stanza dell'Incendio; 1514-17) is named after a fire in the Borgo, which Leo IV apparently stopped with the sign of the cross. The Reception Room (Sala di Constantino, 1517-24) was completed by Giulio Romano after Raphael's death in 1520, and tells the legend of Emperor Constantine's miraculous conversion.

Museo Egiziano

place. Far below lies the alleged site of St Peter's tomb, discovered during excavations in 1951.

Pilgrims head straight for the last pilaster on the right before the main altar, to kiss the big toe of Arnolfo da Cambio's statue of St Peter (c1296), or to say a prayer by the crystal casket containing the mummified remains of Pope John XXIII, who was beatified in 2002.

To be sure to see everything, follow an anti-clockwise direction. Start by joining the tourist throngs making a beeline for the first chapel on the right, where Michelangelo's *Pietà* (1499) is found. Further along, the third chapel has a tabernacle and two angels by Bernini, plus St Peter's only remaining painting: a *Trinity* by Pietro da Cortona (the others have all been replaced by mosaic copies).

Bernini's Throne of St Peter (1665) stands at the far end of the nave. Encased in it is a wood and ivory chair, probably dating from the ninth century but for many years believed to have belonged to Peter himself. To the right of the throne is Bernini's 1644 monument to his patron, Urban VIII.

On the pillars supporting the main dome are venerated relics, including a chip of the True Cross. In the left aisle, beyond the pilaster with St Veronica holding the cloth with which she wiped Christ's face, Bernini's tomb for Pope Alexander VII shows the pope shrouded with a cloth of reddish marble, from beneath which struggles a skeleton clutching an hourglass.

Beneath the basilica are the Vatican grottoes – Renaissance crypts containing papal tombs. The Necropolis, where St Peter is said to be buried, lies under these. The small treasury museum off the left nave of the basilica contains stunning liturgical relics. The dome, reached via hundreds of stairs (there's a cramped lift as far as the basilica roof, then 320 steps to climb to get to the very top), offers fabulous views.

Prati & Borgo

Around the Vatican, the Borgo district grew up to service the burgeoning Dark Age tourist industry. Pope Leo IV (847-55) enclosed Borgo with the 12-metre (40-foot) Leonine Wall, following a series of Saracen and Lombard raids. Pope Nicholas III (1277-80) extended the walls and provided a papal escape route, linking the Vatican to the huge, impregnable **Castel Sant'Angelo** by way of a long *passetto*, or covered walkway. In the 1930s Mussolini's broad avenue, via della Conciliazione, bulldozed through much of the medieval Borgo. A few of the streets remain, however, and salt-of-the-earth Romans mingle here with off-duty Swiss Guards and immaculately robed priests.

The Prati district was a provocation. Built over meadows

In the know
Papal audiences

When he's in Rome, the pope addresses crowds in St Peter's square at noon on Sunday. On Wednesday morning at 10.30am, he holds a general audience, in St Peter's square if the weather is fine, otherwise in the modern Sala Nervi audience hall. Though it's possible to join the crowd at the back of the piazza for outside audiences (there are big screens), you'll need tickets for audiences in the Sala Nervi or for seats close to the pontiff in St Peter's square. Apply well in advance to the Prefettura della Casa Pontificia for tickets (06 6988 3114, open 9am-1.30pm Mon-Sat), which are free and can be picked up the afternoon before the audience.

(*prati*) soon after Rome became capital of the newly unified Italian state in 1871, its grand *palazzi* housed the staff of the ministries and parliament. But its broad avenues were named after historic figures who had fought against the power of the Papal States, and the largest of its *piazze* – nestling beneath the Vatican walls – was named after the Risorgimento, the movement that had destroyed the papacy's hold on Italy.

A solidly bourgeois district, Prati has a main drag – via Cola di Rienzo – that provides ample opportunities for retail therapy. Imposing military barracks line viale delle Milizie, and the bombastic Palazzo di Giustizia (popularly known as *il palazzaccio*, 'the big ugly building') sits between piazza Cavour and the Tiber. On the riverbank is one of Catholic Rome's truly weird experiences: the **Museo delle Anime in Purgatorio**.

Sights & museums

Castel Sant'Angelo
Lungotevere Castello 50 (06 6819 111, castelsantangelo.beniculturali. it). Bus 23, 34, 40Exp, 87, 280, 926, 990. Open 9am-7.30pm daily. Admission €10; €55 reductions. Exhibition price varies. Map p161 F7.
Begun by Emperor Hadrian in AD 135 as his own mausoleum, Castel Sant'Angelo has variously been a fortress, prison and papal residence. Puccini had Tosca hurl herself to her death from the upper terraces, from which there are see excellent views. There is much to see: lavish Renaissance salons, decorated with spectacular frescoes and trompe l'oeil; the glorious chapel in the Cortile d'Onore, designed by Michelangelo; and, halfway up an easily missed staircase, Clement VII's tiny personal bathroom, painted by Giulio Romano. In the summer the *passetto* – linking the castle to the Vatican – is occasionally open (to the halfway point) and worth a visit.

Museo delle Anime del Purgatorio
Lungotevere Prati 12 (06 6880 6517). Bus 30Exp, 70, 81, 87, 130, 186, 280, 492, 913, 926. Open Sept-July 7.30-11.30am, 3.30-6.30pm daily. Aug 8-11.30am, 5-7.30pm daily. Map p161 G7.
This macabre collection, attached to the neo-Gothic church of Sacro Cuore di Gesù in Prati, contains hand- and fingerprints left on the prayer books and clothes of the living to dead loved ones, to request Masses to release their souls from purgatory. Begun just over a century ago, the collection includes a handprint supposedly left by Sister Clara Scholers on the habit of a fellow-nun in Westphalia in 1696, and scorched bank notes left by a dead soul outside a church where he wanted a Mass said.

Restaurants

Osteria delle Commari €€
Via Santamaura 23, Prati (06 3972 9557, www.osteriadellecommari. it). Metro Ottaviano/bus 23, 70, 492, 913, 990. Open noon-11.30pm daily. Map p161 C6 ❶ *Trattoria*
Good, honest food in a convenient location makes Osteria delle Commari a cut above the, mostly, rip-off restaurants nearby. There are some great fried *antipasti* while Roman staples such as carbonara and *saltimbocca* (veal with prosciutto and sage) are cooked with care. Prices are the norm for the area. The wine list has some local gems from Lazio and plenty of by-the-glass options. Open non-stop from noon until late it is a handy address if you find yourself hungry outside of the usual Roman dining hours.

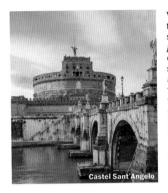
Castel Sant'Angelo

❤ **Pizzarium €**
Via della Meloria 43, Prati (06 3974 5416, bonci.it/portfolio/ pizzarium). Metro Cipro-Musei Vaticani/bus 31, 33, 247, 492. Open 11am-10pm daily. ② *Pizzeria*

Rome's revolutionary pizza maker Gabriele Bonci started his astronomic rise to stardom at this unassuming pizza shop and it has consistently remained top of the list of Rome's best *pizza al taglio*. The focus on the perfect dough and only the best, seasonal ingredients along with a creative eye for toppings have deservedly seen the Bonci brand expand across the city. Despite a recent renovation to double the size of the shop, the place is usually heaving so join the throng and eat on the pavement outside. The location near the entrance to the Vatican Museums is ideal for a post-Sistine Chapel carb fix.

Cafés, bars & pubs

❤ **200 Gradi €**
Piazza del Risorgimento 3, Prati (06 3975 4239, www. duecentogradi.it). Metro Ottaviano/bus 23, 32, 49, 81, 492, 590, 990/tram 19. Open 11am-3am daily. Map p161 D6 ① *Sandwich shop*

Walk right by the Vatican tourist traps and head to this little sandwich shop for very decent *panini* at very honest prices. With over 60 types of (generously sized) sandwiches to choose from, there are also plenty of vegetarian and vegan options. Everything is made to order from the immense counter of fillings so the staff are also happy to make up your own creation. Space is tight so grab your order to take away and sit in the adjacent piazza del Risorgimento.

Be.Re
Piazza del Risorgimento 7/A, Prati (06 9442 1854, www.facebook.com/ BeRe-541249312716140). Metro Ottaviano/bus 23, 32, 49, 81, 492, 590, 990/tram 19. Open noon-2am daily. Map p161 D6 ② *Pub*

A newcomer on the Prati pub scene, Be.Re brings the craft beer trend to the Vatican area with this modern drinking den which was opened under the expert guidance of beer guru Manuele Colonna (of Trastevere's lauded craft beer pub Ma Che Siete Venuti a Fà). The immense bar serves over 20 different beers and ales on tap, hailing from both Italy and the rest of the world. To accompany your brew there is also the, now ubiquitous, *trapizzino*, a pizza dough pocket stuffed with Roman stews.

Il Sorpasso
Via Properzio 31, Borgo (06 8902 4554, sorpasso.info). Bus 23, 32, 49, 81, 492, 590, 990/tram 19. Open 7.30am-1am Mon-Fri, 9am-1am Sat. Closed 3wks Aug. Map p161 E6 ③ *Café/Bar*

Far enough from the Vatican to escape the crowds (and rub shoulders with some locals), Il Sorpasso is still within an easy stroll of St Peter's. The shabby chic interior of this café-bar creates a cool, relaxed ambience for dining or drinking at any time. Food options range from sandwiches and snacks, including hand-cut prosciutto and cheeseboards, to a full menu at lunch and dinner, while the bar churns out some very passable cocktails. Around 6pm the place gets jammed with young professionals from the nearby offices who swing by for *aperitivo* at the outside tables.

Bakeries, pasticcerie & gelaterie
Dolce Maniera
Via Barletta 27, Prati (06 3751 7518, www.dolcemaniera.it). Metro Ottaviano/bus 23, 32, 70, 81, 492, 590, 990/tram 19. **Open** *24hrs daily.* **Map** *p161 D5* ❶ *Bakery*
Most young Romans are aware of this 24-hour basement bakery as a popular haunt for night owls picking up warm *cornetti* (croissants) on the way home from the clubs in the early hours. As well as freshly baked bread and pastries, there are also fried snacks, sandwiches and *pizza al taglio*, all at excellent prices. The entrance can be easy to miss but just follow your nose as the enticing smell wafts down the street.

Shops & services
❤ Coin Excelsior
Via Cola di Rienzo 173, Prati (06 3600 4298, www.coinexcelsior.com). Metro Lepanto/bus 30, 70, 81, 87, 280, 492, 913. **Open** *10am-10pm daily.* **Map** *p161 E5* ❶ *Department store*
The high-class 'excelsior' version of Italian chain Coin, this department store with its gilt escalators and pristine displays looks right at home in the prosperous Prati district. Here you will find top international brands in clothing, shoes, toiletries and homewares

and, handily, there is also a small supermarket on the lower level.

Franchi
Via Cola di Rienzo 200, Prati (06 687 4651, www.franchi.it). Metro Ottaviano/bus 23, 32, 49, 81, 271, 492, 982/tram 19. **Open** *8am-9pm daily.* **Map** *p161 E6* ❷ *Food & drink*
A dream of a deli, for just about anything you could ever want to eat – cheeses from everywhere, cured meats, and ready-to-eat meat and seafood dishes are freshly prepared.

El Spa
Via Plinio 15, Prati (06 6819 2869, www.elspa.it). Bus 30Exp, 34, 49, 70, 81, 130, 280, 492, 926, 990. **Open** *10am-9pm Mon-Thur; 10am-10pm Fri-Sun; noon-9pm Sun.* **Map** *p161 F6* ❸ *Spa*
Decorated in warm, Middle Eastern style, this spa specialises in holistic treatments. Try the *mandi lulur*, an ancient Indonesian treatment that leaves you with blissfully silky-soft skin.

Entertainment
❤ Alexanderplatz
Via Ostia 9, Prati (06 8377 5604, www.alexanderplatz.it). Metro Ottaviano/bus 23, 34, 49, 81, 492, 590, 982, 1N, 6N, 11N/tram 19. **Open** *8.30pm-1.30am daily.* **Admission** *free with monthly (€15) or annual (€45) membership.* **Map** *p161 C5* ❶ *Live music*
The pioneer of jazz in the Eternal City, and *the* jazz club in Rome, is still the Alexanderplatz. This venue offers nightly concerts with famous names from the Italian and foreign jazz scene. Live music starts at 9, 9.30 or 10pm, depending on the gig. Booking is strongly advised. Call ahead or email prenotazioni. alexanderplatz@gmail.com.

St Peter's square

Rome
Essentials

Accommodation

Once a city of polar-opposite accommodation options – exorbitantly expensive luxury hotels on the one hand, cheap *pensioni* of dubious cleanliness on the other – Rome now has the range of hotels you might expect in one of the most-visited destinations on the planet. But they are, on the whole, considerably more expensive than in other tourist hubs. For a dirt-cheap hotel bed these days – and even that concept is relative – you may have to accept a less salubrious part of town, or even an out-of-the-way convent. On the positive side, though, the general standard of accommodation has improved in recent years. At the top of the market, chic boutique offerings are creating fierce competition to the large, often soulless, luxury chains, while older-style mid-range hotels and *pensioni* have been forced to upgrade to keep pace. Small, stylish B&Bs are ever more numerous, and some great deals are to be found in this sector.

Where to stay

The area around Termini station in the **Esquilino** district has a slew of five-star hotels, but the vast majority in the area are cheap *pensioni* swarming with budget backpackers. It's not Rome's most picturesque corner, and almost certainly not what you dreamed of for your Roman holiday. Unless you snag the smart budget offerings at little gems such as **Casa Romana** (see p177) or the **Beehive** (see p177) it's well worth considering looking further afield, even if it costs you a bit more.

For atmosphere and convenience, go for a room in the historic centre, around **piazza Navona**, the **Pantheon** or **campo de' Fiori**. A shower between sightseeing and dinner and a wander (rather than the bus) back to the hotel afterwards can make all the difference.

Moving distinctly up the price range, Rome's top-end hotels have traditionally clustered around **via Veneto** – though bear in mind that it's not as lively as it was in its much-hyped *dolce vita* heyday, and there's a strong whiff of expense account in the air. The **Tridente** area near the Spanish Steps, hub of designer

In the know
Price categories

We have included a selection of the best hotels in the city in four pricing categories. Categories are based on a standard double room per night including taxes and breakfast (not including seasonal offers or discounts).

Luxury	€400+
Expensive	€250-€400
Moderate	€100-€250
Budget	up to €100

shopping, is full of elegant hotels at the upper end of the price scale.

If you're looking for some peace, the **Celio**, just beyond the Colosseum, offers a break from the frantic activity of the city centre while residential **Prati** offers some great deals just a short walk from the Vatican. The trendy neighbourhoods of **Monti** and **Trastevere** are becoming ever-more popular bases, thanks to their picturesque streets and abundance of bars and restaurants.

Booking a room

Always reserve a room well in advance, especially at peak times, which now means most of the year, with lulls during winter (January to March), and in the dog days of August. If you're coming at the same time as a major Christian holiday (Christmas or Easter) it's wise to book weeks, or even months, ahead and expect to pay full whack.

Many of Rome's hotels now model their pricing policy on low-cost airlines: the same room in an empty hotel may cost you less than half what it does in heavily booked high season. It is worth shopping around and contacting the hotels directly for deals.

Stars & standards

Italian hotels are classified on a star system, from one to five. The more stars, the more facilities a hotel will have, but bear in mind that a higher rating is no guarantee of friendliness, cleanliness or even decent service. B&Bs, on the other hand, can sometimes prove to be very pleasant surprises: some offer unexpectedly chic accommodation at very low prices. While, up until relatively recently, internet access in hotels came at an extra cost, free Wi-Fi is now the norm for all except the most basic accommodation.

Aside from the large, more expensive hotels, accommodation in Rome can be on the cramped side, especially in the historic centre where ancient buildings have limited space and many lack a lift. Although staff are generally very willing to help, guests with mobility difficulties

should check before booking to avoid problems with accessibility.

Staying with kids

Parents with babies will find most hotels happy to provide a cot on request, though it is worth checking the accessibility if you are planning to use a pushchair. Extra beds for older children are usually available at a small additional cost and many hotels have triple or quadruple rooms for families or even separate adjoining rooms if more privacy is required. Many of the larger hotels may also offer a babysitting service. However, the most popular choice, particularly for larger families, is to rent an apartment (*see p177*).

Luxury

Eden

Via Ludovisi 49, Villa Borghese (06 478121, www.dorchester collection.com). Bus 52, 53, 61, 63, 80, 83, 150, 160. **Map** *p102 K6.*

Originally opened in 1889, a recent 18-month restoration project has upped the Eden's opulence level to a new high. Glitzy gold and marble abound alongside the original art nouveau features and the result is one of Rome's most sumptuous hotels. The 98 rooms and suites are adorned with bespoke furniture, rich fabrics and Murano glass light fittings in a refined palette of warm neutrals. The brand new spa offers state-of-the-art treatments while the top-floor restaurant affords spectacular views across the Roman rooftops.

Hassler

Piazza Trinità dei Monti 6, Tridente (06 699 340, www.hotelhasslerroma.com). Metro Spagna/bus 117. **Map** *p102 K6.*
Looking down from the top of the Spanish Steps, the Hassler remains the *grande dame* of Rome's deluxe hotels – ageing a little, but still charming. With acres of polished marble and abundant chandeliers, the relentless luxury may make your head spin, but the attentiveness of the staff distinguishes this place from the impersonal service

often found at Rome's top hotels. A stay in one of the 92 rooms includes top-notch amenities (including a spa, Michelin-starred restaurant and several bars) as well as spectacular views over the Roman rooftops.

JK Place Roma

Via Monte d'Oro 30, Tridente (06 982 634, www.jkroma.com). Metro Spagna/bus 70, 81, 117, 492, 628, 913. **Map** *p102 H7.*

Art-deco-inspired JK Place opened in 2013 following its sister branches in Florence and Capri. The elegant, townhouse feel, complete with original fireplaces, wooden bookshelves and leather-bound chairs, is far more intimate than many of the sprawling luxury hotels usually found in Rome, and the 23 rooms and seven suites all offer wireless internet and bucketfuls of opulent charm. The lack of outside space is compensated for by the excellent location just a short walk from the Spanish Steps.

Portrait Suites

Via Bocca di Leone 23, Tridente (06 6938 0742, www.lungarnocollection.com/portrait-roma). Metro Spagna/bus 117, 628, 913. **Map** *p102 J6.*

Portrait Suites is one of the luxury boutique hotels owned by fashion designer Salvatore Ferragamo. Black and white photos and memorabilia from the designer's archives decorate the hallways, yet the rooms themselves carry little clue of the hotel's fashion pedigree (though eagle-eyed fans might spot the designer's *gancino* emblem on the curtains). A black-and-slate colour scheme is offset with touches of pink and lime, and the 14 studios and suites all have spacious marble bathrooms, as well as walk-in wardrobes and even a glamorous kitchenette. Breakfast is served in the rooms or outside on the spectacular terrace.

Rome Cavalieri

Via Alberto Cadlolo 101, Suburbs: Monte Mario (06 35091, romecavalieri.com). Bus 913.

Although situated a little way out of the action, the Cavalieri's majestic position on top of the leafy Monte Mario hill north of the Vatican is worth the extra travel time (there is a free shuttle bus for guests), especially if you like to spend time away from the bustle of central Rome. However, with almost 400 rooms and suites, this is more about palatial extravagance than intimate escape. Amenities are what you would expect from a hotel of this grandeur: three swimming pools, a full spa and fitness centre and Rome's only three Michelin-star restaurant, La Pergola (*see p112*) to name but a few.

Villa Spalletti Trivelli

Via Piacenza 4, Quirinale (06 4890 7934, www.villaspalletti.it). Bus 40, 60, 64, 70, 71, 117, 170, H. **Map** *p78 L8.*

The aristocratic Spalletti Trivelli clan has turned its family home – with views across a little park to the *manica lunga* of the Quirinale palace – into a sumptuously elegant 12-room hotel with such high-class extras as an historic library with a preservation order, a formal garden where breakfast or *aperitivi* can be served, and a marvellous spa in the basement. Some of the large rooms can be linked together to form immense suites. Service is charmingly discreet; and there's a chef on hand to whip up special meals on request. Across the garden, two large and similarly elegant suites offer all the same services plus self-catering facilities and gorgeous private terraces.

In the know
ID

When you book into an Italian hotel, the receptionist will ask you to present photo-ID. Your document will generally be given back to you immediately, or the first time you come back down to reception to leave your key. If it isn't (and this happens sometimes, generally in cheaper hotels) ask for it back: you are required by law to carry photo-ID with you at all times.

Expensive

Crossing Condotti

Via Mario de' Fiori 28, Tridente (06 6992 0633, www.crossingcondotti.com). Metro Spagna/bus 117. **Map** *p102 J6.*

A short stroll from Prada, Bulgari and other fashion heavyweights, Crossing Condotti is remarkably central. The owner's gorgeous antiques are set against a cool contemporary background, and attentive staff are unfailingly helpful. It is more Roman hideaway than fully fledged hotel, though; there are just eight rooms and public spaces are limited to a handy kitchenette with coffee-making facilities and a fridge stocked with (free) soft drinks.

Donna Camilla Savelli

Via Garibaldi 27, Trastevere (06 588 861, hoteldonnacamilla savelli.com). Bus 115, H/tram 8. **Map** *p150 F11.*

This former convent, designed by Borromini, has been transformed into an upmarket hotel by an Italian chain – though there's still a slight air of nunnery around the echoing corridors. The position – in a quiet corner beneath the Gianicolo hill but a short stroll from Trastevere's lively alleyways – is great, there's a pretty garden, and the view from the roof terrace is quite spectacular. A few of the 78 rooms are very pokey so specify your needs when booking.

Grand Hotel Via Veneto

Via Veneto 155, via Veneto (06 487 881, www.ghvv.it). Bus 52, 53, 61, 63, 80, 83, 150, 160. **Map** *p102 L5.*

Award-winning Grand Hotel Via Veneto is just as flashy as you'd expect, with an art deco theme worked to the hilt in the striking public spaces, and given a slightly more contemporary modernist bent in the 116 bedrooms and suites, even the smallest of which are spacious by Rome standards. The huge bathrooms are done out in Carrara marble and the walls are dotted with the hotel's own art collection. The street-level bar-restaurant Time buzzes at cocktail hour with great *aperitivi* and there is also a 500sq m wellness centre with hammam.

Hotel Art

Via Margutta 56, Tridente (06 328 711, www.hotelart.it). Metro Spagna/bus 117. **Map** *p102 J5.*

On a street famed for its arty, crafty studios, the Hotel Art sticks to its theme throughout. The lobby area – with white pods serving as check-in and concierge desks – sets the modern tone; only the ceiling retains a touch of the classic (the building was once a chapel). Hallways are in acidic shades of orange, yellow, green and blue, while the rooms themselves are decorated in a serene palette of neutrals, with parquet floors and chunky wood furniture. Free Wi-Fi (and a wireless keyboard) can be found in each of the 46 rooms.

Inn at the Roman Forum

Via degli Ibernesi 30, Monti (06 6919 0970, www.theinnattheromanforum. com). Metro Cavour/bus 51, 75, 85, 87, 117. **Map** *p118 L10.*

The location of this boutique hotel, close to the Forum but on a picturesque street that is comfortably off the tourist trail, gives the place an exclusive feel. The 12 rooms are a suave combination of rich fabrics and antiques; the spacious deluxe double rooms – some of which have fireplaces – have canopied beds and marble bathrooms. Breakfast is served on the roof terrace or in a cosy room with open fire in the winter. An ancient *cryptiporticus* has been excavated on the ground floor.

Sole al Pantheon

Piazza della Rotonda 63, Pantheon (06 678 0441, www.hotelsolealpantheon. com). Bus 30, 40, 46, 62, 64, 70, 81, 87, 130, 190, 492, 628, 916. **Map** *p78 H8.*

Dating back to the 15th century, this – management will tell you – is the oldest hotel in Europe. The 32 rooms have been painstakingly restored and are fresh and uncluttered, with tiled floors and frescoes. All bathrooms have whirlpool baths. Ask for one of the rooms at the front for superb views over the Pantheon; otherwise console yourself by seeking out the glorious roof terrace, where breakfast is served in the warmer months.

Moderate

Abruzzi

Piazza della Rotonda 69, Pantheon (06 9784 1351, www.hotelabruzzi.it). Bus 30, 40, 46, 62, 64, 70, 81, 87, 130, 190, 492, 628, 916. **Map** *p78 H8.*

The splendid location is really this hotel's selling point. Most of its 26 rooms have breathtaking views of the Pantheon (specify that you want a view when you book), and all are outfitted in bright white decor with splashes of vivid colour. Guests are provided with a complimentary smartphone with unlimited local and international calls. Breakfast is taken nearby, in a café in piazza della Rotonda.

Capo d'Africa

Via Capo d'Africa 54, Celio (06 772 801, www.hotelcapodafrica.com). Metro Colosseo/bus 51, 75, 81, 85, 87, 117, 118, 673/tram 3. **Map** *p118 N12.*

Artfully arranged bamboo? Tick. Pastel armchairs? Tick. The Capo d'Africa is perfect for the design-conscious, and the hotel's location, on a quiet street near the Colosseum, is another thing in its favour. The 65 rooms are spacious and comfortable, and the rooftop breakfast room and terrace has knock-out views of the Colosseum and the fourth-century basilica dei Santi Quattro Coronati.

Daphne Trevi

Via degli Avignonesi 20, Fontana di Trevi (06 8953 8471, www.daphne-rome. com). Metro Barberini/bus 52, 53, 62, 63, 80, 83, 85, 160, 492. **Map** *p78 L7.*

Owned by dynamic Italo-American couple Elyssa and Alessandro, Daphne Trevi sets the standard for inexpensive but stylish accommodation in Rome. The hotel is decorated in modern, earthy tones throughout, and the seven tastefully furnished bedrooms have high ceilings, terracotta or parquet floors and decent-sized bathrooms. Guests are lent a smartphone for the duration of their stay and staff are endlessly helpful. Adjoining rooms can be arranged to create a significant range of family and group accommodation.

Hotel Santa Maria

Vicolo del Piede 2, Trastevere (06 589 4626, www.hotelsantamaria trastevere. it). Bus 23, 280, H/tram 8. **Map** *p150 G11.*

Just off piazza Santa Maria in Trastevere, the Santa Maria stands on the site of a 16th-century convent. Each of the 19 bedrooms has a tiled floor, colourful decor and a spacious bathroom, and they all open on to a charming, sunny central courtyard planted with orange trees. Complimentary bicycles are available for guests to use for exploring Trastevere's winding alleys.

Teatro Pace

Via del Teatro Pace 33, piazza Navona (06 687 9075, www.hotelteatropace. com). Bus 30, 40, 46, 62, 64, 70, 81, 87, 130, 492, 628, 916. **Map** *p78 G8.*

This 16th-century former cardinal's residence lies down a cobbled alley near piazza Navona. An impressive Baroque stone spiral staircase winds up four floors (no lift). The 23 rooms are spacious and elegantly decorated with wood floors, heavy drapes and marble bathrooms. The original, wood-beamed ceilings are intact in all rooms, but higher on the top two floors. Breakfast is served in the rooms.

Torre Colonna

Via delle Tre Cannelle 18, Capitoline (06 8360 0192, www.torrecolonna.it). Bus 40, 60, 64, 70, 117, 170, H. **Map** *p66 K9.*

Quirky little Torre Colonna is just what the name implies: a medieval tower. Five stylish, comfortable bedrooms, with painted wood-beamed ceilings and jaunty artwork, are stacked one on top of the other and crowned with a leafy roof terrace complete with hot tub and a dramatic view across a huge swathe of the *centro storico*. Miraculously, they've also managed to squeeze a lift into this difficult space. The Forum and Palatine are short strolls away. Owner Sarah Hawker and her English-speaking staff are fabulously informative and helpful.

Apartment Rentals

Great options for family stays and longer visits

Apartment rental agencies have been around in Rome for a while, utilised mainly by larger families needing more room and for those staying longer than a few days. However, the market has boomed in the last few years due to both competitive rates compared to pricier hotels and an increasing number of tourists looking to 'live like a Roman'. **Airbnb** (www.airbnb.com) undoubtedly leads the pack, offering a huge range of accommodation choices for all budgets and directing tourism to lesser-known outer areas such as Pigneto and Ostiense, where bargains abound.

Unique, high-end rental properties can also be found in beautifully renovated historic buildings, such as the 17th-century **Palazzo Olivia** (www.palazzo-olivia.it) near piazza Navona, while the UK's **Landmark Trust** (www.landmarktrust.org.uk) rents an apartment in the **Keats-Shelley Memorial House** (see p108) overlooking the Spanish Steps that sleeps up to four. It's full of lovely details including the original painted wooden ceilings.

Elsewhere the **Bed & Breakfast Italia** agency (www.bbitalia.it) has hundreds of chic Roman options on its books, including luxury accommodation in *palazzi*.

Budget
Arco del Lauro
Via dell'Arco de' Tolomei 27, Trastevere (06 9784 0350, www.arcodellauro.it). Bus 23, 125, 280, 780, H/tram 8. **Map** *p150 H12.*
On a picturesque Trastevere backstreet, Arco del Lauro has four rooms, all with private bathrooms, decorated in modern, fresh neutrals. Budget accommodation is hard to find in chi-chi Trastevere, so the Arco del Lauro, with its airy and spotlessly clean rooms and free Wi-Fi, is all the more of a find. Breakfast is taken in a bar in a nearby *piazza*.

Beehive
Via Marghera 8, Esquilino (06 4470 4553, www.the-beehive.com). Metro Termini/bus 40, 64, 75, 492, 910, H. **Map** *p118 O7.*
American owners Steve and Linda Brenner mix design-icon furnishings with reasonable rates and basic amenities, to create a 'youth hostel meets boutique hotel' vibe with both dormitory beds and private rooms scattered throughout the main building and in equally stylish nearby structures. All have internet access, air-conditioning or ceiling fans and use of the communal areas including the sunny garden with comfy patio. Breakfast (at an extra cost) is served in their own organic restaurant.

Casa Romana
Via dei Mille 41a, Esquilino (329 228 0626, www.myromeapartment.com). Metro Termini/bus 40, 64, 75, 492, 910, H. **Map** *p118 P7.*
Simply stylish, this three-room B&B hideaway not far from Termini station offers excellent facilities for this price bracket and each room has internet and air-conditioning. The welcome is friendly, the breakfast is excellent and owner Fulvia's many years of experience in the travel sector make her expert advice consistently spot-on.

Colors

Via Boezio 31, Prati (06 687 4030, www. colorshotel.com). Metro Ottaviano/ bus 23, 34, 40, 49, 492, 982, 990. **Map** *p161 E6.*

A short walk from St Peter's and the Vatican Museums, Colors offers bright, clean dormitory and hotel accommodation that's well above the average quality for this price bracket. The first two floors, decorated in zingy colours, have self-catering facilities, with cornflakes and coffee provided for guests to make their own breakfast. More neutral tones have been used in the superior rooms on the third floor (all with private bathroom, flat-screen TV, air-conditioning and breakfast). There's a sunny terrace, and members of staff are multilingual and very friendly.

La Finestra sul Colosseo

Via Labicana 72, Monti & Esquilino (389 126 4301, www.lafinestrasulcolosseo. com). Metro Colosseo or Manzoni/bus 51, 85, 87, 117/tram 3. **Map** *p118 O11.*
The very white, very stylish accommodation in this five-room B&B is surprisingly spacious for Rome, and the well-equipped, mosaic-tiled bathrooms are similarly large. On a busy artery leading up to the Colosseum, the B&B lives up to its name: two of the rooms do have windows overlooking the ancient arena. All rooms have internet, air-conditioning and striking arched brick ceilings and the price includes breakfast at a nearby café.

Pensione Panda

Via della Croce 35, Tridente (06 678 0179, www.hotelpanda.it). Metro Spagna/bus 117, 301, 628, 913. **Map** *p102 J6.*
Panda's excellent location, just west of the Spanish Steps, is its main selling point. Rooms are very basic but clean; ask for one of the more recently renovated rooms, which have terracotta floors and high, wood-beamed ceilings. There's no lift and you'll have to go elsewhere for your morning cappuccino, but bargains in this area are hard to come by and Panda's 28 rooms are usually booked solid in high season.

Hotel Eden

Getting Around

ARRIVING & LEAVING

By air

Rome has two major airports:
Fiumicino, about 30km (18 miles) west
of the city, handles scheduled flights;
Ciampino, 15km (9 miles) south-east of
the city, is for low-cost airlines and for
charter flights.

Aeroporto Leonardo Da Vinci, Fiumicino
*Via dell'Aeroporto di
Fiumicino 320 (06 65 951, information
06 65 951, www.adr.it).* **Open** *24hrs
daily.*

There's an express rail service between
Fiumicino airport and Termini railway
station (run by **Trenitalia**, *see p180*).
It takes 31mins and runs every 30mins
from 6.23am until 10.35pm daily
(5.35am-10.35pm back to Fiumicino).
Tickets in either direction cost €14. Note
that at the Termini end, the airport train
departs from platform 23 or 24, a good
10-min walk from the main concourse;
tickets bought at the departure
platforms cost €15. For security reasons,
you must have a ticket to access the
platform area.

The regular service from Fiumicino
takes 25-40mins, and stops at
Trastevere, Ostiense, Tuscolana
and Tiburtina stations. Trains leave
about every 20mins (less often on
Sun) between 5.57am and 11.27pm
(5.05am-10.33pm back to Fiumicino).
Tickets cost €11.

You can buy tickets for both these
services with cash or card from
automatic machines in the airport
lobby and rail stations, and the
airport *tabacchi*. Some carriages
have wheelchair access (*see p187*
Transport). You must stamp your
ticket in the machines on the platform
before boarding.

SIT (06 591 6826, www.sitbusshuttle.
it) runs frequent buses from Fiumicino
to Termini railway station (in front
of the Hotel Royal Santina on via
Marsala, Termini exit near platform
1, 8.30am-12.30am) and vice versa
(5am-8.30pm). Tickets cost €6 each way.

Terravision (www.terravision.eu;
journey time 55mins) covers the same
route, and leaves from via Giolitti (*map
p118 O8*, Termini exit near platform
24); tickets booked online cost €4 one
way; bought on the bus, they cost €6.

A **COTRAL** (www.cotralspa.it) night
bus service runs between Fiumicino
(Terminal C) and Termini and Tiburtina
railway stations in Rome. Tickets cost €5
from newsstands or €7 on the bus. Buses
leave Tiburtina at 12.30am, 1.15am,
2.30am and 3.45am, stopping at Termini
railway station 10mins later. Departures
from Fiumicino are at 1.15am, 2.15am,
3.30am and 5am. Neither Termini nor
Tiburtina are attractive places at night,
so it's advisable to get a taxi from there
to your final destination.

Aeroporto GB Pastine, Ciampino
*Via
Appia Nuova 1650 (06 65 951, www.adr.
it).* **Open** *24hrs daily.*

The most hassle-free way to get into
town from Ciampino is to take the
Terravision coach service (www.
terravision.eu) to Termini station
(journey time 45mins). Buses leave
from outside the arrivals hall after
each arrival. Buses from Termini to
Ciampino leave from via Giolitti (*see
above*). This is a dedicated service for
the low-cost airlines, so you will need
to show your ticket or boarding pass.
Bus tickets (€4 online, €6 at the airport)
can be booked online, or bought (cash
only) in the arrivals hall at Ciampino or
at the Terravision office in the Termini
forecourt (next to Benetton) or on
the bus.

SIT Bus Shuttle (www.sitbusshuttle.
it) also does the Termini (via Marsala,
map p118 O7) to Ciampino route (€4

one way). Tickets can be purchased on the bus or online.

Alternatively, **Schiaffini** buses (800 700 805, www.romeairportbus.com) runs a service between the airport and Termini (€4.90 one way). Buy tickets on board the bus, which leaves from in front of the arrivals hall; at Termini, it departs from via Giolitti. The same bus goes to Ciampino station from where frequent trains depart for Termini; this costs €1.20.

COTRAL (www.cotralspa.it) buses run regularly between the airport and Anagnina metro station (€1.20 one way), between the airport and Termini station (€3.90 one way) and between the airport and Ciampino town's railway station (€1.20 one way). The onward trains from Ciampino station to Termini cost €1.30.

After the last bus has departed, getting into the city is well-nigh impossible, as taxis don't bother to pass by the airport. If you are arriving late, phone ahead and organise a taxi before your arrival (see p182).

Major airlines
Alitalia 89 2010, www.alitalia.it.
British Airways reservations 02 6963 3602, www.ba.com.
Easyjet 199 201 841, www. easyjet.com.
Ryanair 899 552 589, www.ryanair. com.

By bus
The long-distance bus station in Rome is **Autostazione Tibus**, an easy walking distance from Stazione Tiburtina, in largo Guido Mazzoni. Most services terminate outside these (metro) stations: Saxa Rubra (routes north); Cornelia, Ponte Mammolo and Tiburtina (north and east); Anagnina and Laurentina (routes south). For more details, see p182.

By train
Mainline trains are operated by **Ferrovie dello Stato (FS)/Trenitalia** (892 021, www.trenitalia.it). Most long-distance trains arrive at Termini, the hub of Rome's transport network (and its pickpockets, so beware). Night trains

arrive at Tiburtina or Ostiense, both some way from the *centro storico*. If you arrive after midnight, take a taxi.

Some daytime trains bypass Termini, while others stop at more than one station in Rome.

Stazione Ostiense *Piazzale dei Partigiani, Testaccio. Metro Piramide/ bus 30Exp, 80Exp, 83, 175, 280, 719, 9N.* **Map** p135 K17.

Stazione Piazzale Flaminio (Roma Nord) *Piazzale Flaminio, Veneto & Borghese. Metro Flaminio/bus 61, 89, 120, 150, 160, 490, 491, 495, C31N, 25N/ tram 2.* **Map** p102 H4.

Stazione Termini *Piazza dei Cinquecento, Esquilino. See below Transport to Termini.* **Map** p118 O7.

Stazione Tiburtina *Circonvallazione Nomentana, Suburbs: south. Metro Tiburtina/bus 71, 111, 120, 135, 163, 168, 211, 309, 409, 443, 448, 490, 491, 492, 495, 649, C3, 2N, 17N, 23N.*

Stazione Trastevere *Piazzale Biondo. Bus 170, 228, 719, 766, 773, 774, 780, 781, 786, 871, H, C3, 8N, 14N, 16N/tram 3, 8.*

---

in the know
Transport to Termini

For convenience, we have indicated 'Transport to Termini' in the listings in this guide, as all of the following services pass by (or terminate at) Termini rail station.

Metro Termini; Repubblica is also within easy walking distance.

Buses 16, 38, 40Exp, 64, 70, 71, 75, 82, 85, 90Exp, 92, 105, 150, 170, 175, 217, 310, 360, 590, 649, 714, 910, C2, C3, H, M.

Night buses 2N, 5N, 7N, 8N, 9N, 13N, 15N.

Trams 5, 14.

Trains & tickets

For bookings and information on Italian rail services, see **Trenitalia** (892 021, 199 166 177 from mobiles, 24hrs daily, www.trenitalia.it). Tickets can be bought at stations (over the counter or from machines; both accept cards), from travel agents with an FS sign, or online; many trips booked online are ticketless (see right). Under-12s pay half fare; under-4s travel free. For wheelchair access, see p187 Transport.

Train timetables can be purchased at edicole (newsstands) but are best checked online. Slower trains (espressi, regionali and regionali veloci) are cheap; faster services – InterCity (IC), EuroCity (EC), Eurostar Italia (ES) and the new super-fast Alta Velocità (AV) – are closer to European norms. Advance seat reservation is automatic on most faster services; check and obtain reservations at peak times to avoid standing in packed corridors. If your plans change, partial refunds are given (phone Trenitalia).

Queues at Termini ticket desks can be lengthy; speed things up by using one of the many automatic ticket machines (all accept cards). You'll often find an unofficial 'helper' by the machines, keen to show you how it's done for a euro or so; if they seem threatening, report them to the station police.

Trenitalia's Ticketless service allows you to book tickets with a card online (www.trenitalia.it) or by phone up to 10mins before the train's departure time. Either way, you'll be provided with a carriage and seat number, and a booking code. The service is available on all AV, ES and some IC trains. Seat reservation is obligatory for all passengers using this service.

Note: with paper tickets, you *must* stamp your ticket and supplements in the yellow machines at the head of the platform, before boarding. You risk being fined if you don't.

PUBLIC TRANSPORT

Rome's transport is operated by **Atac** (06 57 003, www.atac.roma.it). The bus, tram, metro and urban train services of the city centre and inner suburbs are relatively easy to use and as efficient as the traffic-choked streets allow. Pickpocketing is a problem on buses and metros, particularly major tourist routes, notably the 64 and 40 Express between Termini and the Vatican.

Children travel free on Rome's city transport until their tenth birthday; older children pay the full price for single-journey and one- or three-day bus passes.

Information

Atac's website has a handy route-planner for bus and metro travel, and detailed downloadable transport maps.

For real-time information on bus movements as you wait at a stop, go to muovi.roma.it and key in the stop ID number (a five-digit code at the bottom left corner of the information panel); alternatively key in the bus number for which you need information.

Tickets

The same tickets are valid on all city bus, tram and metro lines, whether operated by Trambus, MetRo or regional transport authority COTRAL, but not on airport services (see p180). Tickets must be bought before boarding, and are available from Atac ticket machines, information centres and all tabacchi (see p191). Newer buses have ticket dispensers on board, requiring exact change.

BIT (biglietto integrato a tempo): valid for 100mins, during which you can take an unlimited number of city buses, plus a metro trip; €1.50.

ROMA 24H: valid for one day, until midnight, and covers the urban network; €7

ROMA 72H: 3-day pass, covering all bus and metro routes, and local mainline trains (second class) to Ostia; €18. (Before purchasing, consider whether the 3 day Roma Pass might not be better value; see p24.)

BIRG (biglietto integrato regionale giornaliero): valid for 1 day on rail journeys in the Lazio region. Depending on the zones covered, it costs €2.50-€10.50, and is valid on metro, buses and local mainline trains (second class), but not Fiumicino airport lines.

CIS (*carta integrata settimanale*): valid for 7 days; it covers all bus routes and the metro system, including the lines to Ostia; €24.

Abbonamento mensile: valid for unlimited travel on the entire metropolitan transport system during the calendar month in which the ticket was bought; €35.

Note: when you get on, you *must* stamp tickets in the machines on board.

Under-10s travel free; older kids have to pay the adult fare, as must pensioners. Discounts for students, the disabled and pensioners are only available for residents. Fare-dodging is common, but if caught without a validated ticket, you'll be fined €51 on the spot, or €101 if you pay later at a post office.

Buses

Buses are by far the best way to get around the city for tourists. Bus routes are added or suspended and numbers change with some regularity: regularly updated bus maps can be bought at news kiosks. The Atac website (*see p181*) has a journey planner and maps to download.

Regular bus services run 5.30am-midnight daily, every 10-45mins, depending on the route. The doors for boarding (usually front and rear) and alighting (usually centre) are clearly marked. A sign at each bus stop displays the lines and routes they take.

Note that the 'Express' buses make few stops along their route: check before boarding so you don't get whisked past your destination.

Metro

Rome has three metro lines. Line A runs from south-east to north-west; Line B runs from EUR to the north-eastern suburbs; the interchange is beneath Termini mainline station. Line C runs from the eastern suburbs as far as Lodi,

but will eventually link with Line A at San Giovanni and with Line B at Colosseo.

Trams

Tram routes mainly serve suburban areas. An express tram service – no.8 – links largo Argentina to Trastevere and the western suburbs. The first stop is now in via delle Botteghe Oscure, on the corner with piazza Venezia.

Tour buses

The red **City Sightseeing Roma** (www.roma.city-sightseeing.it) buses can be seen throughout the city (9.30am-7.40pm daily), taking in the major basilicas and pilgrim sites. Options include 24, 48 or 72hr tickets. A 24hr stop-and-go ticket is €28 (reductions €14, free under-5s). Wheelchairs welcome.

The **Roma Cristiana** service (06 698 961 www.operaromanapellegrinaggi.org/it/roma-cristiana/open-bus) departs from Termini and St Peter's regularly through the day (9.30am-6.30pm daily). Tickets can be bought on board at Termini, San Giovanni in Laterano or at piazza Pia near St Peter's. A 24hr stop-and-go ticket costs €20 (under-10s free).

TAXIS

Licensed taxis are painted white and have a meter. Touts are rife at Termini and other major tourist magnets; ignore them if you don't want to risk an extortionate fare.

Fares & surcharges

When you pick up a taxi at a rank or hail one in the street, the meter should read zero. As you set off, it will indicate the minimum fare – currently €3 (€4.50 on Sun and public holidays; €6.50 10pm-7am).

Each kilometre (half mile) after that is €1.10. The first piece of luggage put in the boot is free, then it's €1 per piece. Tariffs outside the GRA, Rome's major ring road, are much higher. There's a 10% discount for trips to hospitals, and for women travelling alone 10pm-6am.

Fixed airport tariffs from anywhere inside the Aurelian walls (ie most of the *centro storico*) are €48 to/from Fiumicino; €30 to/from Ciampino. This is for up to four people and includes luggage: don't let taxi drivers tell you otherwise.

Taxi ranks

Ranks are indicated by a blue sign with 'Taxi' written on it in white. In the centre, there are ranks at largo Argentina, the Pantheon, piazza Venezia, piazza San Silvestro, piazza Sonnino (Trastevere), piazza di Spagna and Termini station.

Phone cabs

When you phone for a taxi, you'll be given the taxi code-name (always a location followed by a number) and a time, as in '*Bahama 69, in tre minuti*' ('Bahamas 69, in three minutes'). There's a set call fee of €3.50 from 6am until 10pm Mon-Sat; €4.50 Sun and holidays; €6.50 from 10pm until 6am after which radio taxis start the meter from the moment your phone call is answered. There's a city-run single phone cabs service: 06 0609. Or else try one of the companies below.
Cooperativa Autoradio Taxi Roma 06 3570, www.3570.it.
Cooperativa Samarcanda
06 5551, www.samarcanda.it.
Società la Capitale Radio Taxi 06 49 94.

DRIVING

Think twice before bringing a vehicle to Rome. Most of the *centro* is off-limits to all but permit holders, and on-street parking (if you can find a space) in most areas costs €1–€1.20 per hour, depending on the area.

Then there are Roman drivers: if you don't have nerves of steel and lightning-quick reactions, then the Eternal City is not somewhere you should be driving.

Short-term visitors should have no trouble driving with their home licence, but if it is in a less common language an international licence can be useful. All EU citizens are obliged to get an Italian licence after being resident for one year.

• You are required by law to wear a seat belt at all times, in both front and back, and have a reflective jacket and warning triangle in the car.
• Outside urban areas, you must drive with headlights on at all times.
• You must keep your driving licence, vehicle registration and personal ID on you at all times.
• Do not leave anything of value in your car. Take all luggage into your hotel when you park.
• Flashing your lights in Italy means that you will not slow down (contrary to British practice).
• Traffic lights flashing amber mean stop and give way to the right.
• Beware death-defying mopeds and pedestrians. Pedestrians assume they have the right of way in the older, quieter streets without clearly designated pavements.

Restricted areas – ZTL

Large sections of the city centre (marked ZTL – *Zona a Traffico Limitato*) are closed to non-resident traffic during business hours, and sometimes in the evening. Police and video cameras guard these areas; any vehicle without the required pass will be fined €84 if it enters at restricted times.

Breakdown services

Before taking a car to Italy it's advisable to join a national motoring organisation, like the AA or RAC in Britain or the AAA in the US. They have reciprocal arrangements with the Automobile Club d'Italia (ACI), offering breakdown assistance and giving general information. Even if you're not a member, it's still best to call the ACI if you have any kind of breakdown.

Manufacturer dealers are listed in the phone book under *auto*, along with specialist repairs such as *gommista* (tyres), *marmitte* (exhausts) and *carrozzerie* (bodywork). The *English*

Yellow Pages has a list of garages at which English is spoken.

Automobile Club d'Italia (ACI) 803
116 (free of charge), www.aci.it.
The ACI has English-speaking staff and provides services for all foreign drivers. Members of associated organisations get basic repairs for free, and other services at lower rates; non-members will be charged, but prices are reasonable.

Parking
A system in which residents park for free and visitors pay is in place in many areas of the city. It's efficiently policed, so watch out for the tell-tale blue lines. Buy parking tickets (€1-€1.20/hr) at pay-and-display ticket dispensers or *tabacchi*. In some areas parking is free after a certain time (usually 8pm or 11pm) or on Sun.

Your vehicle may be clamped if it's improperly or illegally parked. If your car's in a dangerous position or blocking trams and buses, it will be towed (call the municipal police on 06 67 691 and quote your number plate to find out which car pound it's in).

In zones with no blue lines, anything resembling a parking place is up for grabs, but with some exceptions: watch out for signs saying *Passo carrabile* ('access at all times') or *Sosta vietata* ('no parking'), and disabled parking spaces (yellow stripes on the road). The sign *Zona rimozione* ('tow-away area') means no parking. If a street or square has no cars parked in it, assume it's a strictly enforced no-parking zone. In some areas, self-appointed *parcheggiatori* will 'look after' your car for a small fee; it may be illegal and an absurd imposition, but it's probably worth paying up to preserve your tyres.

Villa Borghese Viale del Galoppatoio
33, Veneto & Borghese (06 322 5934, www.sabait.it). Metro Spagna/bus 61, 89, 116, 120, 150, 160, 490, 491, 495, C3, M. **Open** 24hrs daily. **Rates** Cars €2.20/hr, max 24hr rate of €18 **Map** p102 K5.

Vehicle entrances are on via del Muro Torto (both sides of the road). The car park is linked to the Spagna metro station, with 24hr pedestrian access to piazza di Spagna.

Car hire
To hire a car you must be over 21 – in some cases 23 – have held a licence for at least a year. You will be required to leave a credit card number or substantial cash deposit.

Avis 199 100 133, 06 4521 08391, www.
avisautonoleggio.it.
Europcar 199 307 030, 06 488 2854,
www.europcar.it.
Maggiore 06 2245 6060, 199 151 120,
www.maggiore.it.

CYCLES, SCOOTERS & MOPEDS FOR HIRE

To hire a scooter or moped (*motorino*) you need a driving licence, photo ID, credit card and/or a cash deposit. Helmets are required on all motorbikes, scooters or mopeds. For hiring bicycles, you can usually leave ID rather than pay a deposit.

Bici & Baci Via del Viminale 5, Monti
(06 482 8443, www.bicibaci.com).
Metro Repubblica/bus 40Exp, 60Exp, 64, 70, 170, H. **Open** 8am-7pm daily.
Rates (per day) €11 bicycles; €28-€35 mopeds (50cc); €45-€72 scooters (125cc).
Map p118 N8.
This friendly outlet also offers hourly and weekly rates. Another branch is in vicolo del Bottino 8, piazza di Spagna. Metro Spagna. Open 8am-7pm daily.
TopBike Rental Via Labicana 49,
Celio (06 488 2893, www.topbikerental.
com). Metro Colosseo or bus 87. **Rates**
(per day) €19-€45 bicycles. Bike tours in Rome and outskirts. **Map** p118 N11.
Scooters for Rent Via della
Purificazione 84, Tridente (06 488 5485, www.rentscooter.it). Metro Barberini/bus 52, 53, 62, 63, 80Exp, 83, 85, 116, 160, 175, 492, 590. **Open**
9am-7pm daily. **Rates** (per day) €12 bicycles; €40 mopeds (50cc); €50-€70 scooters (125cc). **Map** p102 L6.

Resources A-Z

ACCIDENT & EMERGENCY

Emergency numbers
Ambulance *Ambulanza 118.*
Fire service *Vigili del fuoco 115.*
Police *Carabinieri (English-speaking helpline) 112; Polizia di Stato 113.*

A&E departments

If you need urgent medical care, go to the *pronto soccorso* (casualty department). All the hospitals listed here offer 24hr casualty services. If your child needs emergency treatment, head straight for the excellent Ospedale Pediatrico Bambino Gesù.

Ospedale Fatebenefratelli *Isola Tiberina, Ghetto (06 68 371, www. fatebenefratelli-isolatiberina.it). Bus 23, 63, 280, 780, H/tram 8.* **Map** *p78 H11.*

Ospedale Pediatrico Bambino Gesù *Piazza Sant'Onofrio 4, Gianicolo (06 68 591, www. ospedalebambinogesu. it). Bus 115, 870.* **Map** *p150 G12.*

Ospedale San Giovanni *Via Amba Aradam 8, San Giovanni (06 77 051, www.hsangiovanni. roma.it). Metro San Giovanni/bus 81, 85, 117, 650, 673, 714, 717.* **Map** *p118 O12.*

AGE RESTRICTIONS

Cigarettes and alcohol cannot be sold to under-18s. Over-14s can ride a moped or scooter of 50cc, but 14-18s are required to pass a practical test and obtain a pre-licence first (*see p183* Driving). The age of heterosexual and homosexual consent is 14.

CLIMATE

Spring and autumn are the best times to see Rome; the weather's pleasantly balmy and the city is bathed in a glorious yellow light. To visitors arriving from chillier climes, the weather in May, June, Sept and Oct may seem like a fairly convincing approximation of summertime, but the actual Roman summer is a different matter altogether: searing, 40°C heat and energy-sapping humidity mark July and Aug, when the city empties as Romans scurry for the hills and sea.

Between Nov and Feb the weather in Rome is very unpredictable: you might strike it lucky with a run of crisp, bright, sunny days, maybe punctuated by the odd icy blast of wind buffetting in from northern Europe... or you may arrive in the midst of a torrential downpour that shows no sign of letting up, putting a

Travel Advice

For up-to-date information on travel to a specific country – including the latest on safety and security, health issues, local laws and customs – contact your home country government's department of foreign affairs. Most have websites with useful advice for would-be travellers

Australia
www.smartraveller.gov.au

Canada
www.voyage.gc.ca

New Zealand
www.safetravel.govt.nz

Republic of Ireland
www.dfa.ie

UK
www.fco.gov.uk/travel

USA
www.state.gov/travel

dampener on your sightseeing plans. But there is some compensation: you'll find there's a relative scarcity of other tourists.

CUSTOMS

People travelling between EU countries are not required to declare goods imported into or exported from Italy if they are for personal use. For those arriving from non-EU countries, these limits apply:

• 200 cigarettes/100 cigarillos/50 cigars/250g of tobacco.
• 1l of spirits (over 22% alcohol) or 2l of wine.
• 1 bottle of perfume (50ml), 250ml eau de toilette.
• Gift items not exceeding €175 (€95 for children under 15).

Anything above that will be subject to taxation at the port of entry. For further information, visit www.agenziadogane. it. For tax refunds, *see p38* Shopping practicalities.

DISABLED

Narrow streets, cobblestones and bumper-to-bumper parking make Rome a difficult city for wheelchair-users. You'll almost certainly have to depend on other people more than you would at home. Off the streets, old buildings tend to have narrow corridors and the lifts (if any) are usually too small.

Blind and partially sighted people often find there's no kerb between the road proper and the bit of street pedestrians are entitled to walk on (the one exception is a smooth brick walkway laid into the cobbles leading from the Trevi Fountain to piazza Navona, with Braille notes about landmarks on bronze plaques along the way).

Wheelchair-accessible public toilets are found in many central areas... but there's no guarantee they'll be either in working order or open.

Information for disabled people is available from **PIT** information booths (*see p192*), from the 06 0608 general information line and www.060608.it.

Climate

Average temperatures and monthly rainfall in Rome

	Temp (°C/°F)	Rainfall (mm/in)	Sun (hrs/day)
January	8 / 47	71 / 2.8	4
February	9 / 48	62 / 2.4	4
March	11 / 51	57 / 2.2	6
April	13 / 55	51 / 2.0	7
May	18 / 64	46 / 1.8	8
June	21 / 70	37 / 1.5	9
July	24 / 76	15 / 0.6	11
August	25 / 77	21 / 0.8	10
September	21 / 70	63 / 2.5	8
October	17 / 63	99 / 3.9	6
November	13 / 55	129 / 5.1	4
December	9 / 48	93 / 3.7	4

Sightseeing

Well-designed ramps, lifts and toilets have been installed in many attractions.

Museum 333 396 3226, 338 148 5361, *www.assmuseum.it.*

This volunteer group offers tours of some galleries and catacombs for individuals or groups with mobility or, especially, sight problems. Their museum guides – some speak English; if not, an interpreter can be arranged – have Braille notes, copies of paintings in relief, and permission to touch artefacts. Guides also make works of art comprehensible to the non-sighted with music cassettes and recorded text. A voluntary donation to cover costs is requested.

Transport

Rome's buses and trams have been made more accessible, with most buses plying central routes able to accommodate wheelchairs.

On the metro, most of the central stations on line A are no-go. All stations on line B have lifts, disabled WCs and special parking spaces, though work on the third metro line means that access at some stations is closed off. The www.atac.roma.it website lists wheelchair-accessible stations.

Most taxi drivers will carry (folded) wheelchairs; when you can, phone for a cab rather than hailing one (*see p182*).

To ascertain which trains have wheelchair facilities, call 06 3000, or consult timetables on the **Trenitalia** website (www.trenitalia.it): there's a wheelchair symbol next to accessible trains. For international journeys, call 06 4730 8579. To secure assistance, you must phone the numbers given above or make a request by email (SalaBlu.ROMA@rfi.it) 24hrs prior to departure. Reserve a seat when buying your ticket, and make sure you arrive at least 45mins early.

This also applies to trains to and from Fiumicino airport; in theory, you must call your airline to arrange assistance the day before arrival; in practice, you'll be helped on to the train anyway.

Both of Rome's airports have adapted toilets and waiting rooms.

Wheelchair hire

Ortopedia Colosseo *Viale Carlo Felice 93, San Giovanni (06 7047 4187, www.ortopediamazzotta.it). Metro San Giovanni/bus 360/tram 3.* **Open** *9am-1pm, 3.30-7pm Mon-Fri.* **Map** *p118 Q12.*
Hires out all kinds of wheelchairs, which can be delivered by taxi.

DRUGS

Anyone caught in possession of narcotics of any kind must be taken before a magistrate. The severity of the punishment – which can extend to years in prison – depends upon the quantity of drugs, and whether they are deemed *leggera* (light) or *pesante* (heavy).

Sniffer dogs are a fixture at most ports of entry into Italy; customs police are likely to allow visitors entering with even negligible quantities of narcotics to stay no longer than it takes a magistrate to expel them from the country.

ELECTRICITY

Most wiring systems work on 220V – compatible with UK-bought appliances (with a plug adaptor); US 110V equipment requires a current transformer. Adaptors can be bought at any electrical or hardware shop (*elettricità* or *ferramenta*).

EMBASSIES & CONSULATES

For a full list of embassies, see *Ambasciate* in the phone book.

Except where indicated, consular offices (which provide the majority of services of use to tourists) share the same address as these embassies.

Australia *via Antonio Bosio 5, Suburbs: north (06 852 721, www.italy. embassy.gov.au). Bus 60, 62, 82, 90Exp.*

Britain *Via XX Settembre 80A, Veneto & Borghese (06 4220 0001, ukinitaly.fco. gov.uk). Bus 16, 60Exp, 61, 62, 75, 82, 90Exp, 492.* **Map** *p102 O5.*

Canada Embassy: *via Salaria 243, Suburbs: north (06 854 441, www. canadainternational.gc.ca). Bus 53, 83, 93, 168. Consulate: via Zara 30, Suburbs: north. Bus 60, 62, 82, 88, 90Exp, 140/tram 3, 19.*

Ireland *via Giacomo Medici 1, Gianicolo (06 585 2381, www.ambasciata-irlanda. it). Bus 44, 75, 115, 870.* **Map** *p150 G12.*

New Zealand *via Clitunno 44, Suburbs: north (06 853 7501, www.nzembassy. com). Bus 53, 83, 93, 168.*

US *via Vittorio Veneto 119, Veneto & Borghese (06 46 741, it.usembassy.gov/ it). Metro Barberini/bus 52, 53, 61, 63, 80 Exp, 83, 160, C3.* **Map** *p102 L5.*

HEALTH

Emergency healthcare is available through the Italian national health system; hospital A&E departments (*see p185*) treat all emergency cases for free. If you are an EU citizen, the EHIC (**European Health Insurance Card**) entitles you to free consultation with any doctor. Non-EU citizens are advised to obtain private health insurance (*see right*).

EU nationals with an EHIC can consult a national health service doctor free of charge, and buy drugs at prices set by the Health Ministry. Non-EU nationals who consult a health service doctor will be charged a small fee at the doctor's discretion.

Condoms (*preservativi*) are on sale near checkouts in supermarkets or over the counter in pharmacies; the pill is available on prescription.

For serious dental emergencies, head to a hospital casualty department (*see p185*).

ID

You are required by law to carry photo ID with you at all times. You must produce it if stopped by traffic police (along with your driving licence, which you must carry when you're in charge of a motor vehicle) and when you check into a hotel. Smaller hotels may try to hold on to your passport/ ID card for the length of your stay; you are within your rights to ask for it back.

INSURANCE

EU citizens are entitled to reciprocal medical care in Italy provided they leave their own country with an **EHIC** (European Health Insurance Card), which has replaced the old E111 form. In the UK, you can apply for an EHIC online (www.ehic.org.uk) or by post using forms available at any post office. If you use it for anything but emergencies (which are treated free anyway in casualty departments), you'll need to deal with the intricacies of the Italian state health system. For short-term visits, it is advisable to take out private travel/health insurance. Non-EU citizens should take out private medical insurance before setting off.

Visitors should also take out adequate insurance against loss or theft. If you hire a car, motorcycle or moped, make sure you pay the extra for full insurance cover and, for a car, sign the collision damage waiver (CDW).

LANGUAGE

Romans always appreciate attempts at spoken Italian, no matter how incompetent. In hotels and all but the most spit-and-sawdust restaurants, there's likely to be someone with basic English. *See also p194* Vocabulary.

LEFT LUGGAGE

The left-luggage office by platform 24 in Termini station (06 474 5421) is open 6am-11pm daily. A suitcase costs €6/hr (for up to 5hrs); €1/hr from the 6th to the 12th hour; thereafter, 50¢/hr.

At Fiumicino airport, left luggage in Terminal 3 is open 6.30am-11.30pm daily. Each item costs €6 for up to 24hrs. Hotels will generally look after your luggage during the day, even after you've checked out.

LGBT

There are over 70 gay activist organisations in Italy. Foremost among these are the organisations belonging to the Bologna-based Arcigay network. For up-to-the-minute information on LGBT events, plus gay-friendly listings of all kinds, check out www.friendlyroma. it; it's (kind of) in English too. Another good source for events listings is www. gayvillage.it.

Organisations & resources

Arcigay & Arci-Lesbica Roma *Via Zabaglia 14, Testaccio (06 6450 1102, free helpline 800 713 713, www.arcigay roma.it/www.gaycenter.it/www. arcilesbica.it). Metro Piramide/bus 23, 30, 75, 83, 170, 280, 673, 716, 719, 3N, 9N, 10N, 11N/tram 3.* **Map** *p135 H15.*
The local group gets together on Wed 7-9pm for those over 27; on Fri 6-8pm for those under 27. Arci-Lesbica organises once-monthly women-only meetings (third Tue of mth 9-11pm). Phone or see the website for other events.

Circolo Mario Mieli di Cultura Omosessuale *Via Efeso 2A, Suburbs: south (06 541 3985, 800 110 611 free of charge, www.mariomieli.org). Metro San Paolo/bus 23, 761.* **Open** *10.30am-6.30pm Mon-Fri.*
Named after the pioneer author and thinker Mario Mieli, this is the most important gay, lesbian and transgender group in Rome. It provides a base for debates and events, and offers counselling and care facilities. Its Muccassassina one-nighter (*see p127*) is highly popular, and it also organises Pride events (www.romapride.it) during the summer.

Di'Gay Project *Via Costantino 82, Suburbs: south (06 513 4741, www. digayproject.org). Metro San Paolo/ bus 670, 715, 766, 769.* **Open** *10am-6pm Mon-Fri.*
Hosts the summer Gay Village (*see p57*) as well as a series of other worthy events. There's a welcome group, a film club, a youth group and a theatre workshop.

La Foresteria Orsa Maggiore *Via San Francesco di Sales 1A, Trastevere (06 689 3753, www.orsamaggiorehostel. com). Bus 23, 280.* **Map** *p150 F10.*
The women-only Orsa Maggiore (Great Bear) hostel provides 13 brightly decorated rooms priced at €26-€42.50 per person per night.

Publications

Edicole (newsstands) are often good for gay books and videos; the *edicole* in piazze dei Cinquecento (*map p118 O7*) and Colonna (*map p78 K9*) are treasure troves of porn: discreet amounts are displayed by day, but piles of it come out at night.

The online magazine www. prideonline.it is a great resource for news and key events in the gay calendar.

LOST PROPERTY

Anything lost on Metro lines A and B, on FS trains or at Termini station may turn up at this council-run lost property office.

Ufficio oggetti smarriti *Circonvallazione Ostiense 191, Suburbs: south (06 6769 3214). Metro Garbatella/bus 670, 673, 716, 715.* **Open** *8.30am-1pm Mon, Wed, Fri; 8.30am-5pm Thur.*

MONEY

The Italian currency is the euro, with banknotes of €5, €10, €20, €100, €200 and €500, and coins worth €1 and €2, plus 1¢, 2¢, 5¢, 10¢, 20¢ and 50¢ (*centesimi*). Money from any Eurozone country is valid tender. Vatican euros are a highly collectable rarity.

Banking hours

Opening hours vary, but most banks operate 8.30am-1.30pm, 2.45-4.30pm Mon-Fri. Some central branches now also open until 6pm Thur and 8.30am-12.30pm Sat. All banks close on public holidays, and work reduced hours the day before a holiday (many close by 11am).

Banks & ATMs

Most banks have 24hr cash-point (*Bancomat*) machines. The vast majority accept cards with the Maestro, Cirrus and Plus logos, and will dispense up to a daily limit of €250.

Bureaux de change

Banks usually offer better exchange rates than private bureaux de change (*cambio*). Take a passport or other photo ID. Commission rates vary (from nothing to €5 per transaction). Beware 'no commission' signs: the rate is likely to be terrible.

Many city-centre bank branches have automatic cash-exchange machines, which will accept most currencies (notes in good condition only).

Credit & debit cards

Nearly all hotels of two stars and above now accept at least some of the major credit cards; all but the cheapest local eateries will take them too.

Should you lose a credit or debit card, phone one of the 24hr emergency numbers below.

American Express 06 7290 0347.
Diner's Club 800 393 939.
MasterCard 800 870 866.
Visa 800 819 014.

OPENING HOURS

For information on shop opening hours, see p37.

PHARMACIES

Farmacie (identified by a green cross) give informal medical advice, as well as making up prescriptions. The best-stocked pharmacy in the city is in the Vatican (*see above*): it has a whole range of medicines not found elsewhere in Italy.

Normal pharmacy opening hours are 8.30am-1pm, 4-8pm Mon-Sat. Outside these hours, a duty rota system operates. A list displayed by the door of any pharmacy (and in local papers) indicates the nearest ones open at any time. A surcharge applies when only the special duty counter is open.

Farmacia della Stazione *Piazza dei Cinquecento 50, Esquilino (06 488 0019). See p180 Transport to Termini.* **Open** *8am-11.20pm daily.* **Map** *p118 O7.*
Farmacia del Vaticano *Porta Sant'Anna entrance, Vatican (06 6988 3422). Metro Ottaviano/bus 23, 32, 34, 40Exp, 49, 62, 64, 81, 271, 490, 492, 590, 982, 990/tram 19.* **Open** *8.30am-1pm Mon-Sat.* **Map** *p161 D7.*
Piram *Via Nazionale 228, Esquilino (06 488 4437). Metro Repubblica/ bus 40Exp, 60Exp, 64, 70, 170, H, N7, N8, N9, N15, N18.* **Open** *24hrs daily.* **Map** *p118 M8.*

POLICE

The principal Polizia di Stato station, the **Questura Centrale**, is at via San Vitale 15 (06 46 861, www.poliziadistato. it, *map p118 M8*). Others, and the Carabinieri's Commissariati, are listed in the phone book under Polizia and *Carabinieri*. Incidents can be reported to either. For emergency numbers, *see p185*.

POSTAL SERVICES

For postal information, call 803 160 (8am-8pm Mon-Sat; Italian only) or visit www.poste.it.

Most postboxes are red and have two slots, *per la città* (for Rome) and *tutte le altre destinazioni* (everywhere else).

On the whole, mail arrives swiftly – up to 48hrs delivery in Italy, three days for EU countries and 5-9 days for other countries (in zones 2 and 3). A letter of 20g or less to Italy costs 60¢; to other countries in the EU costs 75¢; to zone 2 costs 1.60¢; to zone 3 costs €2.

There are local post offices (*ufficio postale*) in each district; opening hours can vary, but they are generally 8.30am-6pm Mon-Fri (Aug 8.30am-2pm), 8.30am-12.35pm Sat and any day preceding a public holiday.

Main post offices in the centre have longer opening hours.

Several postal services are available online; visit www.poste.it to avoid the queues.

Posta Centrale *Piazza San Silvestro 19, Tridente (06 6973 7205, information 803 160). Bus 52, 53, 62, 63, 71, 80Exp, 83, 85, 117, 160, 492, 590.* **Open** *8.20am-7pm Mon-Fri, 8am-12.35pm Sat.* **Map** *p102 J7.*
The hub of Rome's postal system has been treated to a facelift: shiny new internet terminals, numerous counters, an information desk... and vastly reduced queues.

PUBLIC HOLIDAYS

On public holidays (*giorni festivi*) virtually all shops, banks and businesses close, although (with the exception of May Day, 15 Aug and Christmas Day) bars and restaurants tend to stay open. There's only limited public transport on 1 May and Christmas afternoon.

New Year's Day *(Capodanno) 1 Jan*
Epiphany *(La Befana) 6 Jan*
Easter Monday *(Pasquetta)*
Liberation Day *(Liberazione)*
25 Apr
May Day *(Primo Maggio) 1 May*
Patron Saints' Day
(Santi Pietro e Paolo) 29 June
Feast of the Assumption *(Ferragosto) 15 Aug*
All Saints *(Tutti i santi) 1 Nov*
Immaculate Conception
(Festa dell'Immacolata) 8 Dec
Christmas Day *(Natale) 25 Dec*
Boxing Day *(Santo Stefano)*
26 Dec

SAFETY & SECURITY

Thefts should be reported immediately at the nearest police station (*see p190*). Report the loss of credit cards immediately to your credit card company (*see p190*), and of passports to your consulate/embassy (*see p187*).

Muggings are fairly rare in Rome, but pickpocketing is rife in the main tourist areas. Below are a few basic precautions:
• Don't carry wallets in back pockets, particularly on buses. If you have a bag or camera with a long strap, wear it across the chest.
• Keep bags closed, with your hand on them. If you stop at a pavement café or restaurant, don't leave bags or coats where you cannot see them.
• When walking down a street, hold cameras and bags on the side of you towards the wall – you're less likely to become the prey of a motorcycle thief.
• Avoid groups of ragged children brandishing pieces of cardboard, or walk by quickly keeping hold of your valuables. The cardboard is to distract you while accomplices pick your pockets or bags.

SMOKING

Smoking is prohibited in all public places in Italy except for those that provide a distinct, ventilated smokers' room. Occasionally you'll find a restaurant or club which has a dedicated smoking room, specifically marked as such, but these are becoming less and less common. Smoking in hotels is almost universally banned.

Tabacchi
Tabacchi or *tabaccherie* (identifiable by signs with a white 'T' on black or blue) are the only places you can legally buy tobacco products.

TELEPHONES

Dialling & codes
There are three main types of phone number in Rome:
• Landlines have the area code 06, which must be used whether calling from within or outside the city. Numbers generally have 8 digits. When phoning Rome from abroad, keep the initial 0.
• Numbers beginning 800 are free. Numbers beginning 840 and 848 are charged at low set rates, no matter where you're calling from or how long

the call lasts. These numbers can be called from within Italy only; some of them function only within a single phone district.

• Mobile numbers begin with a 3.

Mobile phones

GSM phones can be used on both 900 and 1800 bands; British, Australian and New Zealand mobiles work fine, but US mobiles are on a different frequency that doesn't work (unless it's a tri-band phone). The main mobile phone networks in Italy are **Tim** (www.tim.it), **Vodafone** (www.vodafone.it), **Tre** (www.tre.it) and **Wind** (www.wind.it).

Public phones

Rome has no shortage of public phone boxes and many bars have payphones, most of which are readily available as locals are addicted to mobiles. Most only accept phone cards (*schede telefoniche*); a few also accept major credit cards. Phone cards cost €5, €15 and €30 and are available from *tabacchi* (*see p37* Life's Essentials), some news-stands and some bars.

TIME

Italy is one hour ahead of London, six hours ahead of New York, eight hours behind Sydney and 12 hours behind Wellington. In all EU countries clocks are moved forward one hour in early spring and back again in late autumn.

TIPPING

Foreigners are generally expected to tip more than Italians, but the 10%+ that is customary in many countries is considered generous. Some smarter places, however, now include a 10-15% service charge. For drinks, follow the example of many locals, who leave a 10¢ or 20¢ coin on the counter when ordering at a bar. Taxi drivers will be happy if you round the fare up to the nearest whole euro.

TOURIST INFORMATION

For tours, *see p182* Tour buses.
turismoroma.it *information on your mobile*
www.060608 *city council's tourism website*
www.romaturismo.com *plenty of useful information*

PITs (Punti Informativi Turistici) are located in the following places:
Piazza Pia, Vatican & Prati. **Map** *p161 E7.*
Piazza delle Cinque Lune, Pantheon & Navona. **Map** *p78 G8.*
Piazza del Tempio della Pace, Capitoline & Palatine. **Map** *p66 L10.*
Via Nazionale, Trevi & Quirinale. **Map** *p78 L8.*
Piazza Sonnino, Trastevere. Bus 23, 280, 780, H/tram 8. **Map** *p150 H12.*
Via Minghetti, Tridente. **Map** *p102 J8.*
Termini station, platform 24, Esquilino. **Map** *p102 O7.*
Fiumicino airport, Terminal 3.
Ciampino airport, Arrival Hall.

Ufficio Pellegrini e Turisti *Piazza San Pietro, Vatican (06 6988 2350, www.vaticanstate.va).* **Open** *8.30am-6.30pm Mon-Sat.* **Map** *p161 D7.*

VISAS & IMMIGRATION

EU nationals and citizens of the US, Canada, Australia and New Zealand do not need visas for stays of up to three months. For EU citizens a passport or national ID card valid for travel abroad is sufficient; non-EU citizens must have full passports. In theory, all visitors must declare their presence to the local police (*see p190*) within eight days of arrival. If you're staying in a hotel, this will be done for you.

Glossary

Amphitheatre oval open-air theatre in ancient Rome

Apse large recess at the high-altar end of a church

Atrium courtyard

Baroque artistic period in the 17th-18th centuries, in which the decorative element became increasingly florid, culminating in the rococo

Basilica ancient Roman rectangular public building; rectangular Christian church

Campanile bell tower

Cavea step-like seating area found in an amphitheatre or theatre

Chiaroscuro from Italian *chiaro* (light) and *scuro* (dark), juxtaposition of light and shade to bring out relief and volume

Ciborio dome-shaped canopy on columns over high altar

Clivus ancient name for a street on the side of a hill

Cloister exterior courtyard surrounded on all sides by a covered walkway

Column upright architectural element that can be round, square or rectangular; usually structural, but sometimes merely decorative, and usually free-standing; conforms to one of the classical orders

Confessio crypt under raised altar

Cosmati, cosmatesque mosaic technique using coloured marble chips, usually to decorate floors and church fittings

Cryptoporticus underground corridor

Domus Romane city house

Fresco painting technique in which pigment is applied to wet plaster

Gothic architectural and artistic style of the late Middle Ages (from the 12th century), of soaring, pointed arches

Greek cross (of a church) in the shape of a cross with arms of equal length

Insula an ancient multi-storey city apartment block

Intarsio form of mosaic made from pieces of wood of different colours

Largo square

Latin cross (of a church) in the shape of a cross with one arm longer than the others

Loggia gallery open on one side

Matronium gallery (usually screened) where women sat in early Christian and Byzantine basilicas

Mithraeum temple, usually underground, to the deity Mithras

Narthex enclosed porch in front of a church

Nave main body of a church; the longest section of a Latin-cross church

Necropolis literally, 'city of the dead'; graveyard

Nymphaeum grotto with pool and fountain dedicated to the Nymphs (female water deities)

Palazzo large and/or important building (not necessarily a palace)

Piazza square

Pilaster a rectangular column designed to project slightly from a wall

Pillar upright architectural element, always free-standing, but not conforming to classical orders

Rococo highly decorative style of the 18th century

Romanesque architectural style of the early Middle Ages (c500-1200), drawing on Roman and Byzantine influences

Sarcophagus a coffin made of stone or marble

Tepidarium warm (as opposed to hot), steam-filled room in a Roman baths complex

Transept as per the **Latin-cross** shape of a church but with shorter arms

Travertine cream-coloured calcareous limestone

Triclinium dining room

Triumphal arch arch in front of an apse, usually over the high altar; monumental victory arch

Trompe l'oeil decorative painting effect that makes a flat surface appear three-dimensional

Vocabulary

There are two forms of address in the second person singular: *lei* (formal) and *tu* (informal). In practice, the personal pronoun is usually omitted.

Pronunciation

a *as in* a**sk**; **e** *like a in* a**g**e *or e in* s**e**ll; **i** *like ea in* **ea**st; **o** *as in* h**o**tel *or* h**o**t; **u** *as in* b**oo**t.

Romans have a lot of trouble with their consonants. **C** often comes out nearer **g**; **n**, if in close proximity to an **r**, disappears. Remember: **c** and **g** both go soft in front of **e** and **i** (becoming like the initial sounds of **ch**eck and **gi**raffe respectively). An **h** after **c** or **g** makes it hard – *chiuso* (closed) is pronounced 'kiuso'.

c *before* **a**, **o** *and* **u**: *as in* **c**at; **g** *before* **a**, **o** *and* **u**: *as in* **g**et; **gl** *like* mi**lli**on; **gn** *like* ca**ny**on; **qu** *as in* **qu**ick; **r** *always rolled;* **s** *has two sounds, as in* **s**oap *or* ro**s**e; **sc** *like* **sh**ame; **sch** *like* **sc**out; **z** *can be* **ts** *or* **dz**.

Basics

hello/goodbye (informal) *ciao/salve;* **good morning** *buon giorno;* **good evening** *buona sera;* **good night** *buona notte;* **please** *per favore/per piacere;* **thank you** *grazie;* **you're welcome** *prego;* **excuse me/sorry** *mi scusi (formal)/scusa (informal);* **I'm sorry, but...** *mi dispiace...;* **I don't speak Italian** *non parlo l'italiano;* **do you speak English?** *parla inglese?;* **where's the toilet?** *dov'è il bagno/la toilette?;* **open** *aperto;* **closed** *chiuso;* **entrance** *entrata;* **exit** *uscita*

Directions

(turn) left *(giri a) sinistra;* **(it's on the) right** *(è a/sulla) destra;* **straight on** *sempre diritto;* **where is...?** *dov'è...?;* **could you show me the way to...?** *mi potrebbe indicare la strada per...?;* **is it near/far?** *è vicino/lontano?*

Transport

car *macchina;* **bus** *autobus/auto;* **coach** *pullman;* **taxi** *tassì/taxi;* **train** *treno;* **tram** *tram;* **plane** *aereo;* **bus stop** *fermata (d'autobus);* **station** *stazione;* **platform** *binario;* **ticket/s** *biglietto/biglietti;* **one way** *solo andata;* **return** *andata e ritorno;*

Communications

phone *telefono;* **can I make a phone call?** *posso telefonare?;* **letter** *lettera;* **postcard** *cartolina*

Shopping

can you give me a little more/less? *mi dia un po' di più/meno?;* **100 grams of...** *un etto di...;* **one kilo of...** *un kilo/chilo di...*

Eating, drinking & accommodation

I'd like to book a table for four at eight *vorrei prenotare una tavola per quattro alle otto;* **the bill** *il conto;* **is service included?** *è incluso il servizio?;* **a reservation** *una prenotazione;* **I'd like to book a single/twin/double room** *vorrei prenotare una camera singola/ doppia/ matrimoniale;*

Days & nights

Monday *lunedì;* **Tuesday** *martedì;* **Wednesday** *mercoledì;* **Thursday** *giovedì;* **Friday** *venerdì;* **Saturday** *sabatò;* **Sunday** *domenica;* **yesterday** *ieri;* **today** *oggi;* **tomorrow** *domani* **morning** *mattina;* **afternoon** *pomeriggio;* **evening** *sera;* **night** *notte;* **weekend** *fine settimana/weekend*

Numbers

0 *zero;* **1** *uno;* **2** *due;* **3** *tre;* **4** *quattro;* **5** *cinque;* **6** *sei;* **7** *sette;* **8** *otto;* **9** *nove;* **10** *dieci;* **100** *cento;* **200** *duecento;* **1,000** *mille;* **2,000** *duemila*

Menu Reader

Sughi, condimenti e ripieni – Sauces, toppings & fillings

alle vongole *clams;* **al ragù** *minced meat and tomatoes (ie 'bolognese', a term not used in Italy);* **al sugo** *puréed cooked tomatoes;* **all'amatriciana** *tomato, chilli and bacon;* **all'arrabbiata** *tomato and chilli;* **alla carbonara** *bacon, egg and pecorino;* **alla puttanesca** *tomatoes, anchovies, olives, capers, chilli and garlic;*

Carne – Meat

abbacchio, agnello *lamb;* **capra, capretto** *goat, kid;* **coniglio** *rabbit;* **guanciale** *cured pork jowl;* **maiale** *pork;* **manzo** *beef;* **pollo** *chicken;* **prosciutto cotto** *ham;* **prosciutto crudo** *Parma ham;* **tacchino** *turkey;* **vitello** *veal.*

Piatti di carne – Meat dishes

carpaccio, bresaola *thinly sliced cured beef;* **coda alla vaccinara** *oxtail stew;* **ossobuco** *veal shins with marrow jelly inside;* **polpette** *meatballs;* **porchetta** *slow-roasted pork;* **salsiccia** *sausage;* **saltimbocca** *veal strips with ham and sage.*

Formaggi – Cheeses

cacio, caciotta *cow or sheep's milk cheese;* **parmigiano** *parmesan;* **pecorino romano** *hard, tangy sheep's cheese;* **ricotta** *crumbly white soft cheese;*

Pesce – Fish

sarago, dentice, marmora, orata, fragolino *bream;* **alici, acciughe** *anchovies;* **baccalà** *salt cod;* **branzino, spigola** *sea bass;* **merluzzo** *cod;* **pesce San Pietro** *John Dory;* **salmone** *salmon;* **sarde, sardine** *sardines;* **sogliola** *sole;* **tonno** *tuna;* **trota** *trout.*

Frutti di mare – Seafood

astice, aragosta *lobster;* **calamari** *squid;* **cozze** *mussels;* **crostacei** *shellfish;* **gamberi, gamberetti** *shrimps, prawns;* **granchio** *crab;* **mazzancolle** *king prawns;* **moscardini** *baby octopus;* **polipo, polpo** *octopus;* **seppie, seppioline** *cuttlefish.*

Verduri/contorni – Vegetables/sides

asparagi *asparagus;* **broccoli siciliani** *broccoli;* **broccolo romanesco** *green cauliflower;* **carciofi** *artichokes;* **cavolfiore** *cauliflower;* **cicoria** *chicory;* **cipolle** *onions;* **funghi** *mushrooms;* **lattuga** *lettuce;* **melanzane** *aubergine;* **patate** *potatoes;* **patatine fritte** *french fries;* **peperoncino** *chilli;* **peperoni** *peppers (capsicum);* **rughetta, rucola** *rocket;* **zucchine** *courgettes.*

Frutta – Fruit

ananas *pineapple;* **arance** *oranges;* **fichi** *figs;* **fragole, fragoline** *strawberries;* **mele** *apples;* **pere** *pears;* **pesche** *peaches;* **prugne, susine** *plums;* **uva** *grapes.*

Dolci – Desserts

gelato *ice-cream;* **pannacotta** *a very thick, blancmange-like cream;* **sorbetto** *sorbet;* **tiramisù** *mascarpone and coffee sponge;* **torta della nonna** *flan of pâtisserie cream and pine nuts.*

Pizza & toppings

calzone *a sealed pizza pie, usually filled with cheese, tomato and ham;* **capricciosa** *ham, hard-boiled eggs, artichokes and olives;* **marinara** *plain tomato with garlic and herbs;* **margherita** *tomato and mozzarella;* **napoli, napoletana** *tomato, anchovies and mozzarella.*

Index

Picture credits

Credits

Crimson credits
Authors Fulvia Angelini, Agnes Crawford, Luisa Grigoletto, Anne Hanley, Kate Zagorski
Editor Beth Bishop
Proofreader Liz Hammond
Layouts Emilie Crabb, Patrick Dawson
Cartography Gail Armstrong, John Scott, Simonetta Giori

Series Editor Sophie Blacksell Jones
Production Manager Kate Michell
Design Mytton Williams

Chairman David Lester
Managing Director Andy Riddle

Advertising Media Sales House
Marketing Lyndsey Mayhew
Sales Joel James

Acknowledgements

The authors and editor would like to thank contributors to previous editions of *Time Out Rome*, whose work formed the basis of this guide.

Photography credits

Front cover piola666/iStock
Back cover Alexander Mazurkevich/Shutterstock.com
Interior Photography credits, see p199.

Publishing information

Time Out Rome Shortlist 8th edition
© TIME OUT ENGLAND LIMITED 2018
March 2018

ISBN 978 1 780592 59 6
CIP DATA: A catalogue record for this book is available from the British Library

Published by Crimson Publishing
21d Charles Street, Bath, BA1 1HX (01225 584 950, www.crimsonpublishing.co.uk) on behalf of Time Out England.

Distributed by Grantham Book Services
Distributed in the US and Canada by Publishers Group West (1-510-809-3700)

Printed by Replika Press, India.